REINSURANCE FUNDAMENTALS

REINSURANCE FUNDAMENTALS

TREATY AND FACULTATIVE

ROSS PHIFER

Copyright © 1996 by John Wiley & Sons, Inc.

Library of Congress Cataloging in Publication Data:

Phifer, Ross.
    Reinsurance fundamentals / Ross Phifer.
        p. cm.
    Includes index.
    ISBN 0-471-13452-X (cloth : alk. paper)
    1. Reinsurance.   I. Title.
    HG8083.P49 1996
        368'.0122—dc20   95-49717
CIP
Printed in the United States of America
10 9 8 7 6 5 4 3 2 1

to Karen, Brian, and Blair

ACKNOWLEDGMENTS

One who is beginning the study of reinsurance is encouraged to find a mentor. This can help the reader understand this text and perhaps be someone who can provide nuances, subtleties, and colorful anecdotes to enrich the learning experience.

Several individuals helped me learn this business. There have been too many to appropriately acknowledge, but several shall be mentioned here to illustrate the type of help one gathers within a career.

Thomas Dunavant was known to me as a senior officer in the State Filings Department at Allstate Insurance Company. He was a very able devil's advocate. In the 1960s, Tom wrote a manuscript on unearned premium that I saved and used throughout my career. Tom's concepts are part of the fundamentals in Chapter 2.

Arthur Horwitz and *Paul Milliman* were co-workers at American Mutual Reinsurance Company, and currently are senior vice president of Blanch & Company and vice president of Marsh MacLennan, Inc., respectively. Both are people who freely exchanged ideas and tested concepts presented to them. The exposure helped me learn the nuances of the reinsurance field.

Charles C. Hewitt, Jr. was a mentor to me as actuary at Allstate Insurance Company and later as president of Metropolitan Reinsurance Company. Charlie was the author of the pricing of no-fault insurance adopted countrywide during the formative stages of this coverage. Because there were no statistical precedents, the rates were based on modified data and estimated factors. He extended what was known by adaptation to approximate that which would ultimately be developed over time as the actual results were recorded and analyzed. I learned to apply such philosophy in pricing reinsurance, where the existing data often lacks credibility.

Charles L. Niles was president and actuary at General Accident Insurance Company and has retired to very busy, productive work as a consultant and arbitrator. Charlie has made asking questions an art form. He inquires about the core principles of a concept and tests the advocate's preparation. The lesson is in listening to the responses. When Charlie is through asking questions, everyone at the table has a better understanding of the concept. He has been a mentor and friend for many years.

Rudolph A. Zoellner is a retired senior vice president of Fireman's Fund American Insurance Group and my father-in-law. He's been an eminent insurance leader that I have been fortunate to follow. His suggestion started my career in insurance and has been a resource for ideas and advice ever since. Rudy has been a valuable contributor in the writing and editing of this work. I have been most fortunate to have had a mentor within my family.

Contributors. The reinsurance business is not so complex in its fundamentals; rather, it is fertile with options and alternative techniques that may be applied to make an otherwise straightforward application suitable to both the insurer transferring a portion of its exposure and the reinsurer who is taking up a share. The following individuals have taken an active leadership role in insurance and reinsurance. They know how to select from the subtle attributes those that can have significant impact on the reinsurance results. They have made a difference in our business.

Each of the following experts has read and offered suggestions to portions of this work. They hold my sincere gratitude.

Andrew Barile
Virginia M. Bates
Dennis A. Bentley
George H. Crane
Gary J. Curtis
Ronald J. Davies
Stuart H. Grayston
Robert Hestwood
Thomas J. Kennedy
Christian S. McCarthy
Stephen R. Palange
Gary Patrik
Peter J. Tol
Rudolph A. Zoellner

CONTENTS

1

INTRODUCTION TO REINSURANCE

INTRODUCTION

The reinsurance world is like the middle of an ocean. Everyone sees the troughs and crests and senses the ebb and flow. Many sense the drift and currents, while few understand the underlying curvature, that the ocean is not flat. Our emphasis is on the troughs and crests of the reinsurance world. It is important to understand that this world is neither flat nor static.

Reinsurance is constructed from rather simple parts—fundamentals that have stood over time yet are subject to evolution. While the basics remain consistent, tax consequences and other factors need be considered anew in each business cycle and for every reinsurance contract. The application is subject to review and modification when changes brought on by advances in science and technology or changes in applicable law or judicial interpretation produce a material influence upon, or alteration in, the nature of risk to be reinsured.

A solid understanding of the basics is crucial to its application, yet there is more to a successful practice of reinsurance than a slavish application of the fundamentals. Logical analysis and creativity in applying the fundamentals to find solutions for new and constantly changing reinsurance opportunities are the hallmarks of success.

The mission of this text is not to solve particular problems or to show how creativity may be applied in any given situation. Rather, it is to introduce concepts, hopefully with sufficient detail so that the reader can in turn apply principles to real problems. We have attempted to bring a fresh perspective to these topics in an effort to enhance understanding and provide basic knowledge about reinsurance. Moving through the changing exposures, business cycles, and ebb and flow of today's society are challenges that reinsurance professionals must meet in accomplishing the work of reinsurance.

Why Does Reinsurance Exist?

Several thousand years ago, merchants shipping goods on the Yangtze River were concerned about a particularly dangerous stretch of rapids. The merchants would dock and wait until ten junks had arrived. They would then unload the goods and put one tenth of their cargo on each craft. After successfully running the rapids, the junks would continue to their destination. The merchants would receive payment for their surviving goods. Each vessel lost would only result in a loss of 10 percent of the merchant's goods. This was an early version of risk management. Later, the same risk posed by these perils would be transferred to others for a price. That was insurance.

Once insurance transactions became commonplace, an enterprising insurance company surely took some kind of risk management action on its own portfolio of insurance policies. Some of the options considered would be best called prevention activities, as they might modify exposure to, or perhaps eliminate or reduce, some of the perils. For example, giving the captain a better sextant would be one type of risk management. Other actions would be called insurance, a transfer of risk for a price. Insurance of insurance? Obviously, a more appropriate term was needed and reinsurance was the consensus choice.

In its simplest form, reinsurance is insurance passed between insurance companies. (This definition is deliberately simplistic for the sake of introduction at this point in the text.) Surely, in the early years, wealthy individuals participated in reinsurance. However, as insurance is now regulated in some form worldwide, reinsurance has become a commercial transaction between companies or specialized reinsurance syndicates. Reinsurance must meet the basic criteria that distinguish insurance from other types of transactions.

There must be a transfer of risk from one party to another. Insurance is between a buyer and a licensed or approved insurer. Reinsurance is between two such licensed or chartered insurers. The parties must be licensed in order for the reinsurance transaction to be fully recognized by insurance regulators.

The outward transfer is called a *cession*. Single risks or bundled risks are ceded from the primary insurer and assumed by the reinsurer. Historically, some reinsurers chose to restrict the term cession to proportional transfers; in current usage, however, the term applies to proportional and nonproportional transfers alike and to property as well as casualty business. This text shall use the broad context, referring to the department that purchases reinsurance for an insurer as the ceded reinsurance department, which directs reinsurance cessions to reinsurers. In turn, the reinsurers assume the business. So the ceding and assumption of reinsurance cessions are references to the process rather than to the structure of the process.

An insurance company takes up insurance business by writing policies that cover single or multiple risks, and, perhaps, multiple lines or classes of business in a single policy. The collection of an insurer's business is called a portfolio. They must manage the exposures contained within the portfolio.

When they choose to transfer some of the exposure to another insurer, or reinsurer, the transfer is called a cession. As with insurance, the cession can be assumed or taken up by a single reinsurer or shared in part by many reinsurers. The early history of this signing-on practice took place when the initial insurer signed the policy and the remaining shares were subscribed by signatures listed below the first signature, hence the term *underwriter.*

The taking up or binding of a contract of reinsurance is called an *assumption.* The entity that assumes the reinsurance can call itself an insurer or reinsurer, but for the purposes of the specific transaction or assumption, the assuming carrier is called the reinsurer.

Given the complexities of today's business world and the high value of the businesses involved, many commercial insurance policies have very large limits. When the primary insurer seeks to cede portions of its portfolio, few companies can subscribe for the whole amount. Thus it is typical for reinsurance transactions to be ceded by one carrier and assumed in part by several reinsurers. In summary, reinsurance is big business, complex, often global, and it takes many forms.

History of Reinsurance

The first recognized, written maritime code was assembled in Rhodes, Greece, about 916 B.C., which became the basis for the first insurance transaction. The Lombardians began to develop this concept circa 1200 A.D. Surely between these dates there were countless transactions of insurance and likely a great many reinsurance transactions as well; however, since we have no written record, this is supposition.

The year 1370 is the earliest written record of some hazardous marine cargo being "laid off" from one insurer to a second.

After the Great Fire of London, in 1666, there soon arose a significant demand for fire insurance on buildings. This motivated further development of nonmarine insurance. Very likely, such an event would also create awareness among insurers of the control and protection of their portfolio. Yet there is no recorded evidence of reinsurance in this business. During this period, nonmarine transactions were between individuals.

The first fire insurance company was created in 1681, and Lloyd's of London began in 1688. Nonmarine insurance had progressed to the stage where companies existed for the purpose of transacting insurance business. Thus there were now parties between whom reinsurance could be transacted.

In 1746, in England, Parliament enacted a statute with the intent of restricting gambling as well as the practice of reinsurance except against bankruptcy or death. This curbed reinsurance activity in England until the statute was repealed in 1864.

In 1798, The Royal Chartered Fire Company, Denmark, was authorized to seek reinsurance. This is the first reference to fire reinsurance; however, the company did not avail itself of this privilege. There were concerns that reinsurers might interfere in the company's primary operations.

Interestingly, the earliest recorded fire reinsurance transaction took place in 1813 when the Eagle Fire Insurance Company of New York assumed all of the outstanding risks of the Union Insurance Company. It is known that the accompanying premium transaction proved quite profitable for Eagle, with a 15 percent loss ratio on net earned premium with no profit sharing.

An actual reinsurance treaty between the following companies dates to 1821:

Cedent:	National Assurance Company Against Fire; Paris, France
Assuming Reinsurer:	Company of United Proprietors; Belgium

The Supreme Court of New York validated reinsurance as a legal transaction between the following in an 1837 case:

Cedent:	New York Bowery Insurance Company
Assuming Reinsurer:	New York Fire Insurance Company

In 1844, the current system of life reinsurance began. The first life treaty dates to 1858.

The late 1800s brought the formation of the first independent reinsurance companies, including Cologne Reinsurance Company, Germany (1852); Swiss

Reinsurance of Zurich, Switzerland (1863); Reinsurance Company Limited, England (1867); Munich Reinsurance Company, Germany (1880); Nordisk Re of Copenhagen, Denmark (1894); and The First Reinsurance Company of Hartford, United States (1912). The First Reinsurance Company of Hartford was owned by Munich Re. By the time of this formation, several foreign reinsurers were operating in the States under their own names.

How Reinsurance Works

Reinsurance, as defined above, is an insurance transaction between insurance companies. This transaction has the following basic requirements:

1. An insurable interest must exist.
2. Risk must exist at the inception of the contract, although it may change during the period of the contract.
3. The reinsurance must transfer some portion of the risk from cedent to reinsurer.
4. Some consideration must be passed from the cedent to the assuming reinsurer.
5. Reinsurance relies upon the good faith of both the cedent and reinsurer.
6. The agreement is one of indemnity.
7. The reinsurer is liable only to the cedent.

The first four criteria make the transaction one of insurance, distinguish it from speculation, and meet requirements of regulatory and taxing authorities.

The fifth is a standard that has applied throughout the industry since its inception. An insurance policy, particularly a personal lines policy, is a contract between an individual and an insurance corporation. The parties are not considered equals. The policy is written by the insurer, so the terms may be biased. Consumer protection laws have corrected this imbalance so that the individual does have some leverage in court. Reinsurance, however, is between two insurers, considered equals.

Professional ethics, backed by a clause in the agreement, require utmost good faith. Any difference in outcome between the parties is thought to arise from happenstance rather than a lack of good faith by one of the parties.

A contract of indemnity is one that responds to economic loss, not merely damage. The cedent suffers a claim covered by the reinsurance which results in an economic loss; in turn, a portion of that financial loss is transferred to the reinsurer.

A policyholder has no right to take action against the reinsurer. A treaty, or batch contract, rarely specifies any particular policy. A facultative certificate, or single-risk contract, may specify a particular policy. Nonetheless, the reinsurance is not covering the policyholder's risk. Being a contract of indemnity, the reinsurance applies after the insurer has incurred economic damage. It is to the insurer's indemnity that the reinsurance applies.

FUNCTIONS OF REINSURANCE

The functions refer to the motivating needs of the ceding carrier. Each of the functions corresponds to a specific need of the reinsurance buyer arising out of the risk management considerations about the portfolio of business or perhaps an individual policy it has written or plans to write.

Primary Functions

There are four generally recognized primary functions of reinsurance: capacity, catastrophe, stabilization, and financial. Each will be introduced to explain the motivational aspects and later discussed as they apply to specific types of reinsurance.

Capacity
This is perhaps the most obvious need. Insurers cannot afford the potential of a single policy ruining their overall results. They can decline large limit exposures, or they may seek to write some portion of such business, obtaining reinsurance protection which will limit the effect of any single loss on the insurer's results.

Catastrophe
There is a need to limit the impact on an insurer's assets from a single catastrophic event. A catastrophe would be defined as multiple claims or losses arising out of a single same "occurrence." Typically catastrophe relates to property coverage and generally to the perils of storm, flood, earthquake, or conflagration, but it also applies to liability situations if a concentration or flaw exists where multiple accidents result from a single cause. The term "occurrence" has special meanings for property and for liability usage. Part of the semantics stems from the fact that not all casualty events are accidental. This will be discussed in detail later. (Note: There are times when confined interpretations are especially important and times when the usage is intended in a broad context. This happens to be one of the latter cases.)

Stabilization

Insurers strive to produce more or less level results from year to year. Stable results support planning, enable investment in the company by stockholders, and help to meet requirements of lenders from whom some portion of the capital may have been borrowed. Risk assumption is the business of insurance, which surely can be volatile. Thus, insurers are receptive to stabilization products which tend to level results for a fixed cost.

Stabilization should be distinguished from capacity and catastrophe. Surely a capacity problem or a severe catastrophe can affect the company's stability. Yet, volatility can arise from other causes. Instability may be a result of multiple problems arising from multiple policies. It may be the result of a frequency in claims on policies which individually are not large enough to require reinsurance or of sufficient concentration to require catastrophe reinsurance. Instability can also arise from poor pricing of a large class of business or from an unintended or expanded coverage resulting from a judicial interpretation of policy coverage or conditions.

Financial

In modern times, this need has expanded, as companies consider tax implications and related factors in their planning. There are plenty of financial motivations. One company may want to start a new line of business but lack the capital required. Another may be reacting to adverse results or new laws and may want to adjust its business. A third may have secured agreement with an outstanding producer and may be concerned about volume outstripping its conservative capital requirements.

The financial function is a broad concept. The other functions eventually contribute to the company's financial results. There may be multiple needs and to some extent these needs may overlap.

The four primary functions of reinsurance are important to keep in mind. Each time a transaction is consummated, the cedent as well as the assuming reinsurer should grasp the purpose behind the reinsurance, that is what is motivating this transaction. A false purpose may be stated, or the purpose may be misunderstood. The motivations should be known to ensure that the reinsurance contract satisfies the basic needs, is designed correctly, is priced properly, and is a potentially profitable transaction for all parties.

Secondary Functions

In addition to considerations, there are other secondary functions of reinsurance.

Market Intelligence

An insurer may use reinsurance as a vehicle to gain access to the experience of a specialist in a particular field.

Advice

Reinsurance companies do provide support for ceding companies. By laying off a share of the business, the ceding company may secure advice (such as sophisticated pricing) which the reinsurer will offer as part of the package. The reinsurer is motivated to help improve the profitability of its particular reinsureds. If the cedent does a better job, the probability of a profit for the reinsurer is enhanced.

Margin

During certain competitive periods, reinsurance may be offered at very attractive prices. Some insurance companies view the margins as attractive and thus take advantage of production capabilities in the hope of making profit on the expense side of the ledger. If this motivation is one-sided, the cedent is looking for a far greater share of any profit. Thus, it is likely that the reinsurer who enters such a deal will come out a loser.

While attractive commissions and leveraged margins may motivate the purchase of reinsurance, there is a fundamental flaw in such logic. Reinsurance should be viewed with a long-term perspective. Reinsurers may accept loss in one year, with the understanding that the terms will permit a reasonable profit over a reasonable period of time. Deliberate inequity based on greed hinders creation of mutually acceptable long-term relationships. Sooner or later the relationship will deteriorate into a crisis of some sort. Crisis relates to instability, which violates one of the primary functions of reinsurance.

Again, awareness of the needs or motivations underlying a specific transaction is critical to its success. Reinsurance is a negotiation process, so profits may not end up equal for all parties. The test is a reasonable minimum profit for each party, for only on that basis can a successful long-term relationship be established.

REINSURANCE PRIMER

This section is written as a primer for those who are familiar with insurance concepts and want to learn about reinsurance. As such, it is an overview written in simple terms and intended to expand the introduction of reinsurance and initiate the usage of some common reinsurance terms.

We will begin with capacity, the prime motivator pressing the insurer to address the concern that some submissions, while seemingly well priced, have limit requirements somewhat above that typically afforded by the insurer. While the carrier can decline the submission, there are some reasons why the business should be written. Perhaps, the caliber of the insured is outstanding. Perhaps this acceptance will lead to additional business from the source. Perhaps it is simply more attractive than the lower limit business already on the books. The company is in business to accept risk, thus it seeks to write this business, but only if it can manage the higher limit.

The term *relativity* is frequently used in this text to show that comparison is an important factor in reinsurance. For example, the size of an insurer can be viewed in terms of policy count or premium, or its asset base. Therefore, size is a characteristic that can be used to compare insurers as long as the item of measure is known.

Capacity is another relative measure. Company A writes policies with as much as $1 million per policy, while another writes policies only up to $500,000. This measure can be expanded to reveal more information of the two companies. Suppose Company A has a written premium volume of $35 million and Company B has $12 million. The ratio of capacity to premium is calculated as follows:

Company A $= \$1,000,000 / \$33,000,000 = 0.030\%$
Company B $= \$500,000 / \$12,000,000 = 0.042\%$

The latter figure is a ratio or relativity; it compares the two amounts. In this illustration, the relativity shows that Company A has a lower capacity-to-premium ratio, and is thus, more conservative in using its capacity. So a relativity can be employed to learn more by comparison that can be learned by looking at either one of the measures by themselves.

Just as size can be measured in several ways, the capacity relativity can be measured in more than one way. This may seem confusing, but remember that a relativity is simply the quotient between two amounts and that we can learn more by comparing relativities.

Capacity is set upon reflection about the kinds of exposures to be assumed in keeping with the financial base of the insurer. One rule of thumb is to keep the per policy capacity under 1.5 percent of capital, or alternatively, 3 percent of the total written premium volume. (The amount of capital in the company, called capital and surplus for insurers, reflects the net asset base of the company; thus, 1.5 percent is a relatively small portion to expose for any single risk. The total written premium-to-surplus ratio has historically been about 2:1; thus, the translation of that same ratio from a capital or asset base to a premium base shifts the ratio from 1.5 percent to 3 percent.) That would keep the loss from any single claim to a modest portion of the company's financial base. One loss could not put the company out of business.

Consider the following example: A company, Zeus Insurance, has been conservatively writing limits under 1 percent of its surplus. Zeus receives a submission, which while being under the 1.5 percent industry standard, is above the 1 percent corporate guideline and modestly above the typical policy limit offered by Zeus.

This scenario is a normal business quandary, requiring tough choices made day to day. Clearly, if the limit was 25 percent of surplus, the decision would be easy, and this business would be declined. The hard decision arises when the choice is slightly outside the desired area or just beyond the guideline. Before proceeding with reinsurance specifics, let us set some characteristics of the company's portfolio of policies on the books. If Zeus happens to be a brand-new insurer, with just a few thousand policies, its limits distribution might appear something like Exhibit 1.1.

This type of distribution chart displays the profile for business subject to a specific treaty reinsurance contract. Because it applies to a portfolio or batch of policies, the pictorial is not applicable to a facultative cession.

Each vertical column stands for a single policy, although the thicker columns represent more than one policy. The number of policies is not intended to be accurate. The height represents the limit; it is not drawn to scale.

Why use a diagram that has no scale? If you were asked to sketch the boundary of the United States in ten seconds, it would not be accurate. Yet if you showed the sketch to someone, he or she would recognize it. The chart illustrates that reinsurance can be used to alter the shape or profile of the subject business.

We shall always use a triangular distribution for immature portfolios or business of new insurers. A triangle is used because the top is small; a new

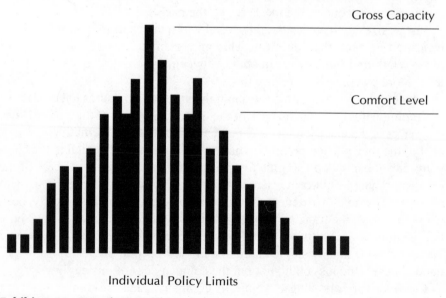

Gross Capacity

Comfort Level

Individual Policy Limits

Exhibit 1.1.   Distribution Chart: Immature Portfolio

insurer would not take up very large limits while it was just getting started. There would be many small and medium-sized limits, but few large ones. A triangular distribution seems to conveys this scenario.

For mature portfolios, where the insurer has been in business many years and has had the opportunity to build consistency into its business, a bell-shaped curve is appropriate. Such a curve is also called a normal curve. It is typical of a profile for a statistically varied, large group. It has the largest limit in the middle and progressively smaller limits spread on either side.

Since our focus is not on the precise number of policies, the triangular or bell curve is displayed without policy detail; it is simply a sketch of the limits profile. Many reinsurers use a box to illustrate these diagrams. This text uses the triangular and bell-shaped curve to demonstrate that one outcome of reinsurance is to alter the basic profile of the insurer's portfolio.

Coming back to our example, Zeus, a new insurer, would likely have an immature portfolio and a triangular limits distribution. The most frequent limit is low and there are just a few higher limits.

The company will naturally have a comfort level, which it typically uses as a limit of choice, sometimes referred to as the amount the company is "willing to lose." In this example, the Zeus comfort level happens to be 1 percent of its capital. On occasion, there will be an exceptional submission requesting greater limits. If the terms and price are right, the company will accept business moderately beyond its general level of comfort. This relates to the offer of a policy with limits at 1.5 percent of the Zeus capital base. (Note: The specific amount of limit has not been mentioned. This technique makes the example more universal. It is more important to stress the relationship of the comfort level to a particular company guideline. Obviously, that guideline and the aggressiveness of the comfort level vary widely from insurer to insurer.)

Being conservative, Zeus may seek to protect itself from those exposures accepted beyond its comfort level. This is one of the classic motivators underlying the purchase of reinsurance. The concern leads Zeus to seek protection in much the same way a family or company seeks protection from exposure to economic loss. In turn, reinsurance companies design reinsurance products to meet specific needs. In short, the ceding company meets an assuming reinsurer and the exposure is transferred for a price. If the price is too high, there is no sale. If the price is too low, there will be no interest on the part of assuming reinsurers in taking up the coverage. The "right" price is reached via negotiation.

If the portfolio contains risks which are dissimilar, presenting a variety of risks with different kinds or types of exposure, the situation may not be conducive to being bundled into one agreement. Under such circumstances, each risk would likely be considered and underwritten individually, in a process called *facultative reinsurance,* and priced on the merits of the specific situation. With just a limited number of risks, there would be no savings in bundling the cessions.

If the risks share a common class or line of business, and if there are enough to amass a fair-sized bulk premium, then they are more likely be ceded in the aggregate. Homogeneity is an important consideration in the bundling or portfolio transferring process. A single negotiation will take into account the minor variances within the group of policies to be protected. Such a contract is referred to as *treaty reinsurance*. Treaties are generally written for a longer term, permitting additional policies to be added, without individual policy approval, as long as they meet the conditions outlined in the original agreement.

Normally, reinsurance treaties do not apply unless there is a large number of policies involved. Under such circumstances the distribution will no longer fit the triangle configuration. Probability forces the distribution to a normal curve (see Exhibit 1.2). The normal or bell-shaped curve is the statistical pattern that emerges when a group is very large and variables (such as policy limits) are being measured. Once a portfolio of business matures it will naturally take this sort of shape. However, selection criteria may skew the curve; the criteria could inhibit high limits, or alternatively, press for full usage of available capacity. While there are always such concerns for the cedent or assuming reinsurer, we will not address them in this example.

With the triangular distribution described above, it is unlikely that there would be a sufficient number of similar policies to allow Zeus to secure a treaty or an automatic reinsurance agreement. Zeus could certainly seek out facultative reinsurers, placing each policy on its merits at an agreed price for the specific policy situation. To manage each policy exposure, the specifications of each policy could be presented to facultative reinsurers for acceptance while the policy is in the initial underwriting stage. Zeus would seek to negotiate the terms of this facultative arrangement before binding each

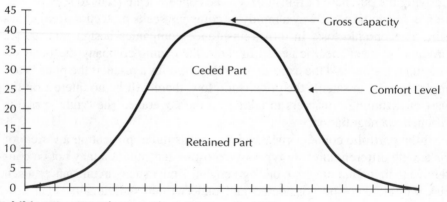

Exhibit 1.2.   Distribution Chart: Mature Portfolio

policy. This would permit Zeus to be certain its large limit exposure was managed prior to final agreement or policy binding.

Some years later, Zeus would be writing thousands of policies each year. Its policy limits distribution would be more mature, and it would likely assume a bell shape, with many small policies and a regular, proportionate number of policies with larger limits. The comfort level may have increased modestly with the growth in volume, but Zeus would continue to have some sort of guideline to control higher limit submissions.

Skewness is a graphical term, used here in reference to an imbalance within the limits that comprise the business written. Clearly, the curve will not be as smooth as displayed above if more lower or more higher limits are sold. Some treaties bend with, or shift as a result of, skewness; others do not. Underwriters are trained to test for aberrations and either adjust the rate or decline the risk if the distribution is uncomfortable.

In this text, we shall continue to apply the bell-shaped or probability curve in diagrams to show the basic reinsurance structures. With a firm appreciation of the fundamentals, one can utilize these or similar diagrams to draw general conclusions; distortions may exist in the diagrams when compared to cases in the real world.

Zeus can accomplish reinsurance of its capacity needs using a number of reinsurance structures. With a mature distribution, it can approach treaty reinsurers seeking an automatic arrangement. The treaty will require a credible number of similar policies. Homogeneous policies is a better term, as they must be similar in more than limit and have consistency in kind, class, pricing, and other characteristics.

Proportional Reinsurance

One way reinsurance can be arranged is on a proportional or percentage sharing basis. The sharing may be fixed or variable.

Quota Share = Fixed Percentage

In this most fundamental type of reinsurance treaty, a common ratio is set when the agreement is bound. This contract cedes a fixed portion of applicable premiums and responds by paying that same portion of all claims and loss adjustment expense (LAE). A $1 claim will be split on this proportion.

The reinsurer has an agreed quota on each and every policy. This *pro rata* or proportional share applies to premiums as well as losses (see Exhibit 1.3).

For example, a 25 percent quota share means 25 percent of all premium is ceded on business applicable to that treaty. It may allow for a commission to the insurer for producing that business and for the continuing work involved in handling that policyholder. If an intermediary is involved, it is paid from

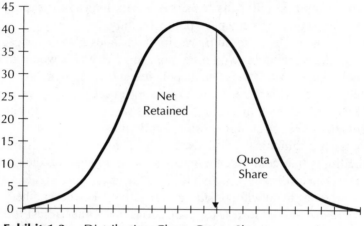

Exhibit 1.3.   Distribution Chart: Quota Share

that premium as well. The 25 percent share applies to additional premiums, (such as may arise if the policy is rated and audited on receipts, sales, or other prescribed variable features) or if a return premium is required. The reinsurer responds for 25 percent of any recognized loss and loss expense applicable to policies which are specifically ceded or automatically ceded as subject business to this contract.

Surplus Share or Surplus Treaty = Variable Percentage

This is not facultative reinsurance, but it does require cession handling on an individual policy basis. The surplus treaty sets protocol for cessions by class or kind of policy (see Exhibit 1.4). The primary carrier sets the portion ceded at the time it binds coverage on each policy. For example, Zeus may have a different maximum and comfort level for homeowner's business as opposed to restaurant business and thus choose ratios appropriate for each line within general guidelines set for the class. The reinsurer has accepted the general tone of writings and permits flexibility in cessions to the treaty.

The surplus treaty requires an extra level of trust. The reinsurer assumes the primary carrier will follow the present standards by class and that homogeneity will be maintained within categories. The reinsurer should undertake specific measurements or audits to ensure that the guidelines have been met. The treaty requires a specific apportionment upon writing or binding each policy. The company should set procedures in writing and exercise control on its underwriters to ensure that this obligation is maintained. It is a two-way street, with extra duties applicable to both parties. The reinsurers should monitor or audit the cessions to be sure the cessions were done properly.

The portion of each premium ceded must follow the preset percentage, and when a claim arises, the cedent should prove the allocation percentage was

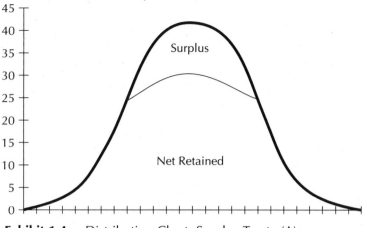

Exhibit 1.4. Distribution Chart: Surplus Treaty (A)

made upon binding and that the appropriate portion of premium was indeed ceded. The reinsurer responds by paying that specific percentage of the loss.

Following guidelines within the treaty agreement, the insurer may cede 25 percent of policy A and 37 percent of policy B. This allocation is made at the time each policy is bound and must be documented within the insurer's policy files. All subsequent premium and loss transactions are split between the reinsurer and insurer according to that original proportion. Policy B would respond for $.37 on a $1 claim to that policy, or $3,700 on a $10,000 claim to that policy.

Note, the above diagram does not clearly indicate how a specific policy is to be split. However, it does indicate the general result desired, that the capacity of the insurer will be limited on a variable basis.

In real terms, the following surplus diagram portrays a more typical distribution (see Exhibit 1.5). Here, the cedent has followed a pattern by class, ceding a different portion and writing a different limit by class or kind of policy.

In every surplus situation, the cedent has the privilege of choosing just how much to cede on each policy. Thus the cedent holds the potential for adverse selection, keeping more of the good business and ceding more of the poorer business. Terms should restrict or limit such freedom and keep the potential for adversity low. The price for a surplus treaty should be more than for a quota share because the reinsured should pay for the privilege of retaining this flexibility.

Excess of Loss Per Risk (Loss Attaching)

This type of treaty does not respond to or attach to each policy. Rather, it responds to claims. As a contract of indemnity, the reinsurance attaches once

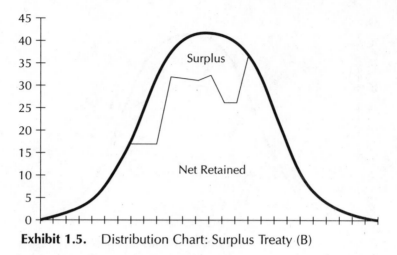

Exhibit 1.5.   Distribution Chart: Surplus Treaty (B)

the claim reaches the preset attachment level. Small losses are paid in full by the cedent. In situations where the loss exceeds the attachment point, the reinsurer responds for only that amount in excess of the attachment point.

The attachment point is like the crest of a dam. Claims reaching a lower point are held net, and that portion exceeding the crest flows over to the reinsurer (see Exhibit 1.6).

Most excess of loss treaties are priced on a rated basis. The rate is determined based on anticipated exposures or perhaps on the insurer's record of losses over the past several years. Some excess treaties set minimum and maximum commissions and a pricing scheme based on loss ratio levels. These concepts will be discussed further in Chapter 5.

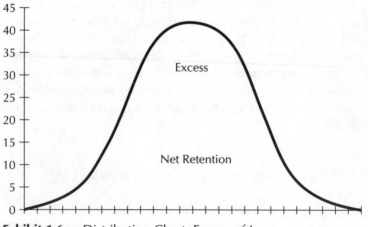

Exhibit 1.6.   Distribution Chart: Excess of Loss

The rate applies to all policies of the specific kind or class listed within the treaty agreement. It may delete certain excluded policies from this basis. The total premium from all applicable policies is called the subject premium. The rate multiplied by the subject premium determines the price for the treaty. We shall also refer to the group of applicable policies as the subject business of the treaty.

The subject premium includes all policies permitted in the kinds or classes listed in the treaty, *regardless of policy size*. It is not necessary that the policy limit exceed the attachment point.

Consider an example of a treaty for $150,000 in excess of $100,000 on homeowner's business, where the insurer agrees not to write any home valued over $250,000. (It is normal to specify the capacity or maximum limit of the subject business.) For the sake of simplicity, let us consider only the property portion of the homeowner's policy. It is possible that the company would not have any loss greater than $100,000 during the treaty term. However, each large loss is individually reported to the reinsurers. If one claim had a $135,000 reserve, the reinsurers would set a $35,000 reserve. The excess reinsurers would not begin to pay claims until after the insurer has paid out the first $100,000. Then too, the cedent first pays amounts above the attachment point and seeks reimbursement from the reinsurer.

Thus, excess treaties do not respond to each and every loss like proportional treaties. They respond once the loss exceeds the attachment point or level and only to those specific losses. They also stop paying once the maximum is reached.

It is important to understand that the price for this type of treaty structure applies to all subject policies, but the coverage responds only to losses which exceed the attachment point. If the above $150,000 excess of $100,000 treaty had a 6 percent rate, the reinsurer would receive 6 percent of all premiums collected on subject policies. Some years might not have any large claims. Other years might have several claims with payments exceeding $100,000.

Skewness

Skewness is the distortion of the bell-shaped curve of a distribution chart when the underlying portfolio contains a greater number of higher or lower limit policies. This would tend to flatten the curve or make it steeper. Other variations might tend to make one side larger and the other smaller. The shape is skewed if it is not the perfect bell shape with which we are familiar.

A quota share participant will suffer on equal terms with the ceding reinsurer if the portfolio happens to be out of balance or skewed. If, for example, there is a preponderance of large limits (or low limits), the quota share reinsurance follows directly and the reinsurers fare in proportion to the cedent. However, excess of loss reinsurance does not follow this course. If there is a preponderance of large limits, the reinsurers may fare worse than the cedent.

If the limits are universally low, the reinsurers may have fewer losses than expected. Happenstance also plays its part; however, if the limits are larger, on average, the losses will also be larger, and the converse also usually holds.

Skewness may exist as an imbalance within the portfolio of business. It may be unexpected or unplanned but materializes in a manner that puts more, or less, of the burden of the exposure on reinsurers. That tendency is the object of underwriting and pricing. The monitoring activity is an attempt by reinsurers to assure themselves that the business is progressing as intended or as outlined in the reinsurance submission.

The bell-shaped curve is an ideal rarely achieved in the real world. Even a mature portfolio will have a distribution that requires analysis by reinsurers. Close review of the actual distribution of limits is most important in determining the need for reinsurance, in assessing the attachment point, in negotiating the price, and in making the acceptability decision of the reinsurer.

The true test of reinsurer profitability is whether the total reinsurance premium collected over several years exceeds the losses paid during the same period, plus a measure for expenses and profit. From the perspective of the ceding carrier, the test is whether the functional need was met and whether the reinsurers paid losses promptly. Subsequent chapters shall attempt to further illustrate that success is viewed and measured in different terms by the cedent insurer and the assuming reinsurer.

2

REINSURANCE FUNDAMENTALS

This chapter will address some fundamental terms and concepts that must be understood for full comprehension of more complex topics in reinsurance. The reader may already be familiar with the terms used in this chapter; however, it is important to read this material before proceeding. The usage is often different for reinsurers and insurers. For example, many statistics, such as unearned premium, are readily available at an insurance company, but might not be reported to reinsurers; thus reinsurers often estimate such numbers. Also, reinsurers may have a concern only if the pattern falls outside that which they have found to hold for many companies. Thus it is not unusual for reinsurers to apply a theoretical formula as they analyze a particular reinsurance contract.

In addition to providing some fundamental definitions, this chapter offers perspective on how reinsurers approach some aspects in common with the rest of the insurance industry.

ACCIDENT, EVENT, AND UNDEFINED TERMS

When a reinsurance contract defines terms, the very first definition must use some words to explain the particular concept. These initial words are not usually defined. *Accident* and *event* are such words.

Most reinsurance contracts apply generally to specific classes or kinds of policies, except as excluded. Basically, permissible claims are determined by the terms of the cedent's policy, subject to special restrictions within the reinsurance contract. Thus, words that refer to the happenings that are covered must be broad and general. Applicability is determined not by defining the event, but by eliminating certain characteristics. For example, facultative reinsurance may require that the loss amount be greater than $25 million and arise at a particular site. Thus *event* and *accident* need not be defined, because other constraints within the reinsurance contract, such as the dollar requirement in the above example, virtually eliminate that which is not intended for coverage.

Although perhaps difficult to explain, the use of *undefined terms* is natural, understood within the law, and actually desired by both buyers and sellers of reinsurance. To be more precise in a contract would serve to limit or constrain the types of occurrences to which the coverage is intended to apply. Then too, the complete list would make the policy far too lengthy. The use of undefined terms, then, is part of the art of contract writing.

Note that some such terms are defined within the cedent's policy language and thus need not be redefined.

Some people use the term *accident* for liability and *event* for property coverages. However, a fire may not be an accident, so at times event is a better word. Libel, slander, certain malpractice occurrences, and other casualty situations may not be accidents either. This text uses the two terms interchangeably. Do not assume such terms always match your understanding.

It is necessary to understand the use of undefined terms when analyzing a reinsurance contract. The terms should be considered by cedent and assuming reinsurer alike, to be certain the basis of the contract is set on appropriate ground. Such considerations require breadth of understanding, for one must be in a position to evaluate flexibility as well as constraint and foresee how these may evolve in the future.

ACCIDENT RECORD KEEPING CONCEPTS

Time of Occurrence

An event or accident happens at a specific point in time. It may require scientific measurement or adjudication, but the timing is critical and must be ascertained. The time and place at which an event happened are key determinants of the application of a specific policy.

The Claim Reporting Process

There is a natural delay between the happening of an event and when that event is reported to the insurer by the agent or policyholder. Most insurers and reinsurers keep records which display both the date the event happened and the date it was *reported.* Such gaps in time also exist between the receipt of the initial advice and the setting of the reserve. The process of taking a reported accident or event and researching to see if the policy does apply is often considered by primary carriers as one step or one process. Reinsurers typically record this in minute detail, being quite precise as to the stage of each claim. The following terms are used in the claim reporting process.

Date of Occurrence
This is the date the event happens. It may be an artificially assigned date, as often happens in aggregate claim situations where the policy inception date is assigned for all claims "batched" within the aggregate.

Insurance Reporting Date
This is the initial reporting date by the claimant to the insurer.

Reinsurance Reporting Date
This is the date the reinsurer first receives formal notice from the insurer.

Recognized Claim
The reinsurer's claim department first tests to see if the reported event is applicable to a particular type of policy and otherwise matches records of the cedent. The process includes checking to see if the event fits within the definitions afforded under the policy and if the event is within the bounds of the reinsurance contract. Reinsurers double check applicability to the policy in this process; they do not automatically assume the insurer has done its review adequately. Thus, when a reported claim is believed to apply to and fit within the terms of the policy and the reinsurance contract, it is recognized by the reinsurer.

"Not Recognized" Claim

If a reported claim does not apply, because coverage does not exist or extend to that claim, it can be dismissed before being recorded; the claim is *not recognized*. A dismissed claim is not opened and should not appear on the reinsurer's books. An example might be a property claim sent in error to the cedent's casualty reinsurer. The reinsurer would not recognize such a claim. Such claims should not exist within the reinsurer's claim counts or data processing system and should not be part of the records reviewed for renewal.

Precautionary Claim

This is a claim which happens to not yet fully meet the terms of the reinsurance contract. For example, the accident may be one with very serious injuries, but in which there is a remote probability that the insured will be held liable. Reinsurers record these as recognized claims and they may or may not be coded as incurred claims within the reinsurer's system.

Denied Claim

These claims are considered disputed events. They are submitted in good faith by the cedent, but not recognized by the reinsurer as falling within the reinsurance terms. On occasion the reinsurer uses this category as a testing stage, where specific questions are formally related to the cedent. It is a higher step in the process because the reinsurer will definitely create a claim file and enter it into the computer system. The claim may reside in this category for years while discussions and research continue. Some reinsurers refer to these as resisted claims, but the denial step is common to the classification.

There are typically not too many denied claims, so some reinsurers deal with them "off the books." This special classification is thought to be necessary in some instances because the reinsurers do not wish to accept the claim formally or tacitly by recognizing the claim. There are some claims that fall into this category after being recognized and reserved by reinsurers, who later learn that the claim was not appropriate.

Incurred Claim

If a claim is recognized and not precautionary, it is recorded in the reinsurer's records as an incurred claim.

The Evaluation Process

An event is unknown until reported and is not incurred until it has been recognized and recorded. The following terms are used in the evaluation process.

Open or Closed Claims

The incurred claim is officially on the books as an open claim. *Open* and *closed* are merely status categories of incurred claims; thus, these terms hold the same meaning in both primary and reinsurance claims, requiring a specific closure action by the reinsurer's claim staff.

Reserved Claim

Reinsurers maintain records for many claims that do not have a reserve. These may be precautionary or simply not reserved. Some insurers routinely assign a $1 reserve to claims that are recognized within the policy, forcing any recognized claim to be a reserved claim. Once reserved, reinsurers pay particularly close attention to developments. If the evaluation process suggests that some liability does exist, an amount is posted. The claim is then referred to as *reserved.* Those claims with nil reserve or which have "zero" posted are *nonreserved.* There are differences between claims evaluated as having nil potential and those just beginning the evaluation process. Some reinsurers do differentiate between nonreserved and nil reserved claims. However, the focus is on incurred cases, where the exposure has been evaluated. The reinsurance processing assumes these nonreserved or nil matters will sort out in time, so most reinsurers classify these together, at least temporarily, as nonreserved.

A reserve does not necessarily imply that the cedent feels the claim is wholly valid. Reinsurers still have the intention to question the claim and perhaps deny coverage or payment. The reserve is a measure of the liability presented within the report but may not totally reflect the reinsurer's belief about the merits of the case. The process of reserving is procedural and important as the reinsurer undertakes its fiduciary responsibility to its owners to be sure the event meets all the terms and conditions of the policy. It is the reinsurer's goal to be sure any amount ultimately paid is warranted, appropriate, and reasonable.

Reserves may be posted for indemnity amounts and also as budgeting of expenses. Reinsurers are particular about separating these categories for reasons that will be explained later in Chapter 10. In fact, reinsurers require that ceded expenses, that is, expenses of the ceding insurer, be split between internal and external expenses. Generally, the reinsurance does not apply to internal expenses such as company claim staff and file maintenance costs. Such costs are covered by any commission allotted in the reinsurance terms.

Those external expenses which are loss adjustment expenses, for example legal costs and expenses to contain the overall claim potential, are considered as applicable to most reinsurances.

Paid

Any payments made toward the claim amount are recorded. The reinsurer controls the takedown of reserves that follow once a payment is made. Typically, reinsurers keep track of claims *closed without payment* separately from those that are closed with payment.

Incurred Amount

The incurred total on a particular claim is the sum of still open reserves plus payments to date. Some insurance carriers use the term *total reserve* for the sum of paid amounts plus unpaid reserves. An alternative is *total compensation amount.* Both are cumbersome logically, but some feel it makes for easier data processing. Reinsurers do not consider payments to be reserves.

Reinsurers normally reduce the reserve by the amount of each payment and periodically reassess the claims valuation to see if the incurred total needs revision. Thus, reserves are considered as outstanding amounts only.

POLICY RECORD KEEPING CONCEPTS

The Offering

Reinsurers call the reinsurance application a submission or offering. There are many cedents, insurers, captives, self-insureds, self-insured groups, and risk retention groups and relatively few reinsurers. Submissions are received in significant numbers. Thus the term "offering" has an "unsolicited" connotation, despite the fact that reinsurers press hard to produce business opportunities.

There is considerable information to be transferred in the submission. Terms and pricing must be negotiated. In a great many cases, the reinsurer will visit the insurer and audit or inspect records. There may be several exchanges in the negotiation process before the terms are set. Thus the offering or submission may include several documents received over an extended period of time.

Binding Business

With the issuance of a binder and confirmation thereon, the account is *bound.* At this point, the account is offered, considered, and consummated. On the insurance level, *consummated* usually means that a deposit or part of the premium has been paid. A treaty or facultative contract is consummated when both companies agree it is bound. In normal reinsurance transactions the initial premium for a contract does not flow for 60 to 90 days. Some contracts are paid "in arears," or after the term or quarter. Thus the term "consummated" has a different meaning at the reinsurance level.

Written

When a policy is bound, it becomes written business. The premium from all policies written in a given period is called written premium. Typically the word *written* is used instead of *consummated*.

In Force

A bound policy is *in force* for its specified term. The binder may be issued a month or so in advance, so it is technically possible for an account to be bound but cancelled before it becomes in force. However this is so rare that the in-force figures are used interchangeably with the binder totals.

There are situations where the insurance and reinsurance statistics are based on rough terms that reduce the number of categories tallied because the policy counts are so large that extended precision is not material. One should be aware of the technicalities for interpretation purposes, but not concerned that some error is introduced.

DEVELOPMENT RECORD KEEPING CONCEPTS

Reinsurers are vitally concerned about the time line of events. Most of the exposures that they accept are time-sensitive. Both premiums and losses must fall within the specified period and meet conditions of the agreement. Premiums are rarely one-payment transactions. Claims are generally evaluated, reevaluated, and handled intensively. The claim counts, reserve, and payment totals that apply to a portfolio of policies must be measured monthly or quarterly. That measurement process continues until all reporting has ceased and all incurred claims are closed. For many kinds and classes of business, that process may extend 15 or 30 years. One example is worker's compensation, where the insurer may be responsible for deterioration in the illness or injury which may develop many years after the event. Another example is injury to a child where the case may not be settled until the child reaches 21 years of age. Other cases that are slow to develop include asbestosis or perhaps accountant's professional liability cases.

Year

It is important to understand the concept of *year* as it is applied to insurance and reinsurance. Coverage questions, measuring and reporting results, allocation of premiums and losses for pricing, and other matters all require understanding of the span of time involved and what is included within the statistics.

Briefly, the term *year* is used by insurers and reinsurers to refer to a fiscal period. It is applied loosely: its duration may not be exactly 365 days but will likely represent an average of about 12 months. Suppose a company wishes to shift its fiscal year from December 15 to December 31 to make its fiscal year a calendar year. It may request a policy term of 365 + 16 days so that upon renewal it will have the desired basis. That 381-day period is considered an *annual* policy. Reinsurers accept odd-length terms as part of the "year."

Some policies are written as continuous or as having an *open* term. Most can be rerated annually. Reinsurers consider these to be a series of single-term policies. Semantics are not held tight in this instance. The reinsurance focus is on policies with terms at or about a year.

A collection of policies by an insurer, a treaty which applies to many policies, or a portfolio of many treaties obviously must contain policies with a variety of terms, the average of which should be about 12 months.

The reinsurance underwriter must inquire whether a specific cedent writes multiple-year policies without the right to rerate on an annual basis. The cedent must not mask this practice and should feel obligated to inform the reinsurer if it varies significantly from the custom and standard of the industry.

Calendar Year

Calendar year refers to the term of a collection or portfolio of policies that are underwritten and have an inception date within a specific calendar or fiscal year. The key is the policy inception date. A specific policy will fall into a calendar year if it has an effective date between the first day of the calendar year and the day specified as the last day.

The *calendar period* is more precise for terms that are shorter or longer, say 15 months; however, one may occasionally find reference to a calendar year with such an odd length. It need not begin on January 1; the term may truly be applied on a fiscal basis. Generally, this term is applied to all matters recorded within an annual or fiscal period.

It is very important to understand that the calendar year term applies to all activity that is recorded during that term. Like tax reports and fiscal year statements, this sweeps in all collections and payments that are booked in the year. In insurance and reinsurance this is the statutory basis that is reported to regulators and printed in the Annual Statement. Generally, premiums reflect activity from only the past few years, since all older years have premiums that are fully earned and collected. All loss activity, whether it be a new report of an old event or a change in reserve on an old claim, is recorded within the calendar year records (see Exhibit 2.1).

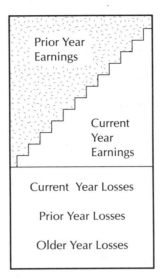

Exhibit 2.1.   Calendar Year

The calendar year is a collection of the current activity. It does not attempt to match losses with the premiums on the same group of policies.

Policy Year

Most insurance policies are in force for a term of one year. However, for various reasons some policies are issued for shorter terms. Some are written for a year plus "odd time," which refers to terms written to adjust the policy so that its expiration date is more appropriate. Odd time may also apply to situations like completed operations that take somewhat longer than 12 months. Typically policies that are written for multiple years are treated as a series of annual terms. The standard is to set new prices on each anniversary. On average, a policy year is considered to be about 12 months.

Obviously, there are variations. Some exposures suit a longer term. Some just do not possess convenient annual break points. Some may have aggregate provisions that apply to longer terms. Longer terms, with particular conditions, require special consideration by reinsurers. These situations should be acknowledged and discussed during treaty negotiations, as the reinsurer needs such information to design and price coverage, and the reinsured wants to be sure such policies are indeed covered. This is a dual obligation; the cedent's to inform and the reinsurer's to ask.

There are some differences between terms of treaty reinsurance and facultative reinsurance that should be addressed first. Normally the term of a facultative certificate follows that of a specific policy. Thus the certificate year and policy year coincide; both start and end at the same time.

Facultative reinsurance can be written for terms that do not match the policy term. For example, suppose one facultative reinsured is cancelled, for any reason. The insurer would seek to replace that coverage and negotiate conditions with another reinsurer. The replacement certificate may be written just for the remaining policy term, or it may extend for a full year plus odd time and cover the upcoming renewal as well as the term left on the original policy.

Facultative reinsurers are much more fluid with the length of term. Their focus is on a particular policy and they can easily understand just what the longer time means. Treaty reinsurers typically deal with great numbers of policies, thus it is difficult to measure and comprehend just how a mix of longer termed policies might affect exposures.

If a treaty has a term of 15 months or longer, it will likely have renewals of some policies within the same treaty period. That can be discomforting, so it usually works best if the policies are annual and the reinsurance is annual.

Aggregate provisions are one of the more complex considerations. A policy may have one limit applicable to each and every loss and another limit applicable to all claims which occur in the given period or are subject to certain conditions. Liability policies often have such provisions. It is difficult, if not impossible, to divide or split such policies into subperiods. Thus reinsurance most often must match or track the term of the policy.

Since treaty reinsurance applies to many policies, it must allow for a fair amount of flexibility in its consideration of year. The starting point is fixed. And while year is a somewhat nebulous concept, generally the renewal of the treaty will pick up coverage for the renewal of the portfolio of policies.

Accident Year

This term implies that the losses all happened during a specific policy or treaty year. The premium will correspond to the loss and will include premiums from policies without loss written during the same period. It does not include incurred developments of losses that happened during previous periods, but are increasing or decreasing at the time. Subsequent developments on recognized losses, or on any subject policy within this period, are included as further measurements are made of the results of this year.

Accident year is a term that applies to a collection or portfolio of policies for either an insurer or reinsurer. Generally, primary carriers will use, for example, accident year 1994 to apply to all policies written in 1994 and to the losses that occur on those policies as a group. Note, many of the policies will extend into 1995, or beyond, or will be exposed to claims beyond the year which collectively refers to the inception dates of the various policies. The term collects policies written during the period and all premiums generated from those policies, and it specifically includes all claims attributed to those policies. The loss amounts are measured as the claims on these policies mature or develop and move through the handling process until they are settled and fully paid. An accident year is a collection of policy years since it applies to many policies effective at various dates within the accident year term.

The corresponding collective term used by reinsurers is *underwriting year*, which applies to all treaties written in a given year and the losses that develop from those treaties. Underwriting year is an accident year concept.

Underwriting Year, Pool Year, and Management Year

These are accident years whose policies have been written during a specific period. This period may be a fiscal year or *underwriting year.*

A managing general agent (MGA) is a person (or corporation) who has been delegated the authority to underwrite on behalf of a reinsurer. The delegation is detailed in a management agreement. Often business written during the year under a specific management agreement is called a *management year.*

A reinsurance pooling arrangement is a collective agreement between reinsurers to write certain business. The underwriting year is then referred to as a *pool year.*

The terms underwriting year, management year, and pool year are interchangeable, except for the additional information they provide about the management structure. The focus in each is on policies written in the period, and all future losses and loss developments on those policies are accumulated as recorded, all subject to a specific agreement or directive. Otherwise, these terms may also be used interchangeably with accident year.

Treaty Year

Typically treaty reinsurers call the accident year for a specific reinsurance contract a *treaty year.* The term is equivalent to a policy year for an insurer, while the term underwriting year, which is a collection of treaty years, is equivalent to the term accident year.

The relationship between the term of a treaty and the applicable policies written within its context is the most basic consideration of a treaty. It determines whether the treaty responds to a given loss. It is also fundamental to considerations of whether or not the insurer "selected against" or ceded in a manner detrimental to the reinsurer.

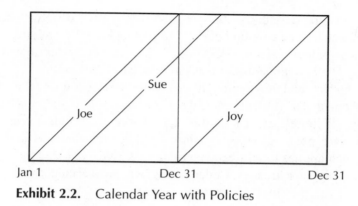

Exhibit 2.2.   Calendar Year with Policies

Exhibit 2.2 displays two calendar years. Policy Joe written on January 1 expires on December 31; its entire term falls within the first calendar year. Another, policy Sue (pun intended), written on April 1, expires on March 31 of the next calendar year. Still another policy, Joy, written on December 31, expires at year-end of the second calendar year. Policy Joy is effective or in force throughout the second calendar year, but is labeled with the group of policies written in the first period. The effective date, or date written, is the key.

If one were to chart a great number of policies, each with its own term written through the year, the diagram would be a parallelogram, as shown in Exhibit 2.3.

Such a diagram can be used for all policies written in a given year; thus it is sometimes referred to as a policy year diagram.

Subsequent years are best diagrammed as in Exhibit 2.4.

Each parallelogram may contain or apply to all policies written under the terms of a given treaty in one year, that is, a treaty year. Thus what an insurer

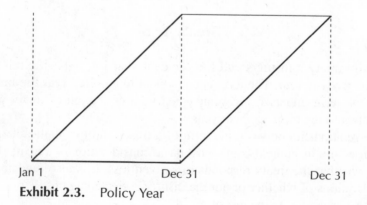

Exhibit 2.3.   Policy Year

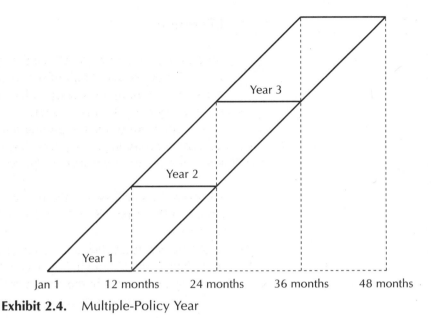

Exhibit 2.4. Multiple-Policy Year

refers to as a policy year is similar to what a reinsurer calls a treaty year. Assuming the same starting date, the difference will be those policies that are excluded from the treaty or written in kinds and classes to which the treaty does not apply.

In this diagram, we assume the policies are evenly distributed throughout the year. In actuality, it is likely that discount periods, regulated terms, and other factors result in distributions that are not spread equally day by day. However, if there are a great number of policies, the distribution works out to be close to that described above. This is a hypothetical model, typical of most situations.

Treaty year written premium refers to the total annual premiums from all policies subject to the treaty. This premium includes additional premiums from endorsements that expand coverages; return premiums from deletions, reductions and cancellations; and premium adjustments resulting from rates applied to receipts, mileage, and the like. It may also sweep in a limited number of "year plus odd time" policies.

Consider the picture at 12 months. All the policies written would be bound. Yet one is not able to state the total written premium as there are always some adjustments in processing or late traveling for one reason or another. The point is, however, that any new policy should not be backdated, to apply at some earlier date. The policy count is fixed or final, but premium and loss totals must be measured in future months as they become progressively more complete and activity closes.

Unearned Premium

The policy year diagram reveals some interesting relationships. Although the total written premium is roughly known at 12 months, about half of the term remains open and exposed to future claims. In our three-policy sample, Joe is complete, Sue has one month remaining, and Joy has just begun its term.

Another way to express this is in terms of open exposure. The premium in which the exposure has passed is called earned premium by insurers. If the policy were cancelled, the insurer would not have to return any of the premium earned to that date.

That portion of the premium still exposed to loss or losses in the future is called *unearned premium.* Thus policy Joe is fully earned, Sue is 11/12 or 92 percent earned and Joy is 100 percent unearned.

Again, earned premium is that portion of the premium allocated to the part of the term that has passed. The losses have happened, although they may not yet be known. The focus is on exposure; if the exposure is in the past, a proportionate share of the premium is earned; if the exposure is to come, the applicable premium is unearned.

Consider the situation at 18 months. The written premium total may be several dollars different from that measured at 12 months due to late traveling items such as endorsements.

The unearned amount can be estimated with a geometric calculation, again based on the assumption that there was a level number of policies written each month (see Exhibit 2.5). The amount unearned is represented by a triangle and we can calculate its area (area = 1/2 × base × height).

Here the base is 6 months or 1/2 year. Since the triangle is a right triangle with equal sides, the height is the same. Thus, area = 1/2 × 1/2 × 1/2 = 1/8 or .125.

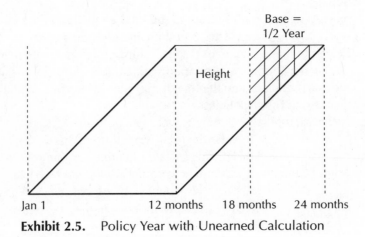

Exhibit 2.5.   Policy Year with Unearned Calculation

The total area of the parallelogram is 1.0 (area = base × height or 1 × 1). Relating the area of the triangle to the whole is therefore easy. It is .125/1 or 12.5 percent, which is 1/8 of the total area. Thus, at 18 months the typical treaty year premium is 7/8 earned and 1/8 unearned. We can calculate earned and unearned premium at several key measurement points (see Exhibit 2.6).

At 18 months, the written premium is likely be quite close to the final number. Depending upon the class and type of primary business, a small amount of premium activity may remain. For example, long-haul trucking business typically is rated on mileage or receipts for transported goods and thus has a premium adjustment after the policy term has passed. A portfolio of reinsurance itself has a different premium inflow pattern. Thus subsequent measurements will have a modestly different written premium total as well as an increasing portion of earned premium. At 18 months, 87.5 percent of the premium has been earned, and 12.5 percent remains exposed to loss over the next few months.

The insurer has been writing new policies and renewing some of those that have already expired. It has been doing so for six months. In fact that subsequent policy period or treaty year is already 12.5 percent earned.

Claims continue to be reported and develop well beyond the in-force period of the treaty. The reasons for this will be addressed in subsequent chapters. An injured child, for example, might not sue till he reaches 21 years of age. Exhibit 2.7 attempts to illustrate this loss development by decreasing the size of the arrow, indicating some decrease in the number of new reported claims. The diagram does not specifically address any deterioration of known claims; that is a factor to be measured as each year ages or develops.

Typically each year is measured quarterly, and depending on the type of business there may be activity for many years, typically three or four years for homeowner's business, perhaps seven or eight years for auto, and more than 20 for certain kinds of professional liability, malpractice, and similar business.

Time	Theoretical Calculation	Percent Earned
3 months	1/2 × 1/2 × 1/2	3.125%
6 months	1/2 × 1/2 × 1/2	12.500%
9 months	1/2 × 3/4 × 3/4	28.125%
12 months	1/2 × 1 × 1	50.000%
15 months	1 − 1/2 × 3/4 × 3/4	71.875%
18 months	1 − 1/2 × 1/2 × 1/2	87.500%
21 months	1 − 1/2 × 1/4 × 1/4	96.875%
24 months	1	100.000%

Exhibit 2.6. Theoretical Calculation of Percent Earned

The vertical lines in Exhibit 2.7 have a particular meaning. The parts of each treaty or policy year between the vertical lines portray or capture a fiscal year period. Thus in rough terms,

a + b = treaty year 1

c + d = treaty year 2

b + c = one calendar year

d + e = next calendar year

Note that in a calendar year measurement, the earned premium need not arise from the same set of policies that determines written premium. Indeed, even when all the exposure has passed, the amount written will not precisely match the amount earned. Note further that the losses reported comprise activity from many older policies, so it is just the incremental changes that are included in the calendar year measurement. Reserve development is included within the measurement of those incremental changes.

Calendar year d + e would include loss developments from year 1 and year 2, as indicated in the schematic by portions of the loss development arrows (see Exhibit 2.7). Plus, there would likely be some early claims advices on year 3 losses.

This schematic can be dynamic. It can be used to illustrate much of the workings of the insurance business. It is important to remember that an insurer can usually turn to a nearby report or check the computer for the amount of unearned premium or other measurements in a given period. A reinsurer is detached and often must make use of the type of approximations discussed above. Reinsurers can, for example, check to see if the amount

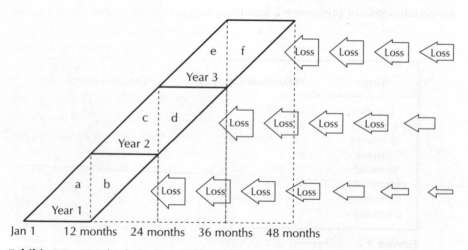

Exhibit 2.7.   Multiple-Policy Year with Loss Development

reported as earned on a particular treaty is following the hypothetical expectation. If the amount is close to the theoretical calculation, the situation is good. However, a significant departure from the expectation should be investigated. Is there some procedure or characteristic of the kind of policy or type of business that causes a different pattern? Just what does this mean to the reinsurer?

Researching abnormal pace, odd distributions, and the like can help the reinsurer understand the business and bolster its confidence that the cessions are conforming to expectations. This sort of information can help a reinsurer spot inappropriate cessions or problems before they develop into major difficulties. Further, this information can support pricing considerations for upcoming renewals.

BULK RESERVES

Insurers and reinsurers alike must maintain bulk reserves. Unearned premium reserve (UPR) is one kind of bulk reserve. It is based on specific policies, although some procedural shortcuts may be made in the calculation, such as collecting the policies in a given week or month rather than performing the calculation policy by policy. The UPR is therefore policy-based. However, because it is not tied to a specific policy but rather held as a reserve for a calendar year period for a group of policies, it is considered to be a bulk reserve.

Case-based claim reserving is another example of a policy-based calculation, that is, tied to specific policies. Insurers and reinsurers must estimate future pay-out potentials arising from existing policies on claims that have not yet been reported. Obviously there should be greater reserves in the current year than the prior year and progressively smaller reserve amounts as one goes back in time. This logic is valid except in special cases such as asbestosis, which may hit a specific group of policies in some past period. In summary, such reserves may have a significant impact on the results of a company, which motivates the establishment of some bulk provision or reserve.

Incurred But Not Reported Reserves (IBNR)

The term IBNR (*incurred but not reported reserves*) is defined as the difference between losses that will ultimately be reported and losses reported to date. It is particularly important to reinsurers for a couple of reasons. First, much of the business selected for reinsurance has a long-term development potential. Secondly, the specific or case reserve information supplied in a submission may not tell the whole story about the development potential of the business. The company may actually know more about the business or hold a theory about the business to be ceded that is not yet evident in the figures recorded at the time of the submission. Reinsurers should be cognizant of any and all information that might affect the profitability of the business they choose to assume. Although the insurer can attempt to set each and every case reserve properly in view of the known situation, the total amount incurred may grow over time. The total may increase due to additional reports of claims, which have occurred in the calendar year under consideration. Alternatively, the growth may arise as bulk net increase due to increases in some case reserves and decreases in others. The net effect is usually an increase, so some provision is appropriate. IBNR includes provisions for claims that are currently unknown, as well as provisions for unspecified developments on known claims. This will be discussed in detail later in the text.

SUMMARY

The above fundamental terms form a very important base for learning about reinsurance. The definitions and usage of these terms are different for reinsurers and insurers. In the course of analyzing materials, for example, the reinsurer will occasionally see statistical headings such as "total reserve amount." This happens to be a term used by one of the industry giants to mean the sum of the incurred amount on open cases. As an incurred summation, it includes payments as well as reserves; thus it is a misnomer. From company to company, there is a great deal of variation in the expression of the terms outlined in this chapter. Failure to clarify definitions can lead to difficulty. Reinsurers must enquire about the definitions, be flexible in acceptance of particular usages, and apply logic to lead to the necessary assessment. Cedents concurrently have a responsibility to maintain terminology in the mainstream of current industry usage. Today's processing capability permits the creation of reports with specific perspectives, such as the total or gross results, results for the ceded portion, and results for the net retained portion.

3

REINSURANCE CESSIONS

FACULTATIVE OR TREATY?
FACULTATIVE REINSURANCE
TREATY ASSUMPTIONS
CESSIONS TO TREATY AND FACULTATIVE
SPECIFIC AND AGGREGATE CESSIONS
SEMIAUTOMATIC CESSIONS
MULTIPLE-LAYER CESSION TRACKING

FACULTATIVE OR TREATY?

The term *facultative* is derived from the concept that the underwriter retains the *faculty* to accept or reject risk on an individual basis. In contrast, treaty reinsurance permits "automatic" or "obligatory" cessions throughout the term of the agreement. A reinsurance contract can be written in such a way as to make each appear to be something it is not, so it is appropriate to take a close look at the differences between these two types of reinsurance.

The right to accept or reject is quite different from the right to cancel. One accepts or rejects a risk before it is bound, that is, before it is in force. Cancellation implies that the risk was bound, covered, or in force at some point in time before the cancellation. Termination and cancellation are synonymous in this discussion.

Facultative means acceptance/rejection in advance of binding coverage, such that the consideration is applied to each single risk or exposure. Treaty reinsurance means the risk or exposure is negotiated and agreed upon on a bulk basis such that once ceded, each risk is accepted for some period of time. Most treaties only permit cancellation of the entire treaty, typically only after a 90- or 180-day notice. Some reinsurance contracts do permit the reinsurer to reject or cancel individual risks on short notice. "Cancel" is the operative word. These are often referred to as semiautomatic treaties due to the feature of individual risk assessment.

Occasionally the reinsurance contract will be set so that each risk will be submitted to the reinsurer with a period of 1–5 days for individual risk review. This can be either treaty or facultative. If the risk is bound by the cedent prior to the decision of the reinsurer, it is a treaty situation. If the risk is not bound until the reinsurer gives the approval, then it is facultative. The distinction between facultative and treaty reinsurance is clear if one applies this straightforward test of rejection versus cancellation.

A specific agreement may not state explicitly just when the risk is bound or in force and if there is an option to reject or cancel individual risks. Beware of situations where the context is not perfectly clear. Avoid final agreement until the understanding is firm. Without clear language, the determination rests upon the pattern of usage, and with that is always subject to debate over just what constitutes the norm.

Most types of treaties require that the ceding company cede all policies that are subject to the treaty. That means most treaties are obligatory. The reinsurer is also obligated to accept risks that meet the terms of the treaty.

Surplus treaties typically permit the cedent to vary the amount ceded to the treaty; usually there is a clause in the agreement that outlines the permissible ranges. These treaties are obligatory in that a cession must be made, but the percentage ceded is variable.

A treaty can be arranged so that it is not obligatory for the cedent, but is obligatory for the reinsurer, to accept. This is commonly called a *facultative obligatory treaty*. Because the reinsurer is obligated to accept the cession, this is a treaty contract. The term facultative is applied to stress the option of cession on a risk-by-risk basis. This illustrates the fact that use of the term facultative does not in itself imply that the *contract* is facultative.

By applying the fundamentals one can test whether the reinsurance underwriter holds the right to accept or reject on an individual risk basis, that is, the test that distinguishes facultative cessions from treaty cessions. One should also understand that a facultative department or facultative underwriter may be in a position to accept business within a contract that meets the definition of a reinsurance treaty. Thus the title and department should not be used as the determining factor in this assessment.

FACULTATIVE REINSURANCE

It is necessary to preface this topic with a discussion of class and type, since the terms used vary by the kind of business. For example, it is common to use the term "risk" in context with property reinsurance. In casualty reinsurance the preferred term is "exposure." Many facultative underwriters avoid use of the term "policy," since their initial selection decision is made from

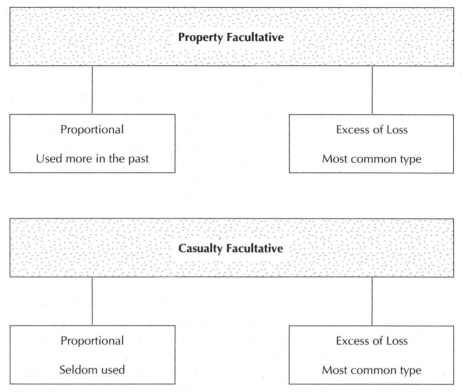

Exhibit 3.1.   Facultative Usage Chart

assessment of the risk or exposure, such that the policy may not become a part of the file until after the business is bound and in force.

Because of the current domination in the use of facultative reinsurance on an excess of loss basis, the focus of this chapter shall be non-proportional excess of loss. Proportional considerations should be considered as quota share cessions of the primary coverage. As such, underwriting, exposure analysis, and pricing track closely to considerations by primary underwriters. As the pricing of proportional facultative business is quite similar to that of a proportional treaty, the reader should refer to the specific treaty section on commissions for pricing of proportional facultative business.

Facultative reinsurance is purchased for the very reasons outlined in Chapter 1 (primary and secondary functions of reinsurance). Facultative reinsurance is also purchased to protect treaties.

Treaties are written on an obligatory basis, which implies that the insurer cedes all risks or exposures falling within the scope or subject matter of the treaty. There are certain situations in which the ceding company wishes to limit or minimize the loss potential to the treaty. Some examples of these situations follow.

The treaties may have tight exclusions, so that borderline exposures are best placed facultatively. The carrier may be forced for competitive reasons to write certain coverages and may prefer to purchase facultative coverage for such business as it may better fit the excess format. Alternatively, it may wish to keep the treaty confined and controlled. Occasionally, the ceding company might find better terms from facultative markets than those available at the time by treaty. Capacity or unusual risk characteristics are common considerations for picking out some business from a treaty to protect the overall cession to the treaty.

It is always wise to determine the purpose underlying the cession when assessing the terms, underwriting (including the net retention of the ceding company), and pricing of facultative business.

The cession specifications should contain significant detail about the particular risk being ceded. A property risk will have dimensions, construction, style, materials, contents, usage, evaluation, fire protection, plus specific safety and prevention attributes. A casualty exposure will be defined in terms of revenues, coverage types, past claim histories, and other factors. In either case, the information is highly individualized with respect to the nature of the specific risk to be ceded.

In addition, facultative underwriters will have considerable market intelligence at their disposal. They will know the specific policy types offered by the markets they service. The information may include preferences about various special clauses or endorsements. Much of this may be supplied by the carriers themselves, overtly or collectively over time. In the course of a year, a reinsurer may see hundreds of submissions from a given cedent, and while it may accept just some portion of these submissions, the collective business opportunities are an exchange of information. Reinsurers must learn from these exchanges. It not only enhances their skills, but also allows them to serve their clients better. This knowledge base should not be neglected; it is significant and the quality of its maintenance helps make some reinsurers better than others.

The keys to successfully writing facultative business lie in the individual policy submission, acceptance, and declination based upon the terms presented, as well as the pricing specific to the risk or exposure.

For example, a fish processing plant that happens to be built on a wooden pier would be a special kind of risk. Even beyond the cooling apparatus, the fact that its foundation might be subject to fire or collapse must be considered by the primary underwriter. If it happens also to be a large structure, the primary carrier might be wary of the loss potential within this risk. While the rate may be commensurate with the exposure, the primary carrier might have a lower comfort level for such a risk. The fact that there are not many such policies in a company's portfolio would make this situation non-homogeneous with other policies. The primary carrier may wish to write such business, or accommodate a profitable source of business, if satisfactory facultative reinsurance can be arranged. Typically, the facultative reinsurance is negotiated prior to binding the specific policy. *Satisfactory* implies good terms and solid financial backing and it will be discussed further in Chapter 14.

Facultative reinsurers underwrite the ceding source in a manner similar to treaty underwriting. The analysis factors of this investigation are included in Chapter 10. It is important to underscore the need for thorough investigation of the financials, management, and processing capabilities of the cedent prior to accepting reinsurance business, whether it is facultative or treaty. A treaty underwriter may see offerings from a given cedent once or twice each year, so the financials and leadership are reviewed by the underwriter in conjunction with the submission. Since facultative reinsurers see numerous submissions from a given cedent throughout each year, the preselection of sources of the business is a critical part of this industry segment.

Accepting business at random from all sources is potentially dangerous for several reasons. The facultative reinsurer may be exposed to pricing by the lowest bidder. There may also be shortcomings in producing and developing the prospect. Good primary carriers hold and require standards that have direct benefit to the facultative reinsurer. Claim handling is also crucial, as a facultative reinsurer does not want to support a weak, inconsistent underlying carrier. Thus the carrier limitation considerations are made in advance, perhaps annually, by the facultative management. The acceptability of primary carrier is normally predetermined and remote from the individual cession considerations.

Yet, one will not find lists of "approved" or "unapproved" business sources. Each submission is either greeted with an expression of interest or a softly worded declination. Clearly, a written list presents an uncomfortable exposure of that list falling into the wrong hands, which in turn can create significant marketing difficulty. It is not uncommon, however, to have virtually all of the submissions from a particular source declined year after year, due to real or perceived shortcomings in that source or in its manner of doing business.

The selection process of a facultative underwriter centers on policy detail, risk characteristics, and price of the specific cession. This assessment, including exposure analysis and pricing, is similar to that which a primary underwriter might undertake on a commercial risk that was not subject to manual rate tables. The essential difference is in the cooperative assessment. The facultative underwriter may help the primary underwriter reach an appropriate rate and perhaps some policy restrictions that make the particular policy mutually acceptable.

The facultative underwriter has the opportunity to review approaches from many primary underwriters. Over time, the more successful approaches are fostered, while those that seemed or proved to be less successful are discouraged. Even though the classes, kinds, and specifics are varied, there are some prevailing characteristics that can be used to improve future terms and conditions.

For example, insurance is a key component of long-haul trucking business. Trucking firms have proven to be shrewd buyers at the primary level. The values hauled are significant and the potentials for disaster are tremendous. Thus it is a business in which insurance is vital and the reinsurance complement is quite necessary.

Often the primary trucking policy premium will be adjustable, with the rate dependent upon miles driven, freight receipts, or routes traveled, as well as prior experience. A facultative reinsurer will know the appropriate questions to ask. Are the drivers responsible for cash or payments? What types of goods are being transported? Is refrigeration involved? Is the cargo flammable, toxic, or dangerous? Are alarms provided for cargos subject to theft or hijacking? The facultative underwriter will know just how to handle these various potential problems. The reinsurance rate may depend on the collective responses, because the acceptance/declination decision must consider these components.

In a more routine case, where capacity is the reinsurance function, the facultative underwriter may set the additional rate for a layer of excess of loss facultative coverage as a percentage of the primary base rate. For example, on an excess of loss basis, the first $1 million of coverage is exposed to small losses, which just penetrate beyond the deductible. The next layer beyond that is exposed to a different frequency and limited severity. The rate assessment, however, should track the lower layer, some factor, say 50%, of the primary, more or less depending on the circumstances. The data for the determination is compiled in the cession offering and subsequent questions asked by the underwriter. The rate setting process varies by reinsurer, but is essentially a judgment based on experience or calculation based on a sampling of existing certificates. Of course, these are trended to be appropriate for the upcoming policy period. That trending may be judgmental or formula-based. This pricing explanation is not specific, since it is intended to apply generally to all classes and kinds of business. However, the more common the kind of risk, the more applicable the rating formula.

Unusual risks, such as the first satellite in space orbit, present interesting problems for the facultative underwriter. The likelihood of success must be assessed. Interestingly, in most cases, as for the satellite case, the insurance buyer will be the source of information about the exposure and likelihood of success. Facultative underwriters are sponges for knowledge. They learn to assess exposure (e.g., what has caused losses in the past?) and adapt that knowledge to new situations.

Facultative underwriters will adopt a different perspective than the rocket scientist (pun intended) and primary underwriter. They are trained to be mindful of potentials and just how things occur. The rocket scientist may build the satellite booster to specifications that contain possibilities of certain events. The facultative underwriter must assess the probabilities of that happenstance or of some unconsidered happenstance. The satellite example is appropriate in that we can observe the different perspectives. In normal business these divergent perspectives exist, but are perhaps not as obvious.

Underwriters secure most of their knowledge from the policyholder. The policyholder's information, which is transferred through the primary carrier, is the basis of most of the facultative underwriter's specific knowledge. To this, it is necessary to add information from outside sources bolstered by the industry segment overview that the underwriter has gained by reinsuring competitors on similar exposures. Like excess and surplus lines carriers, facultative reinsurers are the first to reinsure odd risks, new technology, and developing exposures.

The rate per unit of applicable excess of loss coverage should be greater on a facultative basis than on a treaty basis. This is an important differentiation. Excess of loss treaties apply to homogeneous exposures, collected because of the similarity of risk. The batch concept affords a lower rate per unit. The treaty underwriter has the law of large numbers in its favor. It is unlikely that a loss will occur to each and every policy. This implies that a quantity discount should apply to treaty pricing.

There is a counterargument that favors the excess of loss facultative underwriter on occasion. The treaty rate is an average, a combination of low, moderate, and high rates based on the various risks or exposures. An exceptional quality risk may find greater appeal in the facultative market because of its low exposure, so there is a tendency to apply a reduced rate. In actual practice, there is competition between treaty and facultative reinsurers. Sometimes, the competition is intense and other times it is not.

Suppose a carrier writes property coverages up to $1 million in limit, with treaty reinsurance in place. A small restaurant may have a lesser value, say $500,000, yet be ceded on a facultative basis. Restaurants as a class have a high fire potential. They also have a greater susceptibility to slip-and-fall exposures, due to the clientele and the nature of their service. This is an outgrowth of liquor law liability. In this example, the carrier may have a legitimate interest in protecting itself and protecting its treaty reinsurers from certain exposures that are not common to the portfolio ceded.

On occasion, a facultative reinsurer may afford rates that are actually lower or equal to that afforded by the treaty. The facultative reinsurer may simply be aggressive in building business. It may be motivated by seeking risks that appear to hold lower exposure than its normal offerings. This happens every day in the marketplace.

It is important to understand that one reinsurer is promoting business on a batch or treaty basis and the other on a policy or facultative basis. Theoretically, both cannot always succeed at a given price. For short periods of time, either the facultative or the treaty pricing can get out of line. However, for the long term, homogeneous risks should be ceded to treaties and the individual or specialized risks on a facultative basis.

If a facultative underwriter chooses to price competitively with a treaty reinsurer it will not be successful over the long term. The facultative underwriter will be doing more work, incurring a higher processing expense, and will not be able to sustain a lower price. Thus the facultative reinsurer should not consistently seek business that is appropriately handled on a treaty basis.

If a treaty underwriter sets prices at the facultative level, some other treaty reinsurer will take the business away. If the treaty underwriter chooses to write specialized business, which is more applicable to facultative reinsurance, it will usually fail. There will not be enough of such business to permit batch pricing, batch selection, and batch processing. Bundling different or nonhomogeneous exposures is potentially dangerous.

The costs of handling risks on an individual basis are greater. A treaty may have a quarterly activity monitoring process and a renewal check prior to cancellation notice. The initial and renewal underwriting and pricing may be extensive with thick memorandums and lots of charts, graphs, and projections. Thus, the renewal activity is sometimes intensive, while at other times of the year it is relatively slow.

The single-policy, facultative submission may be just a short facsimile or telex, or it can be as extensive as any treaty submission. Also, each time the primary policy is endorsed for any reason, such as adding or deleting a location, changing limits, or changing a named insured, correspondence flows to the facultative reinsurer. Some endorsements carry changes in premium, others do not. All become part of the facultative file. The point here is that a facultative file is typically handled more often during the year. This is the case even if there is no claim. Space and activity relate directly to handling costs. And because these matters affect the exposure, they must be handled by underwriting personnel with professional credentials and wages.

The policy detail for facultative consideration is far greater than that which is presented to the treaty underwriter. Also, facultative submissions cannot be batch processed. Thus the facultative reinsurer cannot keep up with a treaty reinsurer when presented with large numbers of similar exposures. Likewise, the treaty reinsurer cannot compete for unique, specialized exposures presented with individual policy detail.

Which risk should be placed where depends on the reinsurance function. What is motivating the carrier to cede this risk? Appropriate understanding of that fundamental question keeps the normal flow of business in its appropriate place.

Semiautomatic situations may be confusing, since there are elements of individual policy processing and homogeneous cessions. However, there are distinctive processing components that define the proper classification. We will first discuss treaty assumptions and return to differentials following this.

TREATY ASSUMPTIONS

Most treaties define the line, kind, type, and quality of risk appropriate to cede to the reinsurance cover. The treaty will include a list of risks that are specifically excluded. Usually, surplus, or surplus share treaties (see Reinsurance Primer in Chapter 1) are the only treaties that permit selection or apportionment by the primary underwriter. The object is to respond to a perceived need and to provide coverage to meet specific reinsurance functions. As outlined in Chapter 1 these functions are capacity, catastrophe, stabilization, and financial, as well as several secondary functions. The treaty contract simply outlines all permissible risks and sets the terms intended to resolve that need or needs.

Permitting the primary underwriter to choose whether or not to cede creates a potential for adverse selection. The treaty cannot be successful if the primary carrier cedes all its poor risks and retains all its better risks. Thus treaties are generally intended to apply across a section or class of policies.

A treaty underwriter's main focus is on the capabilities of the ceding carrier. Is the carrier habitually profitable? Does the carrier have adequate leadership? Does it price its business well? Are claims handled smartly and aggressively? Being selective about the ceding companies is vital. Unlike facultative, this determination is rarely preset in treaty underwriting. Some cessions may be acceptable from a particular carrier while others may not. For example, one might consider property exposures of a particular carrier, but not malpractice. The selection depends on the kind, class, and quality of business to be ceded and on the capabilities of the carrier to handle such business.

Typically, the treaty underwriter faces a long-term prospect and thus makes the assessment about management and claims with a long-term view. It is expected that some years will produce loss, but that overall the good years will outnumber the bad years and produce a profitable outcome.

Reinsurance is a business of solving problems. Primary carriers are collecting risk as a business and face serious concerns about capacity, catastrophe, and the other reinsurance fundamentals. If their portfolio becomes skewed or uncomfortable, they take steps to correct the situation.

It takes more than a year to effect an increase in base rates for most lines of business. New rates must be promulgated and tested for appropriateness. Will they drive off good business or attract poor exposures? Should all states get the same increase? Will they be approved on a state-by-state basis? New territories also take time to develop. Retiring from a state is not easy, and the company often faces severe restrictions in personal lines, specifically home-owner's and automobile lines due to insurance department oversight and measures taken to protect consumer rights.

Thus, correcting an uncomfortable situation or effecting reparations have time considerations. Most cannot be accomplished overnight. When a primary carrier perceives a need for reinsurance, the intended time frame is typically several years. Because of this, most treaties are written on a continuous basis, with provisions for cancellation annually and sometimes quarterly.

The rate determined by the treaty underwriter will often be set at a level where one of the previous five years was in loss. Typically there may also be a profit commission, whereby a portion of a very high profit is returned to the primary carrier.

Thus the treaty reinsurer enters into an agreement with sufficient observed volatility such that any year can produce a loss, sometimes a sizeable loss. The insurer plans to adjust rates moderately and work with the cedent to modify or correct aspects of the business that are generating loss severity, loss frequency, or discomfort.

As with facultative reinsurance, competition is keen and involved in most transactions. If the rate is too high, the primary carrier may seek other quotes. If the profit is excessive, the carrier may demand a rate reduction and have competitive pressure to win the negotiation. The goal is for both primary carrier and reinsurer to profit over the long term.

Capacity that is transferred should be appropriately rated to permit adequate flow of premium to the reinsurer and sufficient to be profitable. Catastrophe costs are often amortized over time to allow the reinsurer an appropriate profit while affording the primary carrier the ability to pass off this exposure at a steady or nearly fixed level. The need should be managed to the mutual benefit of both parties.

Treaty underwriting will be addressed in detail in Chapter 8. The underwriting selection process is the method of acceptance and approval of cedents by reinsurers. The converse is reverse underwriting, or approval by cedents of its reinsurers.

CESSIONS TO TREATY AND FACULTATIVE

Let us consider an example: insuring the fire exposure of a 60-story high-rise building worth $120 million.

Such a policy may be written by one carrier. There is no company large enough to be comfortable holding that risk net without reinsurance. Today's giant carriers are likely to hold $10 million to $25 million net. Thus, they must be prepared to handle such exposures long before they quote on the policy.

Let us further assume the carrier is comfortable with a line of $15 million for its own account. Although this is an assumption, there is considerable thought in the decision, both from a general standpoint and from a specific policy consideration. That $15 million represents 12.5 percent of the whole value at risk.

The carrier may set probable maximum loss (PML) estimates. These depend on the nature of the building, its specifications, construction, and location. There are any number of definitions and formulas for PML, but for now we shall just apply some cursory considerations without defining the concept. The carrier may view PML as the number of stories that could burn before the controls held, or the number of stories that might be seriously but not completely burned. In the past, these assessments were based on an estimate of the number of stories that would be affected in a typical fire; obviously one or two floors below would have water damage and a few above would have smoke damage. More recently, insurers consider the values at particular floors, such as the ground floor, and the likelihood that the structure will be weakened, requiring the entire building to be torn down. The PML estimate might involve six or seven stories. The $120 million value for the 60-story building amounts to $2 million per floor. Thus, the PML is $14 million for seven floors. The carrier's net 15 percent exposure of the PML would be $1.75 million.

The logic is that the carrier is considering putting up $15 million on this high-rise building, where the estimated or probable maximum foreseeable loss is $1.75 million. That might fit the carrier's comfort level such that it will accept 15 percent of the whole risk. Of course, this is a simplified view of this decision-making process.

The carrier may have secured automatic treaty capacity of, for example, $30 million on a quota share basis to apply to its prime large account property business; let us assume this was on a surplus share basis. In this case, it chooses to hold its maximum and cede to the treaty its full limit.

The treaty reinsurers might not be advised of this particular cession; after all, it is similar to many others ceded to the treaty. The reinsurers receive the premium supported by a quarterly bordereau, which may not be specific to site or policyholder name. Obviously, if a loss occurs, they will be advised quickly and thoroughly. However, it is important to understand the treaty cession is often made without specific policy detail. The perspective is from a batch or bulk basis, so the detail is not supplied or required.

In order to fill out the remaining capacity, $75 million in this example, the carrier may choose to split that large amount into three layers of cessions to facultative reinsurers: $25 million excess $45 million; $25 million excess $70 million; and $25 million excess $95 million. The facultative underwriters will be advised in great detail about the building, its architect, construction characteristics, site, city fire potentials, sprinkler system, target tenants, and other factors. This information is very specific so that facultative reinsurers can assess the exposure and set prices. This activity takes place before the carrier sets its formal quotation, as the total price will include the cost of reinsurance. The treaty cost is known, and the facultative cost is built on consensus from those that agree to take a portion of one or more of the layers. The quality of support and assessment of security are part of the carrier's decision to move forward.

Exhibit 3.2 illustrates the layoff chart for the above example, which we have chosen to display as a rectangle, since it is a single risk rather than a portfolio with varying limits.

Suppose there was a $50 million loss. It would be split as follows: $15 million net, $30 million treaty, and $5 million to the first facultative layer. The higher facultative layers would not be affected by a loss of this magnitude.

On the other hand, if the loss was $80 million, it would be split as follows: $15 million net, $30 million treaty, $25 million to the first facultative layer, and $5 million to the second facultative layer. The loss is distributed according to prearranged limits. The premium is divided at the onset, according to the amounts each participant agreed was necessary for the exposure they faced.

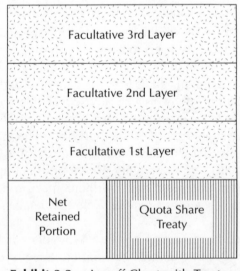

Exhibit 3.2.   Layoff Chart with Treaty
and Facultative

SPECIFIC AND AGGREGATE CESSIONS

Worker's compensation is a line where the norm is to purchase reinsurance on an excess of loss basis. Chapter 1 illustrated an excess of loss cession scheme that applies to specific individual losses. If the carrier's comfort level is $50,000, it may be interested in purchasing reinsurance for losses that exceed $50,000 to the maximum limit offered, say $250,000. That layer would be described as $200,000 excess of $50,000.

Worker's compensation has statutory limits that vary by type of injury and also vary from state to state. The carrier would need to purchase a second layer, on the same basis as above, with a limit of $750,000 or statutory, whichever is greater. This is not an unlimited cover. Rather, the limit applies to the full statutory requirement, which is known to both the carrier and the reinsurers as being applicable to the particular state.

The above pair of treaties would protect the carrier for severity or large losses. This type of treaty is called excess of loss, since it applies to specific losses that exceed the attachment point or full retention of the cedent.

The carrier should also be concerned about a frequency of smaller losses or a combination of many small and a few large losses that produces a poor overall result. Reinsurers offer coverage that applies on an excess basis for the aggregate total of all claims. Suppose, for example, that the anticipated loss ratio was 65 percent, but that the company would be in very serious trouble if the loss ratio exceeded 105 percent. The company might purchase an aggregate excess that attaches when the loss ratio reaches 105 percent and supplies coverage up to the next $1 million of losses of any kind.

This latter cover would be purchased for financial reasons and would only apply to a great many losses. Although the company wrote limits above $1 million, to the statutory limit set by law in the state, it purchased specific excess of loss coverage above $50,000 in two layers. Thus the aggregate excess cover would apply only to losses at $50,000 or less and for the first $50,000 of any larger loss. For this reason, the cover is considered to apply more to frequency of loss than to capacity.

In Chapter 1, we introduced the concept that a company should cap its policy limit at 1 percent of its written premium or 3 percent of its asset base. If that philosophy was maintained, a loss ratio of 105 percent would represent at least 105 large claims, more likely several thousand claims of varying sizes. Because this latter treaty applies to the accumulated loss amount of many claims, it is called an aggregate treaty. Since it attaches above a specific retention, it is also an excess of loss contract or excess treaty. Therefore it is referred to as an aggregate excess treaty.

In the case of worker's compensation it is most likely that any aggregate claim would arise from occupational diseases or exposure to common

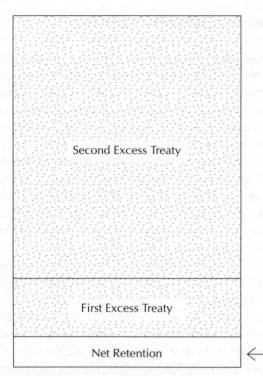

Exhibit 3.3. Layoff Chart with Aggregate Excess Treaty

airborne/waterborne, toxic elements. A chemical exposure could affect many workers at the same plant. Something like poor lighting could cause eye problems in a number of employees at a given location. A conflagration could result in the deaths of several employees. These kinds of potential exposures motivate the purchase of aggregate reinsurance.

Worker's compensation then, is a line in which the carrier often purchases several kinds of coverage. Normally specific treaties are designed to protect for specific situations.

There are many ways to illustrate specific excess of loss cessions, but it is very hard to illustrate how an aggregate excess of loss might apply. Exhibit 3.3 shows the aggregate excess with an arrow, since it protects just the net retention of the cedent and not the treaty reinsurers.

SEMIAUTOMATIC CESSIONS

Having defined and illustrated both facultative and treaty cessions, let us consider a hybrid type of cession, the semiautomatic cession. This is sometimes referred to as semiautomatic facultative while others call it a semiautomatic treaty. Semiautomatic cessions arise naturally. A portfolio of automobile gas or service stations is homogeneous in nature but consists of specialized and hazardous risks. For example, hot engines in proximity to volatile fuels, often self-served by the customer, present severe exposures. There is also the potential of leaks from the underground tanks. Yet, most stations are relatively small, and the risks are common to the class. On the one hand, this situation appears to call for a treaty cession, that is, homogeneous cessions of a large number of policies. On the other hand, the class is high hazard, so the reinsurer may wish to hold individual policy acceptance to maintain close control. Which cession applies?

Often, the industry collects data based on the department handling the cession. Some reinsurers process semiautomatics in their facultative department, while others do so in the treaty department. Thus the question, "which cession applies?" gets confused with the processing location, which is not appropriate as a definition.

Treaties accept all cessions that fall within the terms and conditions of the contract and include a termination provision at some future date. Normally it is bulk acceptance and bulk termination. The treaty reinsurer does not typically hold individual policy rejection privileges. If risks are automatically accepted within terms of the contract, it is a treaty acceptance.

Facultative reinsurers accept individual policy submissions and concurrently hold privilege of rejection on an individual submission basis. They may review numerous submissions of a similar kind or class but do so on a policy basis. If the underwriter must take action to specifically include each and every policy, it is a facultative cession.

If the underwriter reviews each policy but only holds the right of rejection at ten days or some other short term, it is a treaty cession. In the latter case the risk is automatically bound, subject to a policy termination provision. The acceptance is bulk and the termination individual.

It is not the physical act of looking at every policy that distinguishes between these two types of reinsurance. If the underwriting is done on an individual basis, the facultative reinsurer will do it differently than a treaty reinsurer. There are clues within the underwriting that help to identify the process, but the manner of review is not the primary criteria.

Rejection is not the same as termination. Rejection implies the coverage has never been in force. Termination implies that the coverage applied or existed for some period of time. The rejection/termination criteria is the primary determinant in this matter.

It is possible that a facultative underwriter, working in a facultative department, can make a treaty acceptance. Conversely, a treaty underwriter may on occasion take up a facultative risk. Where the transaction is processed is not as important as the mode under which it was accepted.

There are several considerations in determining whether facultative or treaty applies:

1. Was the submission individual or presented as a batch?
2. Was the acceptance bulk or individual?
3. Was the acceptance automatic following an earlier negotiation?
4. Did the underwriter hold a rejection or termination privilege?
5. Were risks cancelled individually or in bulk?
6. Did the contract language match the processing activity?

The fourth consideration is often the key determinant.

Both types of semiautomatic cessions exist with regularity. A semiautomatic facultative contract can be a master certificate applying to a series of individually underwritten acceptances over the period. Alternatively, it can be a treaty acceptance where the underwriter can reject some risks. They appear similar in practice, but are not identical. It is best to adopt definitive wording to make the process quite clear. The reinsurer should audit to be sure that semiautomatic cessions are being processed as agreed at the onset and that the underwriting effort follows the original intent of the contract.

MULTIPLE-LAYER CESSION TRACKING

Carriers are required to report reinsurance cession figures within Schedule F of the statutory, Annual Statement. There is considerable data within this statutory requirement. The database is both large and complex. At this time there is value in illustrating a full, complex, insurance carrier cession chart. The object is to show just how complex the situation can become.

It is possible to chart participation across a ceded program with a loss likelihood by layer and by reinsurer. Some placements are exposed to claim frequency while others are exposed to severity. Some placements aggregate with other placements. Facultative cessions can be categorized by class, kind, and exposure and batched for such analysis.

This mass of data is fertile for analysis. Consider Exhibit 3.4, which displays a single year's portfolio of insurance as a bell-shaped curve, symbolic of the large numbers of policies within the portfolio. A particular layoff scheme has been selected for illustration. Although the scheme for a particular company may be more or less complex, it can be analyzed in the same manner. The analysis can also account for growth from year to year and for change in the cession scheme.

If the business written has complex exposures, large limits, and nuances peculiar to its nature, the reinsurance cession may be as complex as illustrated

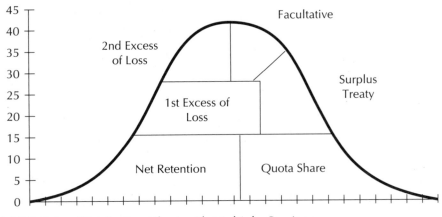

Exhibit 3.4. Distribution Chart with Multiple Cessions

here. The treaty reinsurance capacity may not be sufficient to cover the entire limit. The more remote exposures may be better ceded or less expensively ceded via an alternative type of treaty or facultative cession. If several classes of risk are included, some may require separate reinsurances or different terms. Then too, the fundamental reasons for purchasing the reinsurance may not be the same across the entire portfolio of business. Thus there are many reasons or motivations for handling segments of the reinsurance using different methodologies.

The cedent can use the results from a carefully constructed analysis, which parallels the diagram, as part of its security review. Potential profitability can be calculated for each treaty and in turn for each reinsurer. Each reinsurer's aggregate total can be easily calculated. This information can help assess whether a particular reinsurer is appropriately distributed across the program and match its financial capability against cession potentials.

Knowledge from such analysis can be used to:

- Control Schedule F (The listing of ceded reinsurance contains a sizeable amount of information that can be analyzed.)
- Improve the security review (e.g., monitoring where the reinsurer chooses to participate, perhaps linking some easier business with some harder exposures)
- Help restrict regressive selection by a reinsurer (Surely one should limit cessions to someone interested in taking up only the hard exposures.)
- Help curtail volume ceded to certain reinsurers (since the amount ceded may depend upon the level of security provided by the reinsurer)

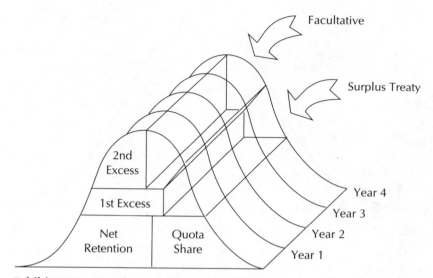

Exhibit 3.5.   Distribution Chart: Multiple Cessions with Multiple Years

- Obtain better terms
- Balance cessions
- Help recognize and solidify relationships

Exhibit 3.5 displays four years with the same cession scheme.

This kind of analysis can be structured to produce limited goals at first and expanded as it proves its usefulness. The point is that insurers collect a good amount of data, which should be used to the company's advantage. If management can enhance the knowledge base upon which decisions are made, suppositions within those decisions will be reduced.

4

CEDING AND ASSUMING REINSURANCE

CESSION CONSIDERATIONS
- **Responsiveness**
- **Fundamental and Supplemental Needs**
- **Cost Effectiveness**
- **Security**
- **Mutual Profitability**
- **Longevity**

DIRECT OR INTERMEDIARY?
- **Agency**

ACCEPTANCE AND APPROVAL OF REINSURERS
- **Tail**
- **Solvency**

MEASURES OF USAGE AND PERFORMANCE
- **Utilization Ratio**
- **Benefit-to-Cost Ratio**

OTHER CONSIDERATIONS IN APPROVING REINSURERS
- **The Tort System**
- **Asbestosis Litigation**

SUMMARY

The insurance industry involves both buying and selling, although those words may seem inappropriate. Insurers are in the business of selling policies, yet they also purchase coverage from reinsurers. In reinsurance the seller pays the buyer and the buyer pays the seller's agent. Buying and selling are confusing terms due to the complexity of the situation; ceding and assuming are better terminology.

Reinsurance was introduced in Chapter 1 as part of a primary insurer's risk management function, that is, when the insurer wishes to transfer some portion of its risk portfolio, motivated by one of the reinsurance functions. Such transfer is called a lay off or cession. The insurer cedes business to the reinsurer. Naturally, some sort of consideration or premium is necessary to effect this reinsurance. Generally the more difficult the cession, the greater the premium.

From the reinsurer's perspective, the above transaction expressed differently. Reinsurers seek to expand their own portfolio by participating in the business of other carriers. The reinsurers review the terms of the cession to see if it is indeed attractive. They assess the exposure and consider whether the premium offered has a profit potential. If the analysis is positive, they determine the amount of the cession they wish to assume.

There is a negotiation period in building the contract of reinsurance, where the terms are set and there is agreement as to which reinsurers will be accepted at which percentage participation. Added value is important here. Reinsurers who bring value and hold secure financials are preferred. Treaty relationships are long-term, so the financial solvency assessment is crucial. This will be addressed further in Chapters 12 and 14.

Consider the following example of a cession: a primary carrier wishes to cede on a quota share basis. As in all cases, there should be a primary motivation (one of the reinsurance functions discussed in Chapter 1). In this case, let us assume the primary carrier is expanding its territory and anticipates a 45 percent growth. Yet, with existing capital it wants to limit growth to about 10 percent. This may seem contradictory, so let us discuss how such apparent conflict might arise. If the new territory happens to be a big state, then the mix of goals, approved pricing, new agency relationships, and so forth can dictate that more than a minimum amount of the business be written at the onset. Agents must be permitted to write a sufficient volume to meet agency profit commission goals, so it is difficult to expand in a limited or contained manner. The attractiveness of this expansion draws the company. Growth provides the carrier with a better diversity or spread of risk and has a favorable impact on the carrier's expense ratios. However, while the positive features of growth seem encouraging, the carrier needs to maintain a conservative ratio of volume to capital.

Reinsurance may be the best way to manage this situation, since it creates an agreement for transferring much of the additional volume and risk. This can be accomplished with the expectation of decreasing the percentage ceded in subsequent years to permit the insurer to grow into the new territory in an orderly fashion, on a net basis.

The desired premium growth is 10 percent, while the anticipated premium level is 145 percent. The desired premium level is 110 percent while the anticipated premium income level is 145 percent. The relativity between these amounts is 110/145 = 76 percent. Thus, if the ceding company retains 76 percent of the anticipated volume, they will generate about 10 percent growth over their current premiums. The carrier may wish to effect a 25 percent quota share reinsurance cession on the combined multistate basis, which would create a net at approximately 75 percent, which meets its plan. The determination of the amount of the cession may not be as simple as illustrated here. However, the cedent will undertake an analysis to determine the appropriate kind of cession and amount to be ceded.

The cedent may wish to cede a greater portion of the new business and retain a greater portion of the existing proven book of business. Although the reinsurer would consider such an arrangement, it would have less interest because the original book may be well seasoned, with predictable loss ratios. Also the entire book offers a better spread of business than just one state. For these reasons, a reinsurer might give a better commission for the multistate book than for a single-state cession.

Further, the cedent may plan to increase its business in both the old and new territories. It may then use the quota share contract to build a steady growth on its net while also watching the totals. The cedent wants both to be under control. Gradually, the cedent may wish to reduce and eliminate the quota share. But expansion into additional states may keep this reinsurance contract in place for many years.

Like all of the cessions described in this text, there is a logical economic motivation that underlies the desire to transfer part of a business to a reinsurer. The rationale will make sense to both cedent and assuming reinsurer. In the above example, a number of reinsurers might compete for the opportunity to assist this cedent in the expansion plans, particularly if the past success was solid and the management was highly regarded.

CESSION CONSIDERATIONS

Initially, the carrier must assess the concerns that motivate it to transfer some of its business. These needs will, in part, dictate just how the cession will be structured.

1. Will the structure selected *respond* to the concerns as intended?
2. Is the need *fundamental* or *supplemental?*
3. Will the cession be *cost-effective* and can the cession be structured to carry its own cost?

4. Are *security* concerns minimal?
5. Will the cession be *profitable* for reinsurers?
6. How *long* will the cession be necessary and will the same structure apply throughout the life of this cession?

Responsiveness

Responsiveness is a combination of the effort in needs assessment and care in designing the program to meet those needs. Such up-front efforts usually have positive results on the program's effectiveness. However, one must remember that losses are fortuitous, so the best laid plans can fall short. Responsiveness is a key goal when creating or designing the cession. If the program is designed and priced with the anticipation of shock losses, but happens to experience unusual frequency, it might not respond as expected. Thus the design must take into consideration a variety of potential happenstances. There are plenty of examples where poor decisions have turned a mess into a disaster.

Fundamental and Supplemental Needs

Whether the particular business to be ceded is core business or peripheral is an important cession consideration. If a supplemental line is not successful, it can be dropped. Reinsurers will consider this in their assessment and may rate the supplemental line higher than the core business. Over a longer term, the reinsurer usually has a better chance for profit on the core business. Since core business will last longer under adverse conditions, both parties consider this in designing the cession.

Cost Effectiveness

Cost effectiveness is an obvious concern. Price is reflected directly as a measure in the assessment of cost within the program and indirectly in reflection of potentials. If the result is not successful, will the cedent be required to contribute funds or somehow make up for the loss sustained by reinsurers? Is it probable that following a disastrous result in part of its program, the cedent will find costs increased on unaffected portions of its program? The linkage may not be contractual. Cost effectiveness has many aspects to consider.

Security

Security concerns are expressed due to the fact that the cedent must post 100 percent reserves and then set credits on its books for receipts from reinsurers. If any of the reinsurers become insolvent, delinquent, or resistive, the cedent can face adverse cash flow and incur carrying costs. This aspect will be discussed later in this chapter.

Mutual Profitability

It is unwise to accept business that knowingly will not be profitable. However, a situation in which the cedent profits and the reinsurer is in loss is critically uncomfortable for all parties. Adjustments can be costly to the cedent. Occasionally, a single large loss may cause such a distortion. Reinsurers will look for ways to build back profitability over time. They may require a greater share of the premium, thereby reducing the cedent's planned margin. They may ask that more profitable core business be included in the mix for this contract. Although these may be negotiated, the effort will be telling on the cedent. The number of reinsurance markets is limited and a cedent cannot survive long by abusing reinsurers or profiting at their expense.

Longevity

The anticipated longevity of the cession should be reviewed. Frequent restructuring or negotiations are costly and potentially disturbing to plans. Thus both cedent and assuming reinsurers pay particular attention to the likelihood and expectation of longevity.

DIRECT OR INTERMEDIARY?

The cedent can approach potential reinsurers directly or market the cession via an intermediary. There are advantages to both methods. *The foremost consideration is trust.* Typically, the primary insurer will have some sort of longstanding relationship with its reinsurance contact. Through this contact, trust can be built over time.

A direct reinsurer offers one-stop shopping. If a claim arises, the cedent can go to just one reinsurer to seek recovery. These reinsurance firms tend to be very large and, in the process of growing, amass considerable expertise and financial capability.

Intermediaries, on the other hand, offer spread of risk. They typically develop rates and terms through a consensus process. Like an independent insurance agent, an intermediary has existing contacts with many experts and often can locate the best terms and prices through such contacts. By maintaining contacts with many companies worldwide, an intermediary can offer flexibility in the design of a specialized program or provide facilities not offered under normal market conditions. For example, they may be able to complete a program for which the direct writer expressed no interest due to the particular kind of exposure.

Currently, the largest U.S. intermediary has a larger staff than the largest direct writing reinsurer in the United States. Since reinsurance is technically complex, the participating intermediaries, the reinsurers who participate as markets for intermediaries, and direct reinsurers all profess and typically possess a variety of specialized knowledge.

Size alone is not the telling criterion. Size does permit varied specialties and multiple focal points. Yet there is a great deal of person-to-person contact in reinsurance. Cedents are often searching for solutions to concerns or festering problems. At times the reinsurance solution is evident to the reinsurer or broker who is closer to the cedent and who has observed the developing situation. Thus the very aspect that builds trust also creates the opportunity to foresee and forestall problems. The point is that close and effective relationships can be built by small companies as well as large ones. The bottom line is added value in helping the cedent achieve its success.

Intermediaries utilize widespread contacts and market knowledge to approach their best markets for a particular program. They seek interest and develop a consensus program, with one or two lead reinsurers setting most of the terms. Intermediaries view this diversity as strength, since the process often permits creative suggestions.

Direct reinsurers view the consensus process as time-consuming. There also maybe a laborious collection process in the event of a claim. In the intermediary market, the cedent does not put all of its trust in a single carrier, and the consensus process has positive results.

An intermediary compiles the terms, presses for good rates, and writes the contract. It acts as a clearing house for rates, terms, and ideas that come from the reinsurer group, the cedent, or its own staff to produce quality products for clients.

In the case of a direct writer, the terms, prices, and contract language are written by the reinsurer and offered to the cedent. A direct writer is typically a large company with diverse specialized in-house expertise.

Perhaps the above considerations are theoretical, as competition often dictates the final terms. A cedent may wish to cede at certain terms and rates, but the market, be it direct or intermediary, may resist and press for other terms. Likewise, if the rate is too high, the cedent will simply find another reinsurer to take up the cession. Thus, the final decision includes many considerations, and the choice of direct or intermediary market becomes just part of the whole decision. There are immeasurables within the decision process, so the intermediary/direct decision usually is based on the trust built over a period of years.

Renewing reinsurers normally have a position of advantage. They have successfully passed the trust criteria when the program was new. They have had the opportunity to further build close contact and thus may hold greater knowledge about the business ceded. Further, if the contract has been successful (profitable to the reinsurer and responsive to the cedent), the reinsurer is holding some profit. This is sometimes referred to as a "bank." The larger the bank and the longer that profit has been held, the more likely the reinsurer will favorably consider modifications, such as removal of exclusions, broadening of the kinds and classes of business permitted, reducing rates, or increasing commissions.

Each renewal includes a renegotiation of the terms and price. If the program has not been successful (again measured by one set of criteria for cedents and another set for reinsurers), there may be discord in the relationship. The cedent and reinsurer may differ as to the best way to repair existing problems. The cedent may resist the price increase. If some of the claims have been disputed there may be misunderstandings about the scope of the contract. There may have been personnel changes at either company which reduce the accumulated trust. Thus, the renewal advantage can turn sour and create opportunities for competitors.

The renewing reinsurer's expansive knowledge about the business ceded may lead to a price increase. A competitor may not be able to amass the same knowledge in its review. Also, the new reinsurer may discount a very large single loss as atypical and not likely to recur and thus reach a lower pricing point.

Every cession or reinsurance deal is unique. This is one reason the industry is not regulated in the same manner as other insurance. In the case of primary insurance, the policy is offered by a sophisticated corporation to a buyer, who may not possess the same level of knowledge, so the regulatory process has built-in protections for consumers. Obviously, this logic is more pertinent to personal lines insurance than for commercial transactions. In the case of reinsurance, both parties are considered to be knowledgeable and sophisticated. Thus rates and terms are not approved by the states, but rather are subject to negotiation. This negotiation takes place in an open, competitive environment. Also, the reinsurance marketplace is worldwide, as spread or redistribution of risk is one of the main industry functions. The sophistication within the process is directly related to the line of insurance. However, all reinsurance should be thought of as complex. The typical reinsurance treaty is over 20 pages in length. The treaty assessments usually are intended for longer periods and thus must consider trends and cycles within the business. Facultative considerations typically involve risks which are beyond the normal comfort level for a net acceptance or a kind of risk that requires special or individual handling. Also, facultative applies if the exposure cannot or should not be bundled with other policies to make a treaty. Adding competition into this process simply makes a hard consideration tougher.

Throughout this text we shall refer to reinsurers, in general, and not direct or intermediary markets. Reinsurers subscribing to a large program may include some of each. All get the same terms. The broker market firms do return a modest amount of brokerage to the intermediary for the production effort. The direct market retains that amount, but has internal account executive expenses to cover.

Agency

Agency is the relationship between a principal and their agent, who in turn affects or creates a transfer of insurance risk. It is a rather easy relationship to understand in an insurance transaction. At the beginning of this chapter we illustrated some points of confusion in buying and selling reinsurance. This confusion serves to make the concept of agency a complex one. Before proceeding further on the matter of agency, consider the three parties involved in this relationship: the agent, the broker, and the intermediary.

Agent
An agent is one who acts for or in place of another. In the insurance business, one is authorized by a carrier to act within the scope of the contract to perform specific functions in a limited territory to bind the carrier/ principal on specific classes of insurance for specified dollar limits and terms.

Broker
The broker arranges deals/contracts between parties or between an agent and a principal/carrier with whom there is no direct contact. Brokers do not have binding authority but submit risks or exposures to an insurer, who in turn binds those submissions that meet selection, terms, and price guidelines. Risks are bound by the insurer.

Intermediary
An intermediary is a reinsurance broker. Intermediaries do not exist in the retail or primary side of the business.

Agency or *implied* agency is a concern when things go right. However, when things go wrong and entities are hurt financially, implied agency becomes the basis of lawsuits and arbitrations.

The reinsurance intermediary usually represents a ceding company by means of a "broker of record letter," which is a formal agreement issued by the ceding company for the intermediary to market the cession, with no authority to bind coverage.

Is the intermediary the cedent's agent, or are they agents of the reinsurer? This is a complex question, but one the reader should understand may be viewed differently by the various participants in this business. There is a very good reason for this divergence of viewpoints. If there is no written contract there is no formal agency for the intermediary. Thus the differing perspectives arise as the several parties assess their own views as to the implied agency.

In most intermediary placements, the intermediary is paid by the assuming carrier or reinsurer. This is a longstanding market arrangement. In essence, the assuming reinsurer is paying the intermediary for bringing business. If the reinsurance is accepted or consummated, an intermediary's commission or brokerage is allowed. The cost is fairly standard, so both parties are aware of the typical amounts allocated to the intermediary. (However intermediaries do not discuss their fees with the cedents, as this information is considered confidential between the intermediary and reinsurer.)

Let us compare this arrangement with that of the independent insurance agent. Being independent, a local agent has secured authority from several insurance companies to transact certain types of business on behalf of each. He holds an agency contract with each of the insurance carriers. The insurer pays commissions once the business is written, and again if renewed. The policyholder, or customer, has no written contract with the agent. So there is a contractual relationship or *agency* between the agent and the insurer.

A reinsurance intermediary has no contractual relationship with the cedent or the reinsurers. The broker of record letter is only permission to market a specific book of business (see Exhibit 4.1). The broker of record letter does not create a formal agency relationship since it lacks terms, conditions, duties, and other important criteria. There are unwritten expectations about this informal relationship, which is referred to as *implied agency*. The cedent, the intermediary, and the assuming reinsurer each view this implied agency from a different perspective. Because it is a somewhat vague relationship, there is some variance in the use and understanding of the term "agency." Typically reinsurers do not afford any sort of binding authority or written authority to intermediaries with whom they choose to do business.

Intermediaries forward copies of reinsurance acceptance authorizations to the cedent. Note that insurance agents issue binders, at times within their authority provided by the agency agreement and at times with specific approval by the carrier. In reinsurance the cedent must decide which of the authorizations it will accept. Brokerage is paid by the reinsurers, initially and again if renewed.

During the 1970s, following the closure of a major domestic intermediary, significant disputes arose over the funds in process between reinsurers, the

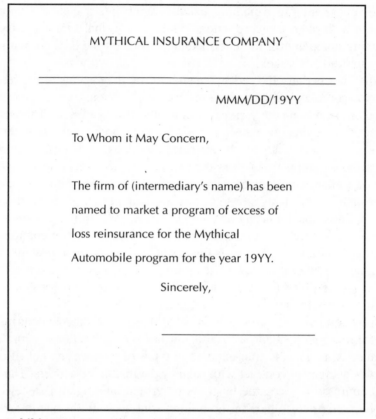

MYTHICAL INSURANCE COMPANY

MMM/DD/19YY

To Whom it May Concern,

The firm of (intermediary's name) has been

named to market a program of excess of

loss reinsurance for the Mythical

Automobile program for the year 19YY.

Sincerely,

Exhibit 4.1.   Sample Broker of Record Letter

intermediary, and cedent companies. Some ceding carriers had forwarded premiums that had not reached the assuming carriers. Some reinsurers had forwarded claim payments to the intermediary that had not reached the cedents. There were a great many contracts involved and confusion abounded. This bankruptcy led to adoption of a standard intermediary clause for reinsurance:

_____, (Intermediary's name) is hereby recognized as the intermediary negotiating this agreement for all business hereunder. All communications (including but not limited to notices, statements, premiums, returned premiums, commissions, taxes, losses, loss expenses, salvages, and loss settlements) relating thereto will be transmitted to the company or the reinsurers through (Intermediary's name, address, city, and state). Payments by the company to the intermediary will be deemed payment to the reinsurers. Payments by the reinsurers to the intermediary will be deemed payment to the company only to the extent that such payments are actually received by the company.

The intent of the intermediary clause is to settle concerns of funds in the hands of the intermediary and to set the requirement that communication goes through the intermediary. Like the broker of record letter, this clause does not create an agency relationship, except at the time of payment. Also, there are no terms, conditions, or duties, except those relating to handling the funds.

Each party involved in the relationship holds its own business perspective with regard to the matter of agency. Intermediaries consider themselves as truly independent companies, providing services to both cedents and reinsurers.

Cedents develop relationships very much like that of the policyholder at the primary level. They chose to do business with the intermediary for some reason, be it convenience or trust. Over time, they seek the advice and opinion of the intermediary. The cedent believes the intermediary is "its agent," just like the primary policyholder believes the agent works in his behalf.

Reinsurers hold longstanding relationships with the intermediary firms. They pay the brokerage. Yet, they do not believe they have an agency agreement with the intermediary. The intermediary collects comments, terms, and conditions from several reinsurers. Almost all of this information is discussed with the cedent, while the reinsurer receives only bits and pieces from the intermediary, as directed by the cedent. Reinsurers also realize that business submissions may contain a certain amount of sales hype. (Please do not misunderstand—"hype" is not necessarily bad, it's not false, it's not lying. It is simply a very real part of all business.) Reinsurers attempt to spot such hype as they read materials.

Let us consider an example. A submission may include the following statement by the intermediary: "I have known the president of this company for ten years, have found him quite knowledgeable about insurance and feel he is the type of individual with whom you would like to do business." That is not a statement of fact. It is an opinion. It is a realistic example of how hype or verbiage is used to foster a positive response. It does not relate how often or how close the observation of this president's leadership might have been. Yet it attempts to describe this individual as a friendly, knowledgeable person.

Reinsurance underwriters do appreciate this kind of statement, and if it is omitted they will enquire. Reinsurers read submissions very closely and attempt to recognize hype and appreciate its merits. Such salesmanship is a necessary part of this business. The reinsurance underwriter expects the intermediary to apply salesmanship within the offering. This effectively positions the intermediary as an agent of the cedent in the mind of reinsurers.

And lawyers hold yet another perspective of the agency relationship. Representations made by the intermediary in placing coverage are considered to be representations of the cedent. And while the intermediary holds no contractual relationship with either party, it accepts duties which last the life of the business. Interestingly there are no specified ways for the intermediary to step aside while activity remains on the business. So even long after the premium has been fully reported and earned and all brokerages are paid, the intermediary still has duties to perform.

These perspectives coexist with little conflict. The client believes he has a "contract" with his agent/intermediary. The intermediary feels truly independent. The underwriter believes he understands the implied agency. All are right, yet all are wrong. While the concept of agency may be difficult to define, it works.

Intermediaries are very real, significant competitors to the direct writing reinsurers. The service they provide is a vital component to the industry. Direct writing reinsurers provide similar services but in a different manner. The differing approaches of a direct reinsurer and an intermediary bring complexity and diversity to the business which should be viewed as positive. It is interesting and it works, though it may not be easy to understand.

Just one further thought. In today's complex marketplace there are a few intermediaries that seek payment by the ceding carrier. The value they emphasize is a clear delineation of loyalty, with no additional cost. Supposedly, the cedent has an even closer relationship with its broker or intermediary. Some intermediaries also tailor their charges to the nature of the service desired by the cedent. This is "unbundled" in that the cedent can choose the aspects of the service that it wishes to purchase. If, for example, the cedent possesses vast computer capabilities, why should it not produce the split payment amounts due to each reinsurer? Indeed, it may do so to prepare its annual statement, so why pay someone else to repeat the process? The submissions to reinsurers do not relate just how much the intermediary has been paid for its work.

ACCEPTANCE AND APPROVAL OF REINSURERS

Procedures for acceptance and approval of reinsurers are as varied as those of assuming the business. Again, the sophistication of the methodology varies directly with the class and kind of business to be ceded and the reinsurance function to be secured. This outline shall be brief and applies to the broad spectrum of classes.

Tail

One of the key reasons why class and kind are critical is the length of the developmental *tail* on claims. Classes with a shorter claim developmental expectancy do not require the same depth of analysis with respect to investment potential as do those classes with extended claim developmental potential. This statement applies to many considerations, not merely tests for solvency and investment. For example, the length of the development tail on claims may be a criterion used in determining the size of line awarded to subscribing reinsurers.

Solvency

Solvency is of course a primary determinant. Premiums flow with minimal delay. The premium is typically in hand before the claims arise and long before claims are paid in full. Therefore, cedents must be careful to make connections with reinsurers who will be active and viable well beyond the in-force term of the specific contract. Reinsurers want to do business with carriers that will remain solvent, have the ability to make all premium adjustments, and make the gross claim payments before coming to them for reimbursement.

Solvency is a tough consideration because it is difficult to determine how long a specific company can last. Cedent companies, reinsurers, and intermediaries devote considerable time to the assessment of solvency. Chapter 14 introduces methods and some considerations in this process. The following are some factors used in the assessment of solvency:

- Premiums-to-policyholder's surplus ratio
- Mix or kinds and classes written in relation to specialty
- Combined and operating ratios for the past two to ten years
- Percentage of business accepted as reinsurance
- IBNR to total reserves related to percent of long tail business
- Ratio of business retained to business accepted
- Reinsurance market reputation
- Results of the National Association of Insurance Commissioners, Insurance Regulatory Information System Tests
- Opinion of corporate management
- Ratings by A.M. Best, Demotech, Duff & Phelps, Moody's Investors, Standard & Poor's, and others.

A systematic approach is important. The statistical detail needs to be consistent and weaknesses should be researched. The opinion of corporate management is vital, not just because they hold final decisions, but because they probably have had contact with leaders of the reinsurer offering its services. Reinsurance is a people business; beyond the statistics it is people who make the decisions that lead to success or failure. The basic trust lies in the capabilities of the company's leadership.

The size of line or amount ceded will vary according to the size of the authorization and according to the security analysis applicable to the specific reinsurer.

Placement of property risks requires assessment of capacity to capital. This should include some consideration of how much the reinsurer might accept on the very same risk or risks being ceded. One simply does not want to cede to a carrier that might be hit by an uncomfortable accumulation from multiple sources. Knowledge about the reinsurer's internal procedures may be part of the decision.

Placement of catastrophe exposures requires a different assessment of likelihood. Has the reinsurer accepted an uncomfortable concentration from an exposed territory? How have they reacted to past catastrophes? Catastrophe business is priced on an amortization basis, such that losses are repaid over an extended period of time. Some companies expand after major losses, having controlled their capacity during prior years, waiting for better rates. Others cut back sharply, hurt by the impact of a major storm. It is a likely assumption that reinsurers in the latter category will be suffering financially and may pay legitimate claims much slower than is required by the cedent. This type of consideration is discussed when selecting reinsurers. Cedents do try to assess financial capability before and after a costly event.

Timely payment of claims is a very important consideration when selecting from a number of reinsurers. Intermediaries keep track of response time by a reinsurer. Direct writing reinsurers attempt to exploit the advantage of being a single source for payment.

Another consideration is where a specific reinsurer might be acceptable on a program. The special expertise and past record of a reinsurer become selection criteria for a cedent. Many reinsurers are oriented toward either property or liability business, and the choice should be made according to the risk or class of the cession.

The key to this analysis is the amount of authorizations received on a particular reinsurance offering. This may change from the original submission to the final terms. Let us consider a case where the cession is huge, thus requiring many reinsurers, possibly a mix of both direct and intermediary markets. If the total subscription is 110 percent, the cedent has some room for choice. If the subscription totals 98 percent, a shortfall exists. In the shortfall case, the cedent must decide whether to take an increased net share. Obviously the decisions about acceptability are harder when the subscription is not ample. It might be possible to improve the terms and draw in additional authorizations, which in turn would permit culling based on the security assessment. The net profitability, indeed, the viability of the program, may rest on these decisions. Given the long term of most reinsurances, these are tough choices.

MEASURES OF USAGE AND PERFORMANCE

Utilization Ratio

Utilization ratio is defined as the percentage of direct and assumed premiums that is spent on reinsurance. The calculation is best measured on an earned premium basis, since a calendar year calculation is desired. The best source of data is the annual statement of the company.

$$\text{Utilization Ratio} = \frac{\text{Total Ceded Earned Premium}}{\text{Direct} + \text{Assumed Earned Premiums}}$$

Some calculate this ratio on a net basis, subtracting reinsurance commissions from the numerator. Such commissions cover a staffing cost rather than an exposure element. However, the denominator should be adjusted by commissions to agents in order to reflect an exposure-to-exposure basis. That precision is not worth the added effort. It is better to use a relativity that is simple and can be calculated routinely than employ a difficult calculation that is seldom used.

The range of this statistic is typically 1 percent to 45 percent. Both 0 percent (no insurance) and 100 percent (100 percent ceded to reinsurers) are possible but unlikely. The average has increased over the years mainly because liability premiums have grown in proportion to property premiums. Liability exposures have traditionally required more reinsurance than property exposures. Most companies average between 16 percent and 24 percent. Larger companies tend to cede more. However, one should not be able to correlate desirability of the reinsurance with utilization. In other words, higher usage does not mean poorer results nor does less usage mean better results.

This utilization measure is important for cedents to track from year to year. It will help maintain consistency in the cessions. If the program is largely excess of loss, it may be a guide to comfort level and the choice of retention level.

Reinsurers should use this statistic more than they have in the past. Reinsurers have intuitive understanding about whether a company is a significant buyer or casual buyer of reinsurance. A measurement such as this utilization ratio may be a way for reinsurers to compare usage from company to company. It also should help them decide if the offer on the table is critical or supplemental in the eyes of the cedent.

Benefit-to-Cost Ratio

The benefit-to-cost ratio is the relativity between recoveries and cost. There are both simple and somewhat difficult calculations for this ratio. The simple calculation uses total loss and LAE recovered as a numerator and the overall cost as denominator. It is like a loss ratio in that commissions, reinsurance costs, and profit make up the remaining percentages.

$$\text{Benefit - to - Cost Ratio} = \frac{\text{Total Loss Recovered}}{\text{Net Cost of Reinsurance (Earned Basis)}}$$

$$\text{Total Loss Recovered} = \text{(Paid Loss + Paid LAE) Recoveries +}$$
$$\text{Ceded Case Reserves + Bulk Reserves}$$

$$\text{Net Cost on an Excess of Loss Basis} = \text{Rate} \times \text{Subject Matter Earned Premium}$$

$$\text{Net Cost on a Proportional Basis} = \text{Ceded Premium} - \text{Commissions Returned}$$

This measure has a few special considerations. First, the bulk reserves, or IBNR, are not often available. Second, some prefer to use net cost as a basis. If the basis of the information is the Annual Statement, ceded IBNR is not available but it can be estimated. Paid losses and paid LAE are supplied in the Annual Statement on both the total and ceded basis. Likewise, ceded case reserves are reported. Bulk reserves are not supplied for the ceded portion and exist only in total. Ceded bulk reserves can be estimated using the following guidelines:

1. If the total bulk reserve is known, it is an upper bound since 100 percent would not be ceded.
2. The ratio of (Ceded Case Reserves ÷ Total Case Reserves) × Total Bulk Reserves will stand as a lower bound for the estimate.
3. IBNR is greater for reinsurance than for primary insurance.
4. It is likely that the ceded bulk reserve estimate will be 1.5 to 4 times the value in item 2 above.

This formula is a base indicator or crude estimate. It should be understood that this fixed formula does not account for the wide variance that surely exists from company to company. Nor does it account for business that may have aged, thus already accruing much of its ultimate development.

There are two ways to approach the fact that the estimate of this portion may greatly affect the benefit-to-cost ratio. One could apply a fixed factor, say 2.00, in every case. Alternatively, one could apply a best judgment estimate for each company. While the fact that one portion must be estimated weakens the credibility of the statistic, it should not preclude use of the ratio. There are ways to mitigate this consideration, but they are beyond the scope of this text.

What should the benefit-to-cost ratio look like? If the calculation is on a net basis, 1.00 is break-even, with nil profit for reinsurers. A ratio above 1.00

puts the reinsurers in loss, while one below 1.00 has a measure of profit. Like the combined ratio for insurance companies, this ratio does not include investment income. If the ratio is calculated on a gross basis, commissions and fees must be considered. Typically with excess of loss reinsurance the contract will be rated with brokerage of 10 percent. That implies $1.00 - .10 = .90$ is the break-even point.

In proportional situations it is necessary to subtract the actual commission ratio and the brokerage ratio. Since the ratio is calculated on an earned basis the deductions should also be measured against earned premium. Typically the commission will be something like .275 and the brokerage .01, so the breakeven ratio will be $1.00 - .275 - .01 = .715$.

How should the benefit-to-cost ratio be interpreted? In an ideal situation both the cedent and reinsurer should be allowed to make a profit on their business. Investment income should be considered, but ideally both should make an underwriting profit.

If the cedent is having a bad year, very likely its reinsurance benefit-to-cost ratio will be above break-even. During a good year, the cedent will profit and the reinsurance benefit-to-cost ratio should be below break-even.

With a break-even ratio, the cedent could expect its rates to go up. This implies that reinsurers have not achieved an underwriting profit, thus the expectation is for upward pressure on rates (or pressure to reduce commissions). If the ratio is above break-even, the pressure from reinsurers may be stronger. However, the decision should be tempered by the total experience over the term of the reinsurance. Increases or decreases in rates or commissions should reflect total experience with due consideration for trends.

If the benefit-to-cost ratio is unusually high or unusually low, change should be expected. An unusually high ratio implies increased rates, higher retention levels, and perhaps a restructuring of the entire reinsurance program. Unusually low ratios mean high reinsurer profits, that is, rates will drift lower, terms will relax, commissions will increase, etc. An unusually low ratio is healthy, as it often means both cedent and reinsurer are building profits. The motivation to change will be increased if one party holds an apparent advantage, so the terms should shift toward a better balance. Balance does not necessarily mean equal. Balance is relative to the amount and kind of exposure held by the parties to the reinsurance contract. They will not always agree as to what constitutes proper balance.

The benefit-to-cost ratio is a leading statistic. Monitoring its movement from year to year can lead both the cedent and the reinsurers to apply pressure to adopt changes in the contract. It can also help reinsurers assess submissions from new clients. If the benefit-to-cost ratio of the cedent is uncomfortable, the reinsurer should not compete for business from this client. Alternatively, with an attractive ratio in the past, the reinsurer might be comfortable in pressing aggressively for business from this cedent source.

OTHER CONSIDERATIONS IN APPROVING REINSURERS

Certain incidents have been material in developing the considerations that ceding companies have in selecting or approving reinsurers.

The Tort System

The U.S. tort system has been in crisis since the mid-seventies. Laws vary sharply from state to state. There is no universally applied rule about how to settle disputes or how to evaluate pain, suffering, and myriad other loss situations. Consider the following example:

CASE STUDY: TANKER TRUCK LOSS

A large tanker truck was traveling through a small town; its speed was excessive. It is not known if the driver fell asleep or if some automobile merging into traffic caused the crash. The tanker jackknifed, flopped on its side, and hurtled down the roadway, until it hit the abutment of an overpass. The tractor and front of the tanker went on one side, while the back of the tanker spewed its flammable cargo, with sparks under and beyond the overpass into more than a dozen people waiting for a bus.

The liability coverages of many companies were affected. The major payee, however, was the manufacturer of the fifth wheel or deadplate. That is the greasy plate that joins the tractor and trailer. In this case, the product did not fail. It was not separated even by the impact of the bridge. This product performed well beyond expectations, and admirably so. Yet this manufacturer and its product liability carrier were the major contributors to the fund split among these injured parties. Fair? Of course not. Others, with some fault in the matter faced lesser consequences.

The deadplate insurer paid the largest single claim in its corporate history in the above example. It was a knowledgeable participant that selected its exposures with containment in mind; however, the system sought the nearest deep pocket, rather than determining true liability. The deadplate insurer asked its reinsurers to pay their part of this claim, per the reinsurance treaties in force at the time.

The following treaty year, this insurer faced extreme pressure from its reinsurers, who had begun to pay this huge loss. Some reinsurers chose not to continue. Other reinsurers demanded increased rates. Filling out the capacity required some new reinsurers. These latter reinsurers enjoyed the much higher rate, better terms, and increased underwriting scrutiny by the primary carriers on this business which naturally followed.

This example is perplexing. The primary insurer (and its policyholder) had no part in causing the event, yet it had to contribute dearly to the loss and also suffered consequences on its cost of business for many years.

Such instances of incalculable pain and suffering seeking redress have led to disproportionate sharing of the costs of reparations in the current tort system, in some cases. Thus, with the system in crisis and no common agreement on how liability should be distributed, liability carriers and their reinsurers continue to apply their best efforts to make things work.

Asbestosis Litigation

In the late seventies, the asbestosis litigation rose to a fever pitch. Asbestosis is a slowly developing disease and several theories were formulated as to when the disease started. One theory was that the disease began on first exposure to asbestos fibers, and since most claims were occupational cases, the cause was referred to as an exposure trigger. A second theory, set the coverage trigger at the time the disease was first diagnosed. The third trigger was a continuous one, where each and every exposure constituted an incremental advance of the disease. A fourth swept in all of the other triggers to apportion coverage.

The story of how the industry faced and worked to resolve these matters is interesting and still controversial. It is related here because these losses were incredibly significant to the insurance industry. Insurance companies took sides defending one trigger mechanism or another. Reinsurers were faced with the prospect of paying one cedent under its theory and another under a different, diametrically opposed theory.

Reinsurers did take part in the debate and pressed for what they believed was the best course of action. The professional performance of the reinsurance segment of the industry was remarkable in that reinsurers responded to each reinsurance acceptance on whichever theory was chosen by the primary carrier. They paid claims under more than one theory.

Recognizing the individual needs of ceding carriers, the reinsurers fully agreed to "Follow the Fortunes" of the cedent. The commitment to do so is an integral part of the business and, in this historical illustration, reinsurers followed the fortunes on a case specific basis, in response to the individual philosophy of the cedent. It was not an immediately adopted practice, there were certain and difficult deliberations before the end was generally accomplished. Reinsurers discussed and informed and participated in developing the necessary underlying claim theory and, ultimately, did respond.

SUMMARY

The selection of a reinsurer (or reinsurers) is a tough choice and an important one. Will the reinsurer respond as required? Will it react logically and professionally to unforseen circumstances? Can they be counted on in the long term?

In this chapter, the object has been to briefly discuss some of the considerations underlying the choice of reinsurer. Every consideration has not been mentioned.

The ultimate decision must weigh the relative impact versus consequences. Price must be weighed against management capability. Solvency must be related to adaptability. While it may be tempting to take the lowest price or most attractive terms, all these other matters (and some not mentioned here) must be taken into consideration when selecting reinsurers.

In summary, there are five critical points in the process of selecting a reinsurer:

1. *Security:* Is the reinsurer financially sound?
2. *Capacity:* Does the reinsurer have sufficient capacity to fill the need?
3. *Leadership:* Can the reinsurer help create profits, give suggestions about problems, and give an overall boost in developing the business?
4. *Claim Handling:* Does the reinsurer have a sound claim paying ability and adequate response time?
5. *Reputation:* Is the reinsurer a good long-term partner?

5

REINSURANCE STRUCTURES

SIXTH LOSS EXCESS
EXCESS OF LOSS TREATIES, PER RISK OR PER OCCURRENCE
CATASTROPHE EXCESS OF LOSS TREATIES
QUOTA SHARE TREATIES
SURPLUS SHARE TREATIES
AGGREGATE EXCESS OF LOSS OR STOP LOSS TREATIES

This chapter outlines some of the basic structures used by reinsurers. The term *structures* may not mean the same thing throughout the reinsurance industry. Here the term refers to the standard statistical types of reinsurance. We often refer to the kind, class, and type of insurance to which the reinsurance is applied. The application of a reinsurance structure will effectively alter the shape of the portfolio held by the ceding carrier. Because of the selected reinsurance structure, the cedent will hold a retention, net after reinsurance, that is different than that held gross.

The insurer writes a portfolio of insurance business, part of which is transferred or ceded to reinsurers. The remaining business will have a different limit, a smaller volume, or perhaps a different mix of components than the original portfolio. The *gross* is the actual writing, while the remainder is referred to as the cedent's *net*.

Structures apply to treaty and facultative alike; however, facultative cessions tend to use the simpler structures because of the type of exposure they involve. Facultative exposures are often quite complex. The cessions involve large or unique risks, such that there are too few in number to bundle together as homogeneous cessions to make a treaty. A complex cession of a complex exposure may be hard to assess as well as price; therefore, simple structures are often better for complex exposures. Typically a facultative reinsurer handles many thousands of facultative cessions or certificates with the focus on the exposures of each one. Complex structures would hinder the flow and make the business less cost-effective, the processing less swift.

SIXTH LOSS EXCESS

This is an unusual cover, one that may have many names. The premise is that there are few very large claims. The six largest claims comprise that portion of the portfolio that has experienced the greatest volatility. An insurer certainly may wish to address such a worrisome potential.

First, let us digress from structures to discuss comfort level, which was introduced in Chapter 1. The comfort level will be that limit which the company typically uses as its policy limit. The insurer may offer higher limits to superior clients, that is, those with nominal exposures. Given a statistical profile of the limits distribution, an analyst can usually spot the area where the insurer has greatest comfort. If the company writes many different kinds and classes, the comfort level may not be visible since the levels differ depending on the class under consideration.

Exhibit 5.1 depicts the limits distribution for a mature portfolio. Compare this to Exhibit 1.1 in Chapter 1, which depicted an immature company. The comfort level here is rather high up on the graph.

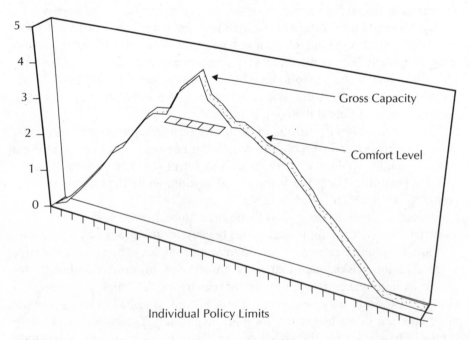

Exhibit 5.1.   Distribution Chart: Mature Portfolio

A specific comfort level may be determined based on financial considerations, such as 1 percent of policyholder's surplus or perhaps 3 percent of premium volume, so that an individual loss would not be material to the bottom line results in a given year. Or it may be judgmental with respect to the types of claims that arise in a given line of business.

Let us now suppose that the chart in Exhibit 5.1 represents claims instead of policy limits. The size of claim is bounded by the policy limits offered. A giant claim cannot happen with a low limit policy. If there are a hundred or so larger limit policies, one cannot predict where the loss will occur or which policy will have the larger claim. Still, there will be many small claims, a moderate number of medium-sized claims, and few large claims.

The shift from limit comfort level to claim comfort level is easy conceptually. The basic principle is to avoid claims above the comfort level.

If a company has experienced many large claims it will take action to reduce the likelihood that such discomfort will arise again. For example, it will be more conservative in allowing high limits, even though the higher limits are acceptable in the printed guidelines.

The sixth loss excess treaty is based on the theory that the sixth largest claim will be very nearly the same size each year. Large claims are unusual. Most claims are small, and the claim count diminishes at higher claim total levels. Six claims should comprise the very largest claims in a given year. There may or may not be a giant claim each year. Occasionally the company may experience two huge claims. Other years it may have three or four big claims, but no giant claim. Consider one example of the six largest claims (Exhibit 5.2).

This type of treaty can be considered a capacity treaty, since the levels to which limits are offered certainly become a determining factor in the cession for both the cedent and assuming reinsurer. Most portfolios generate fairly high claim frequency, so it is likely that in setting up this cession the cedent will expect several hundred or perhaps a thousand claims in all and in purchasing this cover will address the peak of its volatility. In Exhibit 5.2, the sixth excess treaty would cover only the very tip of the exposures.

There is likely to be greater volatility in the very largest claim from year to year than in the sixth largest. The 100th largest may be almost level. However, capturing the largest six encompasses a segment of the greatest volatility. For example, consider the relativity of the largest loss in the five-year period to the smallest such loss in the same period. In this example, year 5 has two bad claims at $975,000. Year 3 also happens to have two claims tied for worst at $650,000. The relativity between the "worst worst" and the "best worst" is $975,000/$650,000 or 150 percent. That would be a high measure of volatility. With such historical volatility, the ceding company might well seek coverage that will level the volatility for a fixed price. The sixth excess treaty is one treaty structure that can provide the desired leveling effect.

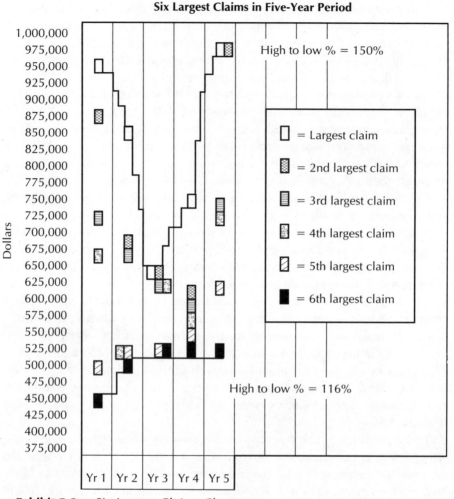

Exhibit 5.2.   Six Largest Claims Chart

The sixth highest claim varies only 16 percent from $450,000 in year 1 to $525,000 in years 4, 5, and 6. Thus in contrast to the ratio for the very largest claim, the latter is a relatively stable situation.

The average total per year of the six highest claims in the above example is just under $4 million. That is a big number, surely enough to create worry for the company. Such worry fuels the need to purchase some reinsurance protection. The average claim over this period is $660,000. For a fixed price, of say $700 × 6 = $4.2 million a reinsurer may take up that exposure. The cedent would be passing off the volatility within its portfolio for a fixed price.

The loading used in this example is just 5 percent, (4.2 million/$4 million). In order to accept that low loading, the reinsurer would have to be supremely confident that the $4 million average would hold and that the 5 percent would cover its cost plus a margin for profit. Given the volatility in these largest claims, 5 percent seems inappropriately small. Here, 5 percent has been used to illustrate a fixed cost and also to demonstrate that judgment is required in setting the loading factor. Such judgment is a complex consideration, but one the reinsurer will have researched.

The price would ultimately be set competitively or perhaps by consensus. The pricing methodology would take into consideration the limits exposing this treaty, the kind and class of risk, the typical payout rate for claims, and the cost of money, that is, the current interest rate.

One of the unusual characteristics of this sixth excess treaty is that one does not know for sure which claims apply until the year is over. They can even develop later such that the seventh largest grows and the sixth largest reduces, resulting in a shift well after the year is over. This treaty also illustrates the faith that often develops between the reinsurer and the cedent. The reinsurer would obviously closely follow developments of the six to ten largest claims to be sure the cedent was properly containing payments.

The sixth excess treaty is an excess of loss treaty since it has a specified retention and applies to the losses that exceed that level. It is an unusual treaty in that the retention level is expressed as a count rather than a specific loss amount. This cover also pays 100 percent of these six largest claims. This unusual type of treaty illustrates many principles and demonstrates that although the number of structures is fairly small, their use can be quite creative.

EXCESS OF LOSS TREATIES, PER RISK OR PER OCCURRENCE

These treaties are structured such that all claims above a specified level are paid by the reinsurers and all claims below it are held net by the cedent. The net portion is called the retention. Reinsurers abbreviate the term as XS for excess, sometimes just X, or XOL for excess of loss. On this basis, each claim that is large enough to exceed the treaty attachment point is theoretically split into the excess portion and net portion, based solely on the size of the claim compared to the preset attachment level. Property excess treaties that apply on a policy or risk basis are called "per risk excesses." That usage has evolved from basic fire insurances, that a building can only burn to the ground once. It is true that property coverages may respond to many claims in a given year. For example, a high-rise apartment building may have a number of water damage claims, several storm claims, perhaps a few smoke damage claims, etc. So while some of the language appears to have evolved from the single claim concept, repeated events can occur under such policies and be applicable to these treaties.

If the buildings are separate and satisfy the agreed definitions of a "risk," then claims are set in the perspective of each of those risks. For example, a group of town house apartments may be considered as multiple risks, if they are sufficiently separated to not be exposed to a common fire hazard. For the property excess of loss per risk treaty, the amount of loss at each site is a separate claim. Catastrophe reinsurance or other reinsurance coverage may also apply to the claim.

Casualty excesses work a little differently. Liability policies allow for and expect any number of claims in a given year. It is therefore possible that one policy could have more than one claim and more than one large claim. Thus the casualty term is *excess of loss per occurrence*. The focus is on the event that caused the damage.

Both property and casualty excess treaties are set on policy limits. They will reflect the comfort levels determined by the cedent (if the reinsurance is available at a reasonable cost at that level). Normally the cedent will secure limits from the comfort level upward. It may top off the very largest capacity with facultative cessions but will plan the treaty limit to handle that portion of the capacity which is used with some frequency.

Since these excess treaties apply on a policy limit basis and do so above a specified level or attachment point, they supply capacity. They permit the company to write some limits above their comfort level, thus providing added capacity. This is accomplished for a fixed cost, or a cost with a modest increase if the results are adverse.

If there is substantial capacity ceded, the cession may be split into layers of excess coverage. Layering is motivated by pricing considerations, the profile of limits, as well as marketing preferences. Some reinsurers prefer to participate on layers where there is a fairly high loss frequency; they hope the pricing will be more credible. Others prefer to participate on high layers, to avoid claim frequency, and to hope for an occasional claim-free year. This is discussed further in Chapter 9.

Exhibit 5.3 is a limits profile for property values in the Mythical Insurance Company Homeowner's Insurance Program, which provides limits up to $1 million on a single residence. Assume in this example that the company's comfort level is $200,000. The table shows that 75 percent of the policies have limits below that level. The company wants to purchase an excess of loss, per risk, property-only reinsurance treaty. It may be advisable to split the $800,000 of further capacity into two layers.

The first $200,000 excess of $200,000 contains the bulk of the higher limit policies. A top layer of $600,000 excess of $400,000 would exist as a true capacity cover. With just over 10,000 policies exposing the top layer, the company may not expect to have a claim most years.

At the very top of the scale, these numbers are rather small to support a treaty, so the cedent may find the cost prohibitive. This is a simplistic example of the type of considerations that underlie the design of such a treaty. Consider that the 10,280 higher limit policies comprise only 2.5 percent of the policies

| | Policy | Exposure Measure | |
Limit Ranges	Count	Subtotal	% Count
900,000 to 1,000,000	10		
800,000 to 899,999	45		
700,000 to 799,999	105	10,280	2.5%
600,000 to 699,999	510		
500,000 to 599,999	355		
400,000 to 499,999	9,255		
300,000 to 399,999	21,333	93,458	22.8%
200,000 to 299,999	72,125		
100,000 to 199,999	145,350		
50,000 to 99,999	110,250	305,600	74.7%
25,000 to 49,999	50,000		
0 to 24,999	0		

Exhibit 5.3. Limits Profile with Layer Subtotals

written. The cedent would consider the relative cost of offering such limits with their attendant cost and other benefits of writing such business.

This example could be structured differently. Note that 9255 of the policies fall into the range of limits from $400,000 to $499,999. The cedent may find it necessary to purchase the first layer excess of loss treaty attaching at $200,000 but having a $300,000 limit. With the higher limit, that layer would cost more; however, the company would have automatic treaty contracts for 99.7 percent of its policies. The remaining high limit situations, 1025 in number, could be managed with facultative reinsurance on an excess of loss basis.

The cedent, intermediary (if such exists), and reinsurers all closely consider the business from several statistical profiles to select the structure that best fits the cedent's needs and to determine the appropriate cost.

During periods of inflation, each renewal would find a greater portion of the limits exposed beyond the layer attachment point. This is natural due to inflation and generally increasing property values. New business would also be affected by the increase in values and the insurance price would rise as well. Under such circumstances, it is unwise to maintain the same retention year after year. The comfort level should expand with growth in the portfolio. That growth should also track growth in the insurer's financials, for if the business growth exceeds growth in the insurer's financials, the insurer's solvency ratios may become out of balance. Because liability claims tend to remain open for many years, inflation has a greater impact on casualty claims. Thus, it is even more important to increase routinely the retention of casualty excess treaties, particularly those with a great number of limits exposing the layer.

Normally, excess treaties are priced with rates against volume rather than on a commission basis. The latter is not unheard of, it is just rare. Rates are straightforward in logic and easy to calculate for an accounting statement. They are set to apply to all policies in the class or kind specified for the treaty, whether or not the limits reach the layer. The premium from all such policies is called *subject premium,* since it is the subject business to which the rate applies.

Subject premium may be written or earned. From a practical standpoint, the difference is one of pace, as earnings typically follow writings by four to six months. The first quarter's written becomes the second quarter's earnings, in rough terms. At times, however, the choice of written or earned may result from the definition of which policies apply to the annual term. This is an important point to review when ceding or assuming a new treaty. Using a basis of earned premium may sweep in activity from prior years. Remember, the calculation of earnings does vary somewhat from company to company. Earnings in a particular calendar year will include earned premium from policies written in the prior year and perhaps some earnings from multiple-year policies written even earlier. It is wise to eliminate such possibilities by specifying that the treaty applies only to new and renewal business and not to all in-force business at the inception of the treaty. That will require that the business be underwritten anew within the term of the treaty and will generally avoid business that may be recognized as substandard in quality or rate, at the time the treaty is being negotiated.

Because the cedent handles its business on a daily basis while the reinsurer only sees quarterly or annual summaries of premium and individually reported claims, the cedent holds a distinct advantage in recognizing the quality of its portfolio and rate adequacy. Business ethics in the industry are usually high enough that such disadvantage is not abused.

Loss Adjustment Expense (LAE) may be handled in a number of ways. Often, as shown in Exhibit 5.4, coverage for LAE is in addition to the amount of loss and is split proportionally by the amount of loss paid by each reinsurer and the net amount held by the ceding company. For casualty business, this is the most often selected basis. In property situations you will frequently find LAE to be included within the limit, by applying the excess to the sum of loss and LAE.

Statistical reporting is set at the time of negotiation. The premium will likely be agreed on one of two bases. A quarterly deposit may be set at 25 percent of 80 percent of the anticipated income, to be adjusted at 15 months at a specified rate and minimum premium. This effectively places the premium at five payments of 20 percent. The minimum is typically set at the 80 percent amount. In addition, the subject premium to which the rate applies may be subject to an annual maximum to hold growth in check. Alternatively, the treaty may require monthly or quarterly reports of subject pre-

Excess of Loss Per Risk/Per Occurrence	
Characteristic	Remark
Type	Excess
Reinsurance functions	Capacity, stabilization, or financial
Pricing	Generally rated based on subject premium written or earned. May also have a profit contingency. Based on past loss activity to the layer, with assumptions about the changes expected for the future. May include a capacity charge.
Premium split	Apportionment related to the developing profit history of the treaty rather than to specific claim sizes.
Claims split	All claims that are large enough to penetrate the treaty, subject to the treaty limit, exclusions, and other terms. Not specifically related to premium share.
LAE split	Proportional split with the amount of loss compared to the total loss.
Layering	Standard practice. This type is quite adaptable to layering. Each layer responds in order, bottom layer first.

Exhibit 5.4. Characteristics of Excess of Loss Per Risk or Per Occurrence Treaties

mium, with payment of the specified rate multiplied by the subject premium. This method effectively secures the full amount in four payments. With the same rate, these two variations would have the same result, except for the timing of the payments.

Losses are reported on an individual claim basis. The first report may be specified in cases that do not exceed the attachment point. The guidelines may require notice as soon as practical (ASAP) on each and every case that meets certain criteria, such as cases with reserve at half the attachment point, any death cases, and serious injury cases without regard to reserve level or judgment about apportionment of negligence. Reinsurers want to receive notice on any case that is likely to reach its layer and seldom complain of too many reports.

CATASTROPHE EXCESS OF LOSS TREATIES

These might be the oldest type of reinsurance transaction. In the 1800s, a transoceanic shipping company might have been smart enough to split the shipment over several ships. It would still be concerned that a single storm might knock all of the ships off course, such that the goods perish or the storm could even sink all the ships. The coverage has evolved since those days, but the storms continue, season by season. Interestingly, the available history of storms with sufficient detail to use for rating dates back only about a hundred years, and the U.S. insurance industry has only been tracking damages since the 1940s.

How does one measure such happenstances? Are they predictable? Is it best to constrain the contract language or provide for flexible pricing to eventually recover claims and provide for profits with a long-term view?

Generally, this type of coverage applies to property business rather than to liability or casualty business. Property coverages are exposed to perils of storm, conflagration, etc., that might affect a great number of policies. Liability coverages are more complex. Asbestos, urea foam, lead paint, and other seemingly common causes do not affect policies simultaneously. A lead paint claim, for example, is likely to arise from multiple coats of old paint not identifiable by manufacturer that are slowly ingested by a child over a period of months. It is difficult enough to consider such an occurrence on an individual claim basis and impossible to track as arising from a single event. The litigation would be mind-boggling. Thus casualty business is often handled by other means and by other reinsurances.

Casualty coverages were included with property coverages prior to 1985, but seldom after that year. Earlier there were so few catastrophic casualty occurrences that inclusion of casualty coverage was not generally considered to be material. Once asbestosis cases and other events of the 1970s and 1980s became visible, the practice of including multiple lines diminished, and catastrophe coverage became essentially a property-only coverage.

Event is defined only in general terms with respect to catastrophe reinsurance. A bad winter is not considered an event, since it comprises multiple storms and periods of rising and falling temperatures. The treaty contract language focuses on the short term. This type of cover provides protection for hurricanes, tornadoes, windstorms, rain, conflagration, earthquake, etc. Flooding is somewhat different as it is normally excluded in the primary insurance policy. This exposure is offered voluntarily and through the federal flood program. Thus the definitions are broad, but not universal. One must be careful in considerations about inclusions of coverage.

For example, in the winter of 1974/1975, New England was hit hard by some severe winter storms, causing roof damage and leakage to residences and the collapse of the Hartford Civic Center. Catastrophe excess of loss treaties did not specifically address how such claims might be bundled or collected in a winter event. Many reinsurers involved themselves in the process of determining the proper language to exclude this sort of event. The damage from the storms seemed to be a result of wear and tear and not applicable to catastrophic loss coverage.

One reinsurance broker suggested that reinsurers should consider an expansion of coverage to cover such an event and that they should demand higher rates for the broader coverage. He suggested further that the current claim would quickly be recovered. It is a type of exposure which can be written at a profit by reinsurers. Still further, those reinsurers not providing the expanded coverage would soon find that someone else would. He was correct. The industry soon came to that consensus and expanded coverage at elevated prices.

Catastrophes are huge events that threaten the very viability of the carrier in some situations. Insurers that failed to purchase sufficient reinsurance have become insolvent due to a single event. In other cases, the insurers have benefitted in the long term. Consider the following real-life case:

CASE STUDY: CATASTROPHE EXAMPLE

A Texas insurer was a debit fire insurer, offering industrial fire insurance. The company offered named peril coverages to low-valued dwellings, generally in amounts of $10,000 to $15,000 per policy. The policyholders remitted a weekly premium to the agent, or fieldman, of about $2.50. The fieldman saw the policyholder 52 times a year. In the 1970s, a hurricane hit hard, and many of these low-valued dwellings were in low-lying areas that suffered tremendously. The loss exceeded the insurer's annual premium volume and very nearly the insurer's equity.

After an emergency call to the reinsurer, funds were wired within hours. The president of the insurance company called all the fieldmen into the office and literally supplied each with a briefcase filled with claim forms and cash. The fieldmen visited the stricken policyholders, assessed the claims, and in many instances paid cash for a signed release. It is often said that claims which are settled quickly are settled economically. The policyholders sorely needed the funds and greatly appreciated the prompt response. This was a cash society, and the quick cash served both policyholder and company well. The overall claim was paid below estimates, and the policyholders passed the word around about their fine insurer. The fieldmen were well known to the customers and came quickly in their time of need. The relationship inspired tremendous growth for the insurer. The company emerged from the crisis, with an expanded business that permitted a faster payback to the reinsurer.

The catastrophe excess treaty contains definitions of some events to limit the collection of claims that are considered to have arisen from a singular event. Normally wind storms are limited to 72 hours. Thus a Gulf of Mexico hurricane could develop into two events: one 72 hours just after landfall at the coast and another 72 hours later when the same storm pours 12 inches of rain in the Northeast. A bad winter is a series of storms where temperature seldom remains below freezing between storms. Each storm is considered to be a singular event. Many winter storms are sufficiently small to be entirely within the deductible or retention of the catastrophe coverage.

Setting the retention amount, or attachment point, and the treaty capacity are critical items. They can be set on the number of maximum policy limits that would be required to penetrate the cover and consume the limit or by the number of average policy limits required to amass those amounts.

The average claim in a hurricane is often less than $3000. Surely, a number of expensive coastal properties will be ruined. However, insurers track properties to avoid severe concentrations. When all the claims are recorded and paid, the average seems nominal. Thus in catastrophe treaties the frequency hurts most.

On occasion a storm is particularly devastating. A giant insurer, which had considerably less than 10 percent of the property market in Kansas had to cover 20 percent of the storm damage from a single tornado. One factor was that a huge tract of garden apartments happened to lie right in the center of the tornado's path. The insurer was well prepared for the risk of conflagration, but the storm proved to be quite wide, resulting in the disproportionate loss to this carrier. This insurer had properly purchased catastrophe reinsurance and thus overcame the big loss.

Some large catastrophes cause considerable movement or activity in the marketplace. Often they cause the insurance cycle to move from low rates and reluctant underwriting to high rates, aggressive underwriting, and swift growth. During periods of rapid change, available capacity is fickle. Some companies find it easier to get coverage, albeit at higher cost, while others are not able to purchase the coverage at any price. This latter situation forces the insurer to reconsider its underwriting strategy, for along with higher nets comes a renewed concern about the proper comfort level.

Many reinsurers react conservatively after a catastrophe and reduce their capacity or retract from certain territories. Other reinsurers exhibit restraint in expansion and conserve capital until a huge loss hits the industry. With rates up, competition reduced, and insurers seeking more capacity, the catastrophe marketplace quickly becomes more attractive. Those reinsurers that were patient can reposition their portfolio of catastrophe business to effect a better result for the long term. These periods of extremely attractive opportunity seldom last long, perhaps one season. Then the marketplace gradually shifts to normal and in time tends to become overly competitive, renewing the pressures underlying a new cycle. A dramatic shift typically does not occur until there is a significant industrywide loss. Events that happen mid-cycle do not appear as significant, while those that happen to occur when the market is poised for change do generate swift reactions across the industry.

Catastrophe Excess of Loss	
Characteristic	Remark
Type	Excess
Reinsurance functions	Catastrophe
Pricing	Generally flat rated based on amortization of the limit.
Premium split	Not related to specific claim size. Rather, this is a function of the developing loss-to-premium ratio.
Claims split	Does not function on an individual claim basis and is not related to the amount of premium.
LAE split	May be excluded. Often applied to indemnity amounts only.
Layering	Standard practice. This type is quite adaptable to layering. Each layer responds in order, bottom layer first.

Exhibit 5.5. Characteristics of Catastrophe Excess of Loss Treaties

There are some good opportunities at every point of the cycle. However, reinsurers that plan to build and improve for the long term generally have superior results. It is most desirable to actively consider new business at all times but at the same time be opportunistic and plan for short periods of faster growth and be conservative as the competition increases.

Catastrophe excess of loss contracts are often reported on a quarterly deposit set at 25 percent of 80 percent of the anticipated income for the layer, or rate multiplied by the subject premium. The annual premium is calculated at 15 months, subject to a minimum premium, typically set at the 80 percent mark.

Losses are few in number, known universally at the time of incidence, and tracked until fully paid. This contract responds as payments are made by the insurer at the level defined for the layer.

QUOTA SHARE TREATIES

This is the simplest type of treaty. It is a proportional treaty, with a fixed percentage sharing for each and every policy that applies to both premium and losses. The reinsurer also shares in the acquisition cost, and is thus in the same position as the cedent. A complex reinsurance cession may be configured so that the exposure is not congruent; however, in straightforward application, this should be considered a true partnership form of reinsurance.

The cedent's costs vary by class and line of business but generally involve agent's commissions of 15 to 20 percent and insurer administration expenses of 7 to 10 percent. To remain on equal footing with the cedent, the reinsurer typically permits a 22 to 32 percent commission. This commission is taken up front and deducted from premiums forwarded to reinsurers. This administration expense allotment includes in-house claims expenses but not ones for which independent experts must be hired. Outside adjusters and unallocated claim expenses are shared at the same fixed percentage as premiums and losses.

Earlier, we introduced the term expense margin as that portion of the commission which exceeds the actual acquisition cost plus true expenses of administering the business. At times reinsurers do permit a modest expense margin. Sometimes it appears as hard-won profit by the cedent who has been able to control the expense budget. At other times it is a motivation to add volume to the portfolio.

A profit commission or sliding scale may be included to motivate good quality business and successful management of the portfolio. These shall be further described in Chapter 9. It is conceivable that the sliding scale may be formulated to cut any expense margin, even produce a negative margin or penalty to the point where the company actually loses money on the cession when the results are not successful.

This last statement is important. In most quota share situations, the cedent retains the major proportion of the business and cedes a minority position to reinsurers. This implies that when the results go sour, the cedent is hurt to a greater extent, simply because it holds the larger share. Thus most quota share cessions are accomplished with just a modest expense margin in favor of the cedent. The reinsurers suffer the same fate as the cedent and experience success or loss as the business develops. They should have the same risk.

Any penalty within the commission scheme looms large to the cedent since it is already experiencing poor results on its own holding. The cedent would already be motivated to take action to correct the results. The sliding scale commission penalty is calculated after the fact, and because of the timing it appears to be punitive. Therefore, analysis of such penalty situations will show that they are quite modest in amount. The object is to motivate but not economically strap the cedent.

Obviously, the reinsurer and cedent discuss developments as they progress and often initiate action before commission penalties are reached. If the reinsurer does not like the direction of the reparations, it can issue cancellation notice and walk away. That is not a swift or definitive type of action. Typically treaty contracts have a 90- or 180-day advance notice requirement. Also, termination stops exposure to future events or to any remaining, unearned exposures. It does not alter the very real exposure that has existed prior to termination.

The reporting for proportional treaties varies considerably from that of the excess contracts discussed earlier in this chapter. Normally both premiums

Quota Share	
Characteristic	Remark
Type	Proportional
Reinsurance functions	Capacity, stabilization and financial
Pricing	Commission, may be flat or sliding scale. If flat might be augmented with a profit contingency.
Premium split	Fixed proportion, applies to all applicable policies.
Claims split	Same fixed proportion as premium, each and every claim.
LAE split	Same fixed proportion as premium, each and every claim.
Layering	Not applicable. May work with a surplus for higher limit policies. Can also function with excess layers above.

Exhibit 5.6. Characteristics of Quota Share Treaties

and losses are reported in a bulk format. Remember that the reinsurer pays a portion of every claim, including those at $1. Thus, by necessity, the loss reporting must be accomplished on a bulk basis. In this case, the bulk reports can be either a summary report or *bordereau*. The summary report supplies only the totals for the period. The bordereau (bordereaux, plural) is generally a computer generated report that contains minimal information and statistics on each account.

A premium bordereau is normally a single line listing by account of premium-generated activity recorded in the month or quarter. The line will supply reference numbers, reason for the premium, and amount of premium accounted for in the quarter, but not much other information.

A loss bordereau will list claims individually, including reference numbers, applicable dates, line and type codes, cause codes, incurred change at this report, incurred total, amounts paid, amounts outstanding, and LAE amount. The loss bordereaux are more detailed and supply both current activity and activity incurred to date.

Payments are forwarded quarterly, premiums less paid losses for the quarter. Thus, some reports will enclose a draft and others will enclose an invoice with payment due as soon as practical.

SURPLUS SHARE TREATIES

This is a variable proportional treaty. It is most often used to generate capacity for the ceding company. The variable aspect is necessary to permit flexibility in completing the placement for large limit, single-policy situations. At times the capacity/flexibility feature appears to be more important than the fact that the variability affords the cedent the potential to keep more of the best risks and less of the worst risks. Our discussion will focus on the later aspect, but keep in mind that this structure generally holds greater capacity than the quota share contract.

A quota share will provide capacity in a fixed proportion to that which the ceding company holds net for its own account. The fixed percentage may cede 25, 40, or 70 percent. In the case of a 70 percent cession, the contract affords 2.33 times the 30 percent held net.

Most surplus treaties permit cessions of some multiple of the cedent's net. It is not unusual to see 300 percent, 400 percent, or even 700 percent for certain kinds and classes. The multiples are often higher for a surplus than for a quota share treaty.

The cession protocol is negotiated with other terms at the onset of the reinsurance relationship. This sets an upper and lower bound for the cessions as well as other requirements for the cession scheme.

As indicated in Exhibit 5.6, the cedent is permitted to keep more and cede less, or reduce its net retention and cede more than its average cession. This requires trust on the part of the reinsurers. It is possible for the insurer to cede to its sole advantage. Thus it is a good idea for the reinsurer to audit the cession patterns as this business develops. It is not wise to merely monitor the claim activity, since this may not reveal the entire picture.

The cession schedule may require that certain kinds or classes be ceded in one manner while permitting other kinds to be ceded in another manner. For

Surplus Share	
Characteristic	Remark
Type	Proportional
Reinsurance functions	Capacity, stabilization and financial
Pricing	Commission, may be flat or sliding scale. If flat, may be augmented with a profit contingency.
Premium split	Variable proportion; the cedent sets the percentage at the time the policy is bound or accepted, according to the schedule negotiated for the treaty. There are upper and lower bounds on these cession percentages.
Claims split	Same proportion as premium, on a policy-by-policy basis.
LAE split	Same proportion as premium, on a policy-by-policy basis.
Layering	Can be layered.

Exhibit 5.7.   Characteristics of Surplus Share Treaties

example, since restaurant business often has a higher loss level than other types of property business, the contract might include a schedule for the two kinds of business. Similarly, the cession scheme might be different for national account risks and regional risks, as the former is developed and controlled at the home office level and the latter probably at the branch level. The cession schedule may set requirements as to the amount to be ceded according to the original policy limit.

The price of the surplus share treaty should be greater than that for a quota share, since the cedent should pay for the privilege of retaining the cession flexibility. Further, reinsurers should minimize any expense margin in a surplus treaty. It does not seem prudent to reward volume with the right to cede with discrimination. Similarly, a sliding scale commission penalty makes more sense for this type of treaty. These remarks should be viewed as negotiating guidelines rather than hard and true principles. Other than this, the commissions are similar in all respects to those outlined for the quota share treaty. Reporting for this contract is also the same as that for the quota share contract.

AGGREGATE EXCESS OF LOSS OR STOP LOSS TREATIES

Aggregate treaties do not apply to individual losses, but rather to a predesigned aggregation of claims that arise from a policy portfolio that has been set to meet agreed specifications. The treaty is structured to apply to that unfortunate year with an overall result that falls well above the norm for the cedent.

The treaty will not be hit by a single claim. The cedent's comfort level reflects that amount of limit it typically holds on any one risk or exposure. Often this is set at 1 to 3 percent for reasons explained in Chapter 1. If we suppose that 2 percent of written premium is the largest amount the insurer is willing to hold net on any risk, it would take 30 claims of that size to amass or aggregate to a 60 percent loss ratio. If 60 percent happens to be the average loss ratio, the *stop loss* or aggregate excess of loss treaty would be set to attach at something higher than 60 percent.

The policy limits profile is known and reviewed closely before the treaty goes into effect. The definition for the aggregation will specify that each loss be cutoff, such that the underlying portion be applicable only to the aggregate. The cut off is often the attachment for the standard excess of loss treaty. Thus the aggregate is often the aggregation of the insurer's net retained line amount per claim.

For example, a homeowner's insurer may purchase an excess of loss per risk for its larger homes. It may also purchase an aggregate treaty just in case it runs into a bad year where many of the losses happen to be small. Such losses would fall below the attachment level of the per risk excess and could substantially affect the net result or the result after the excess of loss protections. Remember also that a catastrophe excess of loss treaty requires that its losses arise from the same event. It too would be a priority deduction, to apply before the aggregate excess of loss treaty.

Thus the aggregate excess is designed to apply to loss frequency arising from multiple events, after the high loss potential has been taken care of administratively, usually through the purchase of reinsurance.

The aggregate attachment point may be set in a number of ways, the primary one being a limit on the loss ratio. Suppose a company plans for a 5 percent profit, with average expenses running 30 percent and a loss ratio at 65 percent. It would not be appropriate to set the aggregate attachment point at 65 percent, because that would virtually guarantee the cedent could not lose money. Setting the attachment at 70 percent puts the combined loss and expense ratio at 105 percent—a very low level. Many ceding companies would like to secure such coverage, but reinsurers avoid such close tolerance. With such low attachment points, the cedent is not motivated to select good business and might press for volume at the ultimate expense of reinsurers. An aggregate that attaches at a 110 percent loss and expense ratio should cost more than one that attaches at a 115 percent ratio.

The limit of coverage might be described as "the first $1 million of loss in excess of 110 percent loss and loss adjustment expense." Obviously a limit of $2 million over the same retention should cost more.

Some kinds, classes, and lines of business are more stable than others. The claims counts and average losses tend to fall in predictable ranges for some business and loose ranges for others. Thus, the kind of business is a significant cost determinant.

The key determinant for pricing is the attachment level. The lower the level, the higher the reinsurance cost. The attachment level may be set, in several ways.

The first is a batch limit, which was used more often in the past. In the case of product liability, an aggregate limit might apply on a batch basis, whereby all the claims that eventually arise from that batch would be measured against the aggregate excess attachment and limit. Batch might mean a production run for a cake mix or a series of similar products. With time, it became difficult to define batch. If you manufacture toasters, when does one batch stop and the other begin? Thus, the industry adopted the annual aggregate concept.

The attachment point may be set on loss plus LAE only or on the total result of the portfolio. It is best to attach on the losses alone, since it is not wise to include the expenses of the cedent. The latter permits inclusion of yet another variable that can elevate the claim total. If a cedent is having a bad year, it could choose to investigate each claim aggressively, even through an associated investigative service, and cover this additional cost with the likely application of the aggregate excess of loss treaty. Obviously, including LAE only is the next best strategy. Including loss, LAE, acquisition cost, and administrative cost is the worst strategy for reinsurers.

The major point is that the treaty should not be structured to guarantee the cedent a profit. While setting the attachment point on a combined loss and expense basis may seem to achieve the goal of assuring that profit does not exist when the cover is hit, it may specifically include costs that should not be covered by the treaty. Thus it is best to measure and review all the components in assessing the treaty while setting the attachment of the aggregate excess of loss treaty on the claim happenstance alone.

An aggregate reinsurer should understand the excess of loss treaties that are in place, since they are priority reinsurances and apply first. This means that the larger individual claims that hit the excess of loss treaty are reduced by recovery from such reinsurances. The aggregate applies after that calculation, whether collectable or not. Thus, it is important that the aggregate reinsurer include references to the excess of loss covers in the contract wording to be sure of the order of priority.

The aggregate reinsurer may also require that the cedent purchase reinsurance when there are a great number of claims arising from a single event. Such catastrophe excess of loss reinsurance would be a second priority. It is important to understand that the aggregate exposure includes so many potential happenings that other functional considerations should be addressed first. The aggregate underwriter should insist that the priorities be listed and the specifications clearly stated before undertaking consideration of the final terms of an aggregate agreement. What position will the cedent be in when this treaty is called upon to respond? That question is a key determinant in considering this type of treaty.

This is not inexpensive reinsurance. Aggregate treaties do not name perils and thus sweep in many potential problems. If the business is not priced correctly, the aggregate will not, perhaps cannot, be profitable. If there is some reason for a multitude of small claims to occur, the aggregate will be hit. In liability coverages, product liability claims might conceivably cause such a result. There will be a few monumental claims that affect the excess of loss treaties and many small claims. These small claims may be cases where, for example, an injured worker loses some time but can return to an active work schedule. Or they can be cases where the exposure happened to be minimal, either through luck, a short period of exposure, or an incidental or minimal exposure. It is a situation where the net loss applies. If the premium was set too low, perhaps pressured to that level by consumer-oriented regulators, the aggregate would be exposed to higher loss likelihood. Premium is the

Aggregate Excess of Loss	
Characteristic	Remark
Type	Excess
Reinsurance functions	Stabilization and financial
Pricing	Generally flat rated. Often priced without a prior loss history, on an amortization basis.
Premium split	Based on the loss activity to the layer or a measure of just how close past aggregated losses have come.
Claims split	Does not function on an individual claim basis and is not related to the amount of premium.
LAE split	May be excluded. Often applied to indemnity amounts only.
Layering	Seldom layered. Quantity available is often limited.

Exhibit 5.8.   Characteristics of Aggregate Excess of Loss Treaties

denominator for loss ratio; it therefore has a direct bearing on the amount of loss that this treaty incurs. Because of the multitude of possible causes of poor results, the cost of aggregate insurance is fairly high. The function of this type of reinsurance is stabilization or financial; the purpose is to trade the overall volatility of the portfolio for a fixed cost. This type of treaty is often priced with a quarterly deposit and annual minimum, adjusted to a preset rate against subject premium.

This is an appropriate time to introduce the term *net net*. The *net result* is the net after the per risk/per occurrence excess of loss and any applicable proportional reinsurance. *Net net* is the result after the stop loss or aggregate excess of loss treaty. The first set of reinsurers would be concerned about the net result. This is the statistic with which they compare their result. Net net is secondary layer of analysis which is pertinent to the stop loss reinsurer. Obviously, the cedent must assess and evaluate the net and net net to judge if it is paying appropriate amounts for the reinsurances at each level.

Consider the following example: Suppose the ceding company purchases a 40 percent quota share treaty and a stop loss that attaches at 75 percent only with respect to the *ceding company's holdings* at a rate of 6 percent. In other words, the reinsurers do not purchase the stop loss coverage. Let us further suppose that the result is an 80 percent loss ratio, which means there will be a recovery from the stop loss treaty. For ease with the calculations let us set the treaty subject premium volume at $12 million. Thus, we have

    Premium   = $12,000,000
    Loss   = $ 9,600,000
    Loss ratio = 80%

The quota share reinsurer's holding is:

    Premium   = 40% of $12,000,000 or $4,800,000
    Loss   = 40% of $ 9,600,000 or $3,840,000
    Loss ratio = 80%

The net after quota share (or *gross net*) is:

    Premium   = 60% of $12,000,000 or $7,200,000
    Loss   = 60% of $ 9,600,000 or $5,760,000
    Loss ratio = 80%

The stop loss reinsurer's holding is:

    Premium   = 6% of $7,200,000 or $432,000 (Note: The subject premium
                for the stop loss treaty is $7,200,000 because this treaty
                only applies to the net part of the quota share.)
    Loss   = 80% of $5,760,000 less 75% of $5,760,000
              = $4,608,000 − $4,320,000
              = $288,000
    Loss ratio = 67%

The net net (occasionally one might see this expressed as "nett") or the cedent's holding after both recoveries, is:

    Premium   = 60% of quota share less cost of stop loss
              = $7,200,000 − $432,000
              = $6,768,000
    Loss   = 60% of total loss less recovery from the stop loss
              = $3,840,000 − $288,000
              = $3,552,000
    Loss ratio = $3,552,000/$6,768,000
              = 52%

Because the year turned out to be a poor one, the cedent was wise in purchasing both kinds of protection. Also remember that the cedent could be considered "wise" if the stop loss was not hit by the claims. It is a good purchase if the cost is appropriate for the risk ceded. The words "over time" should be added because losses are not expected to reach the stop loss attachment level or retention level each year. One should acquire the habit of testing the outcome in each example or situation. Remember always that success is best measured by assessing the goals or purpose of the reinsurance as affected by the results of the period.

6

FINANCIAL REINSURANCE

FINANCIAL REINSURANCE TREATIES
FINANCIAL RISK TERMINOLOGY
TIME AND DISTANCE POLICY

FINANCIAL REINSURANCE TREATIES

Financial reinsurance treaties can be excess or proptional and can take the form of any of the structures discussed in Chapter 5. This type of coverage began in the 1980s. Some may point to earlier historical precedents; however, such connections merely suggest that these former structures possessed some of the financial attributes of the current treaties. The financial evolution that took place during the 1980s created a new set of considerations that had not been previously isolated or analyzed by the reinsurance industry. This evolution led to the creation of specific reinsurance products that differed from how standard insurance policies had been structured up until that point.

The reinsurance industry functions to serve the insurance industry in managing its assumed risk and providing facilities to disperse exposures so that many companies might participate in a broad selection of risks with minimal impact on the solvency of each company. It is also a competitive marketplace. As reinsurers move to better position themselves, new products are created. Many are reapplications of older principles. Others are truly unique products. Financial reinsurance is in the latter category. Its providers have isolated new concerns, formulated new language, and developed new reinsurances to fulfill those needs. It is truly one of the more exciting industry-wide developments of our times.

CASE STUDY: MGM GRAND HOTEL FIRE

One of the early cases that spurred the formation of this class forward was the MGM Grand Hotel fire in 1980. In addition to being involved in a large building fire, the MGM Grand Hotel had thousands of hotel guests. Thus, the fire exceeded the criteria for industrywide tracking at the time, with $5 million in losses and over 1000 affected policies. Opportunists moved to provide retroactive coverages. The initial coverages were purchased by the hotel owners, but they were quickly passed, in part, to reinsurers.

These insurers and reinsurers were confident of the payout patterns for a loss such as this and offered long-term payments for the immediate premiums. The logic was that the funds would generate considerable investment income over time and prior to the eventual payout.

It did not turn out as planned. With funds available, the claim settlements advanced at a far swifter pace than had earlier large losses. Also, the hotel was rebuilt with modern fireproof materials, while the original had been of lower quality. Disputes arose out of the fact the replication was not what previously existed, in violation of the original policy conditions, and the fact that payments were made to escalate construction. The legal technicalities of this situation are beyond the scope of this text. We shall focus on the fact that payments were much faster than expected and ignore the remaining controversy.

Many of the opportunistic insurers and reinsurers who devised these particular coverages ended in loss. They had been wrong in assessing the pace at which the funds were expended. The payout pace had been the core of the coverage afforded. The insurance and reinsurance had been devised to recognize that there was a value related to the pace of payments. The MGM property loss had already occurred. The amount of standard insurance had not been sufficient to cover the entire rebuilding. The owners wished to cap their ultimate cost by purchasing coverage that considered both the pace of payments and the ultimate amount to be paid. These were sophisticated concepts.

Some reinsurers claimed that the exposure was a type of financial guarantee and therefore excluded from existing treaties. Many of these reinsurers were fixed in restricted coverage philosophies that would preclude them from embracing the new coverages even after they were well defined and the class of business was developed. (See Chapter 5, Catastrophe Excess of Loss Treaties, for a similar lesson.) Those that did participate lost in this particular situation, but they were also at the forefront of developing new financial reinsurance products. As is typical in reinsurance developments, some participants moved forward while others receded.

FINANCIAL RISK TERMINOLOGY

The jargon of reinsurance is colorful and rich. It is not always clear and definitive.

Financial risk is different from underwriting risk. Underwriting risk is against the resulting economic damage from a defined peril, which may range from smoke damage to hurricane wind, from slander to malpractice. Financial risk may not specify a peril or perils; instead it focuses on whether a given target on the financial page is met or not met. Both concern economic impact but differ in that one is primarily concerned with causation while the other is concerned with the mere realization of a specific financial measure.

Finite risk and financial reinsurance are synonymous because a very limited amount of risk, underwriting risk, is transferred along with the financial concern. While some insurances are unlimited, almost all reinsurances are bounded and contain an upper limit. Therefore almost all reinsurance is finite. For that matter, most insurance is also limited at least annually if not by event. Thus finite here means having a small limit rather than simply limited. In the dictionary, "finite" is defined as being neither infinite or infinitesimal. It is used in reinsurance to mean "limited" or "small" in financial terms. It is important that one realize the distinction between the literal meaning and that which applies within the context of reinsurance.

It is also crucial to make sure the terms meet accounting standards as promulgated by the Financial Accounting Standards Board (FASB) and the federal tax consequences of the Internal Revenue Service (IRS). Obviously the state and local tax consequences should be investigated, however, they generally follow the federal guidelines. The amount and kind of risk transfer is under the supervision of the FASB and IRS, and it is likely that they will require certain amounts of underwriting risk transfer coincident with finite risk transfer.

There are several types of finite risk. *Asset risk* is the exposure that a specified asset will maintain its value or perhaps grow, given tax and interest consequences. *Credit risk* is the exposure that a recoverable amount, notably a reinsurance recoverable from treaty or facultative cession, will be received in full. *Interest rate risk* is the exposure that the projected rate of interest will not materialize as anticipated. *Payment timing risk* is the exposure that an amount of reserve will generate a specified amount of interest before the necessity of payment.

Financial insurance is coverage afforded by an insurer to an individual or corporation. It is financial reinsurance if the transaction is between two licensed insurance carriers. Each contract or contract is uniquely determined based on the specific needs and circumstances of the cedent.

Normally these contracts feature a success bonus if the fortunes of the reinsurer are more favorable than anticipated. In the case of financial insurance the clause is typically called a "no claims bonus," which returns a portion of the premium if no claims are incurred. A financial reinsurance contract is more likely to have a sliding scale or contingent commission, which are slightly more sophisticated, or gradual success bonuses. They would be similar in design to those illustrated in Chapter 9 for traditional reinsurance contracts.

Financial reinsurance, or finite risk, has several important characteristics. There is a sever limit on the amount of underwriting risk to be ceded, which may take the form of an overall aggregate limit of liability. This creates a low risk situation for the reinsurer, which can in turn create a reasonable cost for the transfer of finite risk. Often the contract will have a cancellation provision, or commutation clause, beneficial to the assuming reinsurer.

The assuming reinsurer will credit the ceding company with an expectation of investment income. This credit is created at the onset of the transaction, which in turn motivates the cedent to undertake the transaction. Remember, they would realize the interest over time, but by virtue of this finite risk transaction, the benefit is consolidated and earned immediately.

Profit commissions or sliding scale commission schedules share the benefit of favorable experience. This is a necessary component of transactions in which the cedent remains in charge of handling and settling claims, which if not done appropriately, can lead to financial problems for both cedent and assuming reinsurer. Existence of the economic benefit provides incentive for the cedent to handle claims properly.

The regulatory concerns are to differentiate financial reinsurance from risk financing or premium financing. It is necessary to take a close look at the contract language and specifically assess just what is being accomplished by the transaction.

One focus of such scrutiny is the contract term. Generally, financial insurance has a fixed term, while financial reinsurance has an indefinite term or a term which is longer than that of the finite insurance policy. Simply spreading payments over a longer term would constitute premium financing. Thus, beyond the term, one also looks for risk transfer. That is, the premium financing would constitute a type of loan and therefore should be booked with a corresponding liability for the amount of the loan. A risk transfer accomplishes the shift of the liability from the insurers to the reinsurer, which is the fundamental point of financial reinsurance.

A true transfer of risk can be supported by the following two conditions: a transfer of significant risk, including both financial risk and underwriting risk; and a *reasonable* potential for the assuming reinsurer to incur a *significant* amount of loss.

Financial Reinsurance	
Characteristic	Remark
Type	Both excess and proportional.
Reinsurance functions	Stabilization and financial
Pricing	All types used.
Premium split	Generally like that of a stop loss treaty.
Claims split	Claim follows terms of treaty, not related to premium share.
LAE split	LAE generally included with incurred claim total.
Layering	Certainly possible; similar to stop loss treaties.

Exhibit 6.1.   Characteristics of Financial Reinsurance

The emphasis is on significant and reasonable, which may at times be subjective. The ambiguity of this measurement is a significant concern to regulatory and tax authorities, who are working to develop guidelines for this business and tools for assessing such matters.

In assessing the risk transfer, one usually focuses on the timing risk and underwriting risk, because timing risk often represents the greater financial risk exposure.

The following case studies will illustrate the workings of financial reinsurance. The examples will also demonstrate how the structures outlined in Chapter 5 can be applied in an actual reinsurance situation.

CASE STUDY: FINANCIAL INSURANCE AND FACULTATIVE REINSURANCE CERTIFICATE

This case is adapted from a case study in *A Practical Guide to Finite Risk Insurance and Reinsurance,* by R. George Monti and Andrew Barile, published by John Wiley & Sons, Inc.

This is an example of a case with a financial insurance product, backed by a standard quota share facultative reinsurance certificate. The reinsurer participates in the financial insurance on an individual-risk, proportional sharing basis.

Superior Screw Company is a healthy, growing company with steady cash flow. The company faces nonrenewal of its director's and officer's liability insurance because of several potential claims arising over the past year. The company was concerned that its board might not continue to serve without the protection of insurance and sought a broad form of coverage on a long-term basis.

This situation was resolved by Deity Assurance Corporation, a licensed carrier in Superior's home state. Deity offered Superior a manuscripted broad form excess director's and officer's policy with a ten-year term. The aggregate limit of liability over the ten-year period is $20 million with a $1 million self-insured retention, also aggregate over the period. Superior must pay $20.6 million premium at inception. The insurer has a minimum margin of $3.1 million, that is, 15 percent of the premium plus 5 percent of any loss payment. A profit sharing is credited to Superior based on the 12-month Treasury bill rate, to be paid 30 days after the end of each year, based on the unpaid balance.

Deity is a recent participant in financial insurance and thus wished to begin slowly. They secured the help of a direct writing reinsurer, Guardian Angel Reinsurance. Guardian participates on a facultative, quota share basis through a standard reinsurance certificate tailored to accept only financial insurance business. Guardian offers Deity help with pricing and because most situations are tailored to the policyholder's needs, Deity must approach Guardian before binding, to obtain acceptance of the terms and conditions of its policy. In the case of Superior Screw, Guardian agreed to participate on a 50/50 basis, on equal terms with Deity.

As a quota share reinsurer, Guardian shares on a fixed percentage basis with all premiums, commissions, and losses. The certificate itself contains only standard clauses, in this case. So the reinsurance is not financial reinsurance, but rather standard reinsurance tailored to the primary class of business, which happens to be financial insurance.

CASE STUDY: FINANCIAL REINSURANCE
QUOTA SHARE TREATY

Cupid Insurance Company is a regional insurance carrier licensed throughout the Southwestern Sun Belt, specializing in residential property and personal automobile business. It currently writes $48 million annually. For the past few years it has averaged 32 percent in expenses and 68 percent in losses. For the sake of simplicity, let us further assume the business has just a two-year developmental profile. The current year results appear as follows:

Cupid Insurance Company
Financial Statement: Gross Displaying Two-Year Development

	Current Year	Next Year
Written premium	$48,000,000	$ 0
Change in unearned premium	$24,000,000	($24,000,000)
Earned premiums	$24,000,000	$24,000,000
Incurred loss at 68% of EP	$16,080,000	$16,080,000
Expenses at 32% of WP	$15,360,000	$ 0
Statutory profit/(loss)	($ 7,440,000)	$ 7,920,000
Surplus at start of year	$48,000,000	$40,080,000
Surplus at end of year	$40,080,000	$48,000,000
Written premium-to-surplus ratio	1.20	
Two-year premium-to-surplus ratio		1.0

On a statutory basis, Cupid suffers a 20 percent penalty at the 12-month measurement. In a normal situation, the insurer would have the second half of the prior year coming in to offset the second half calendar year delay. If a company is experiencing rapid growth, the prior year carryover will be significantly less than the new year delay. This could be problematic if the insurer needed to hold level financial ratios to maintain or improve its financial ratings. The company may not wish to post a statutory loss during a period of growth, in order to maintain a positive image in the marketplace.

With a financial reinsurance quota share the picture can be significantly different:

Guardian Angel Reinsurance Company
Financial Statement: Gross Displaying Two-Year Development

	Current year	Next year
Written premium	$24,000,000	$ 0
Change in unearned premium	$24,000,000	($24,000,000)
Earned premiums	$ 0	$24,000,000
Incurred loss at 68% of EP	$ 0	$16,080,000
Expenses at 32% of WP	$ 7,680,000	$ 0
Statutory profit/(loss)	($ 7,680,000)	$ 7,920,000
Two-year profit/(loss)		$ 240,000

Guardian's written premium-to-surplus ratio is not significant in this situation, because this contract is one of many for Guardian Angel. Yes, it will have to maintain industry acceptable ratios, but its situation may be significantly different from that of Cupid I. C. It can undertake this sort of transaction as long as its bottom line meets industry benchmarks.

For Cupid I. C., the situation with financial reinsurance quota share will change:

Cupid Insurance Company
Financial Statement: Net Displaying Two-Year Development Restated
with the Benefit of the Financial Reinsurance Quota Share

	Current year	Next year
Gross written premium	$48,000,000	$ 0
Ceded written premium	$24,000,000	$ 0
Net written premium	$24,000,000	$ 0
Change in unearned premium	$ 0	$ 0
Earned premiums	$24,000,000	$ 0
Incurred loss at 68% of EP	$16,080,000	$ 0
Expenses at 32% of WP	$ 7,680,000	$ 0
Statutory profit/(loss)	$ 240,000	$ 0
Surplus at start of year	$48,000,000	$ 0
Surplus at end of year	$48,240,000	$48,240,000
Net written premium-to-surplus ratio	1.0	
Two-year net premium-to-surplus ratio		.99

The benefit of the deal is obvious: Cupid I. C. grows and is able to maintain its financial ratios, which in turn help maintain its ratings. The cost has not been included in this example.

This example makes the attractive assumption that the loss plus cost is break-even. With that expectation the cost can be fairly modest. If the underwriting result worsens, or has the potential to get worse, the cost should be significantly greater. It is incumbent on the financial reinsurer to contain the underwriting risks, so that its cost can be held low and attractive.

CASE STUDY: FINANCIAL REINSURANCE OF A LOSS PORTFOLIO TRANSFER

This case is a financial reinsurance quota share situation. The structure may not be entirely evident because the amount ceded is 100 percent, rather than a fixed proportion.

Deity I. C. is an insurance carrier licensed in a single mid-Atlantic coastal state. Deity discontinued its commercial auto line following Hurricane Hugo, in which it experienced significant physical damage losses. Upon reaching the decision to discontinue the line, the Deity management also wanted to significantly reduce its expenses. The auto line was serviced by a large portion of its staff, including a significant number of claims specialists. On an ongoing basis, the company would not need the commercial auto liability claims specialists, since its focus would now be on property coverages.

Deity Insurance Company
Before Purchase of the Loss Portfolio Transfer Reinsurance

Balance sheet	
Cash	$ 6,000,000
Assets	$18,000,000
Total assets	$24,000,000
Outstanding losses—commercial auto liability	$ 4,800,000
Outstanding losses—all other classes	$ 5,000,000
Other liabilities	$10,600,000
Total liabilities	$20,400,000
Policyholder's surplus	$ 3,600,000
Total liabilities and surplus	$24,000,000

Income statement	
Written premiums	$ 9,000,000
Earned premiums	$ 9,000,000
Outstanding losses	($ 5,900,000)
Incurred expenses	($ 3,600,000)
Underwriting profit/(loss)	($ 500,000)
Investment income	($ 1,200,000)
Operating result	$ 700,000

Operating Ratios		
Premium to surplus	= $9,000,000/$3,600,000	= 2.5
Loss to EP	= $5,900,000/$9,000,000	= 66%
Expense to WP	= $3,600,000/$9,000,000	= 40%
Combined ratio		= 106%
Investment income to WP	= ($1,200,000)/$9,000,000	= (13%)
Operating ratio		= 93%

These operating ratios indicate that the company is currently in good shape. The expense ratio is high, at 40 percent, mildly motivating the company to address its internal costs. Its decision to discontinue based on the hurricane losses is no longer evident in today's statistics, except perhaps to the extent that the loss development may also be a concern. This example illustrates that the motivations may not be currently evident by a cursory analysis and that a company need not be in financial difficulty in order to purchase finite reinsurance.

Deity has $4.8 million in commercial auto liability case reserves. Let us assume that it did secure a portfolio transfer as of January 1 of the current year, and let us review the cost versus benefits of such financial reinsurance. Obviously in an actual case the costs may be higher, or the benefits better.

In calculating the cost, the financial reinsurer assesses the probabilities that the up-front premium will grow faster than the projected loss settlement payout. The reinsurer will compare past patterns of Deity reserves as well as industry norms for the class and type of business. In this case the reinsurer requests payment of $4.2 million at the inception of the contract.

The faster the claims are expected to settle, the greater will be this up-front charge. Obviously the determining factor is the amount of interest expected compared to the amount of claim development. In this case, the reinsurer has allowed a credit from $4.8 million to $4.2 million based on the assessment that interest will cover that credit plus expected loss development, the cost of new reports, and a margin for the reinsurer's expense and profit.

The loss payout pattern, or developmental pace of the incurred claims, constitutes the timing risk assumed by the financial reinsurer. If the interest is high the reinsurer benefits. If interest rates drop, or if the loss payments accelerate faster than expected, the reinsurer loses. Thus, there is both interest rate risk and timing risk. The total finite risk amounts to $600,000 or 12.5 percent at the onset of this deal.

The underwriting risk to be transferred is that which constitutes the potential for new claims. IBNR was introduced in Chapter 2 as either development of known claims or subsequent reports of claims that already happened but as yet have not been reported. This latter aspect is the underwriting risk in this transfer.

Having both underwriting risk and timing risk within this transfer should satisfy regulators and tax authorities that the transfer is acceptable. Let us return to the financial exhibits for Deity and restate them with the financial reinsurance treaty applied.

Deity Insurance Company
After Purchase of the Loss Portfolio Transfer Reinsurance

Balance Sheet

Cash	$ 1,800,000
Assets	$18,000,000
Total assets	$19,800,000
Outstanding losses—commercial auto liability	$ 0
Outstanding losses—all other classes	$ 5,000,000
Other liabilities	$10,600,000
Total liabilities	$15,600,000
Policyholder's surplus	$ 4,200,000
Total liabilities and surplus	$19,800,000

The reinsurance premium paid to the reinsurer, $4.2 million, is deducted from cash; thus, assets drop by $4.2 million. On the liability and surplus side of the ledger, the loss portfolio transfer of $4.8 million is deducted from outstanding losses. The net result is an increase of $600,000 in Deity's policyholder's surplus. This also creates positive cash flow for Deity, so it earns interest on the $800,000 that it retains, estimated to be $48,000 in this example.

Deity Insurance Company
After Purchase of the Loss Portfolio Transfer Reinsurance

Income Statement

Written premiums	$9,000,000
Earned premiums	$9,000,000
Outstanding losses	($5,100,000)
Incurred expenses	($3,600,000)
Underwriting profit/(loss)	$ 300,000
Investment income	($1,248,000)
Operating result	$1,548,000

Operating Ratios

Premium to Surplus	= $9,000,000/$4,200,00	= 2.1
Loss to EP	= $5,100,000/$9,000,000	= 56%
Expense to WP	= $3,600,000/$9,000,000	= 40%
Combined ratio		= 96%
Investment income to WP	= ($1,264,000)/$9,000,000	= (14%)
Operating ratio		= 82%

These are dramatic improvements, perhaps slightly unrealistic due to the simplicity of this example, the low level of premiums, and the relative size of the amount transferred. The WP/Policyholder's surplus ratio drops from 2.5 to 2.1, which is significant. This also happens to make a profitable year even better.

The transfer also accomplished another benefit. The reinsurer assumed responsibility for handling the claims. This enables Deity to reduce its staff and thereby lower its expense ratios. This reduction was not illustrated in the above calculations.

The loss portfolio transfer is accomplished by a quota share contract, one in which the cession is 100 percent and the retention nil. If, for example, the company also cedes any existing or in-force business, a quota share treaty can adapt for the entire transfer.

TIME AND DISTANCE POLICY

This coverage is an application of an aggregate excess of loss reinsurance structure, applied to reinsurance recoveries in the future which arise out of past business. It is called a retroactive cover. This type is further characterized by a specified payout schedule. Thus the recoveries constitute a financial transaction where premiums are returned on a scheduled basis that does not necessarily correspond to the actual loss payout of the ceding company. In the United States regulators do not accept this as meeting conditions of a financial reinsurance transaction, because there is no timing risk. It is a method of improving the cash flow, and it happens to meet Lloyd's of London's definitions for financial reinsurance. Thus this is reinsurance employed by Lloyd's Syndicates.

This transaction is a stop loss treaty that effectively limits the aggregate amount of losses incurred on the subject business and thus possesses an underwriting risk transfer. This transfer is on an aggregate excess basis, so it stands as a cap or limit to losses. It is not indefinite, so the cedent holds that portion of the risk for its net retained portion plus that portion which exists if losses exceed the aggregate limit of the reinsurance treaty.

In simple terms, a Time and Distance Policy is a mix of premium financing coupled with some underwriting risk transfer. Because this type of policy does not possess timing risk, it is not recognized within the United States as financial reinsurance.

7

REINSURANCE MARKETS

INDUSTRY SEGMENTS
LICENSES
- **Insurance License**
- **Nonadmitted Insurance License**
- **Captive License**
- **Risk Retention Groups**
- **Reinsurance License**

FOREIGN VERSUS DOMESTIC
LEVELS OF BUSINESS
TYPES OF REINSURERS
- **Departments of Insurance Companies**
- **Professional Reinsurance Companies**
- **Lloyd's of London**
- **Reinsurance Pools**
- **Front Companies**
- **Managing General Agents**

SUMMARY

INDUSTRY SEGMENTS

It is necessary for perspective to examine the insurance industry along with the reinsurance industry. There are about 2800 licensed insurance companies. Of these, about 2500 are substantively active. This active segment comprises about 1200 organizations. The giant organizations hold multiple, licensed entities, many consisting of a group, or fleet, of a dozen or more insurance companies.

The total written premium of the U.S. insurance industry is currently in excess of $410 billion:

Direct written insurance premium	$255,000,000,000
Reinsurance assumed	$155,000,000,000
Total written premiums	$410,000,000,000

It is not accurate therefore to conclude that reinsurance comprises 38 percent ($155 billion/410 billion) of the combined industries. The companies cede over $165 billion in premium. Thus, the net written premium total for the domestic industry is about $245 billion.

The assumed reinsurance total comprises reinsurances assumed from affiliates and nonaffiliates.

Assumed from affiliates	$121,000,000,000
Assumed from nonaffiliates	$ 34,000,000,000
Total reinsurance assumed	$155,000,000,000

Note that $34 billion is about 13.5 percent of the $250 billion in direct writings. This is one measure of the open market reinsurance in a given year. Cessions to affiliates do constitute transactions of reinsurance but are of a different nature than open market reinsurance. For example, many groups create an internal pool of business and simply divide it among the various corporate entities. Some groups pool the general business and keep specialized segments within individual entities.

The limitations of the various categories make the measurement of the reinsurance market elusive. A better way to measure this is shown below:

Direct written insurance premium	$255,000,000,000
Premiums ceded within primary group	$125,000,000,000
Premiums ceded to nonaffiliates	$ 43,000,000,000
Percentage ceded to nonaffiliates	17%

A.M. Best's report, *Aggregates and Averages,* supplies statistics compiled from carriers that predominantly write reinsurance and from those considered "professional reinsurers." There is a component in common, so one cannot simply combine the statistics, which are displayed here in approximation (Exhibit 7.1).

Of the top 50 reinsurance entities, approximately 80 percent are broker markets and 20 percent are direct writers of reinsurance. Many reinsurers write both directly and through brokers, using various companies within their group to access both areas of the market. The direct writers tend to be

	Predominantly reinsurance	Professional reinsurers
Reinsurance entities	29 groups	48 companies
Unaffiliated companies	59 comapnies	59 companies
Subsidiaries of others		38 companies
Total	88 entities	145 companies
Direct written premium	2,000,000,000	1,000,000,000
Assumed premiums	16,000,000,000	20,000,000,000
Ceded premiums	5,000,000,000	5,000,000,000
Net written premium	23,000,000,000	26,000,000,000

Exhibit 7.1.   Domestic Reinsurance Industry Statistics

somewhat larger and probably write more than 50 percent of the premium volume.

The collective statistics above are some indication of the size of the reinsurance industry. However, the size is still ambiguous because some is ceded within owned groups and some is ceded to others. The total amounts listed as ceded do not exactly match those given as assumed. For example, some business is ceded net of commissions, while other business is ceded 100 percent with a return of commission. The statistics are calendar-year figures, which implies that the current term is ceded on a provisional commission, while adjustments to prior terms are recorded in this year (see Chapter 2).

In Chapter 1, reinsurance was introduced as the transfer of insurance liabilities from one insurer to another in return for compensation. Thus the parties in a contract of reinsurance are insurance companies. Yet reinsurers have many forms, structures, and capabilities. This chapter will outline the distinguishing characteristics of each type of entity participating in the reinsurance business.

LICENSES

An entity cannot legally transact insurance if not properly licensed. There are three types of licenses available in the United States: insurer, nonadmitted insurer, and reinsurer. The license is secured on a state-by-state basis. The regulatory requirements are fairly complex, with some variances from state to state. This text shall not relate the requirements for such licenses; the interested reader is encouraged to contact the National Association of Insurance Commissioners (NAIC) for further information on this topic.

Generally, a license held in one of the larger states may have automatic recognition in some smaller states or may facilitate the process of obtaining a license in the smaller state. Regulators know that common law holds, so that in the event of trouble, policyholders have access via the courts to insurers domiciled in other states.

The states permit certain types of business to be transacted within their domain by licensed companies. Some licenses are "grandfathered" to licensed insurers in other states who request a license in the particular state.

Insurance License

The insurance license carries the greatest versatility, since insurers can participate in a variety of lines and classes, including both insurance and assumed reinsurance.

Nonadmitted Insurance License

Generally this business is excess of primary coverage insured through a licensed carrier, or surplus to such business. In this respect, Surplus means that it has been passed over or rejected by one or more licensed carriers; note that it is not surplus as in surplus share treaties. Thus, such business is termed excess and surplus lines, or XS & SL and tends to follow the primary coverage. It may exist as additional policy capacity. Alternatively, it may be an umbrella policy that covers above several other policies and may incidentally pick up some coverage in gaps between primary policies. It is not reinsurance. The carrier has the same relationship with the policyholder as does the primary carrier, namely, exchange of the policy contract for premium, with responsibility to pay covered claims and covered expenses.

Remember, reinsurance is protection afforded to the insurer and happens to be done in a manner such that the policyholder has no right of access to the reinsurer. The primary insurer or XS & SL carrier remains responsible for the entire limit of liability stated in the respective policies. Reinsurance is a transfer mechanism for primary insurers and XS & SL carriers alike to protect their portfolio of business from happenstances motivated by the functions of reinsurance (see Chapter 1).

Surplus lines carriers can be either "approved/nonadmitted" or "nonapproved/nonadmitted." Some states, such as Texas, make the broker responsible for the payment of claims, as the broker is recognized as the last entity within the state to touch the premiums before they leave the state. Surplus lines carriers write nonstandard business, such as coverage on oil rigs, pipelines, refineries, pollution liability, professional liability, medical malpractice, hole-in-one insurance, weather insurance for amusement parks or ski resorts, and almost anything one can imagine that has an insurable interest.

Captive License

A captive license permits the owners of a company to incorporate an insurer, or reinsurer, to write solely the risks of their owned company. There are approximately 2500 captives in existence worldwide, with about 300–350 incorporated in the United States. There are 13 states that have captive insurance regulations, including Vermont, Hawaii, Illinois, Georgia, Tennessee, and Delaware. Such companies are able to write, with certain restrictions, throughout the United States.

Risk Retention Groups

These groups are permitted by a federal law, the Risk Retention Act of 1989, enacted to permit a risk retention group (RRG) to be incorporated in a single state to write certain classes of insurance in any other state, without interference from other state authorities. These companies can be easily identified as they must include the letters RRG in their name. Many have used this law to write specialized covers such as products liability, pollution liability, professional liability, and medical malpractice. This legislation was enacted to encourage the injection of new capital into the insurance industry and to focus it toward areas of business that needed such capacity most at the time. Consequently, property risks are specifically excluded under the act. The law also allows the formation of risk purchasing groups, or RPGs, used in the main by industrial associations, to buy insurance as a group without forming their own insurance company to accomplish that task.

The RRGs and RPGs are vehicles used to create discounts through group purchasing. Such group purchasing is a massive undertaking, so insurers who write these normally secure sizeable amounts of reinsurance to support their policy. The laws that define RRGs and RPGs do characterize them as insurance entities and, therefore, allow them to negotiate and purchase reinsurance with some limitations.

Reinsurance License

A reinsurance license is usually termed "reinsurance only" as it does not permit the carrier to write primary policies or insurance of individuals or corporations who are not themselves licensed or recognized insurers or reinsurers.

Since this is transfer between licensed carriers motivated by the functions of reinsurance, it is considered to be business between equals. The consumer protection advocacy does not exist. The contracts tend to be tailored to specific situations. Thus such business is not regulated in the same manner as are primary policies, or, for that matter, XS & SL policies.

FOREIGN VERSUS DOMESTIC

The states hold different levels of recognition, with different taxes, for insurers domiciled within the United States and elsewhere. Those holding a U.S. license achieve a higher level of recognition than those who do not have such a license, enabling domestic licensed insurers to write a better selection of risks.

Foreign companies do not hold the same rank or privilege as domestic carriers. There are giant insurers and reinsurers who possess recognized financial solvency and industry expertise. However, if they do not have a licensed branch in the United States, they are not viewed in the same manner as domestic carriers. The laws and access to funds are not as simple for an aggrieved policyholder trying to gain compensation from a foreign-based carrier who is not licensed domestically.

U.S. regulations are set on consumer advocacy concepts. The insurer, who is deemed to be knowledgeable, writes the contract, sets the price, and offers coverage to the public. The regulators view the typical insurance buyer as not being as sophisticated or knowledgeable as the carrier about insurance. Thus the contract of insurance is not viewed as being between equals. Therefore, the regulators adopt a consumer advocacy role. As such, they hold more power over companies licensed specifically in their own state, modestly less control over those licensed in other states, and considerably less control over foreign carriers who are only licensed in other countries. Thus the regulators restrict the types of insurance/reinsurance transactions such companies write for policyholders within their jurisdiction.

LEVELS OF BUSINESS

An individual policy is a complex contract. The coverage tends to be rather basic: the house, the car, medical needs, liabilities to others, objects in one's care/custody/control, compensation for injuries on the job, etc. XS & SL policies tend to be broader, perhaps covering larger overall limits or coverages that are difficult to obtain because of unusual characteristics of the exposure. Such business is set apart because of its specificity and uniqueness.

A self insurance group can be formed in some states with as little as $250,000 in policy premium and $1 million in collective net worth of the corporate membership. An insurance carrier is required to hold more capital; a minimum of $5 million exists in some states. XS & SL carriers tend to be somewhat larger on average. Reinsurers face similar regulatory requirements as to assets, but within the industry it is difficult for a reinsurer to hold recognition or wide acceptance when it has less than $100 million as an asset base. These are not all regulatory minimums, nor is there any consistency from state to state. However, this is another way to illustrate the levels of business.

Still, the world's largest property and casualty insurer is generally recognized because of its auto and homeowner's insurance volume. This particular company, like many giant carriers, participates in most levels, kinds, and types of insurance and reinsurance. Thus, carriers build their own expertise and are recognized by regulators, competitors, business partners, and the public for that portion which is visible to each observer. Advertising can help the carrier demonstrate its expertise and business interest. All these things together comprise the world of insurance.

TYPES OF REINSURERS

Departments of Insurance Companies

There are many reasons why an insurer will form a division to write reinsurance. For example, a regional carrier may attempt to secure geographic spread by writing business in states where it is not licensed to write insurance or where it lacks an agency force. Interestingly, the business sought may be either similar to that in which the insurer holds special knowledge or complementary to such business.

The business assumed by the department may be shares of opportunities secured by participating in the open market or very specific situations that arise as reciprocity. Reciprocity is a trading of business between carriers. Each may need to lessen its capacity for a given kind of business and may arrange to do so by ceding shares of its own business in exchange for shares of the other carrier's business. Often this is core business over which each carrier wishes to maintain control. Occasionally it involves remote attachments of high capacity risk. Typically they are of similar kinds; however, in reciprocity there is often an exchange of premiums to further equate the exposures.

In many instances the business focus of a department is one-dimensional. The department is conceived as a profit center, created to build an underwriting profit. Since it does not hold an allocated amount of surplus, it often has no mechanism to assess investment income generated from its particular accounts. Thus, departments generally avoid financial reinsurance and many concentrate on property risks. Obviously, departments of giant insurers may participate across a wide spectrum of business.

Professional Reinsurance Companies

These are entities dedicated to reinsurance as their major line of business. Perhaps a decade ago there were small specialized professional reinsurers, formed to write single classes. Today professional reinsurers tend to be very large. As such they tend to write a diversified portfolio of business. Obviously, some do specialize in certain classes or kinds of exposures.

Lloyd's of London

The collective underwriters at Lloyd's represent a special part of the reinsurance scene. It is among the oldest of the reinsurer markets. It has also been a market leader for more than a century. Lloyd's holds insurance licenses, secured by virtue of a very significant trust account deposited in U.S. banks. This trust account satisfies the regulators' concern for funds availability. Lloyd's holds licenses as an insurer. As it is a diversified group of underwriting syndicates, it is known for writing almost every kind and class of insurance and reinsurance.

Lloyd's requires that its syndicates collectively sign contracts that are separate from all other reinsurers. Thus one would not see a Lloyd's participation within an interest and liabilities agreement alongside other reinsurers. In this instance there will be separate contracts for portions of the cession, one specifically for the various Lloyd's syndicates and one with interest and liabilities for the other participants.

Reinsurance Pools

The pooling concept has had an inconsistent history. It is a reinsurance operation where several entities collectively take on business and internally distribute the premiums and losses on a quota share basis. Keeping the group together is sometimes difficult. Commonly the pool is formed to satisfy a particular need within the industry. When that need has been satisfied, or when alternative sources are created, it becomes problematic to keep the pool together. There have been stellar examples of successful pools. And there have been many that existed only for short periods of time.

There are two types of pools. One is led by a licensed entity that provides the license for 100 percent of the business assumed, for a fee. This technique is called fronting. In a fronting situation, one might not know the respective shares of the companies that support the issuing carrier. The second type makes its capacity available on a subscription basis, where each company signs for its respective share. In some cases a designated administrator holds authority to sign for all participants. In a subscription situation the respective shares are listed.

Front Companies

The fronting technique is applied in pools and in many other situations, where licensing is purchased by other entities that wish to partake in the business but lack the license themselves.

Fronting is not always considered in positive terms. In the past overly aggressive carriers viewed the technique as a method for leveraging their business. In several such situations the carriers wrote significant amounts of business but were careless in reviewing the security of those that supported their capacity. When their reinsurers failed to pay promptly, or did not respond at all, these carriers suffered greatly. A number of them went bankrupt.

Collectability of reinsurance is a significant concern. When troubles occur, it spills over, giving the industry a bad name. Insurance is an industry that requires the highest financial capabilities.

Managing General Agents

Managing general agents administer the business for an insurance or reinsurance company. In many cases the arrangement has been created because the producing agent holds special expertise in a line, class, or type of business. The insurer or reinsurer delegates the authority to produce, underwrite, and administer the business. Generally this service is supplied on a fee basis, and the insurer may or may not own a part of the MGA.

The MGA receives its authority through a management agreement, which will stipulate the various duties delegated in the situation. Claim handling is an area that many insurers prefer to retain; on occasion it is also a delegated duty.

There is an obligation of the carrier to monitor the business of the MGA. The insurer or reinsurer has delegated the authority to underwrite, but not the responsibility for the business. At times in the past the monitoring was neglected, and significant problems arose. MGAs became a major topic of concern within the reinsurance industry during the 1980s, and many such organizations were closed or restructured. One type of restructuring was the outright purchase of the MGA by the contracting company, which reinforced the corporate ties and in essence created a "departmental" type of situation.

Insurance MGAs do still exist in significant numbers. Reinsurance MGAs that are not at least partially owned by the carrier are substantively extinct.

SUMMARY

The business of reinsurance is transacted among all these types of entities. Some companies are heavier buyers of reinsurance than others. While there are certain kinds of companies that are heavier users of reinsurance, there is a great amount of variance. Thus, corporate strategy is more indicative of the tendency to purchase reinsurance than is the corporate structure or type of business. If the company is set or leveraged such that its financial, capacity, stabilization, or catastrophe needs are high, it will be a significant buyer of reinsurance. If those fundamental functional needs are low, the company will retain greater portions of its business.

The business is dynamic, with complex cycles and trends. These exist within the types and kinds of companies doing business in reinsurance, as well as in the structures and amounts of reinsurance purchased.

8

REINSURANCE UNDERWRITING

There is some debate as to whether underwriting is an art or a science. In fact, it is neither. Like science, it involves a great deal of quantitative analysis. Like art, it is also subjective. Judgments, whether subjective or objective, are made within a structured context. Each judgment is unique, but the thinking process and options are limited. There is an interesting mix of gut feeling and exposure analysis in each decision. Because of the guidelines and constraints, underwriting lacks the freedom of an art form. Because many parts of the process lack definition and cannot be measured

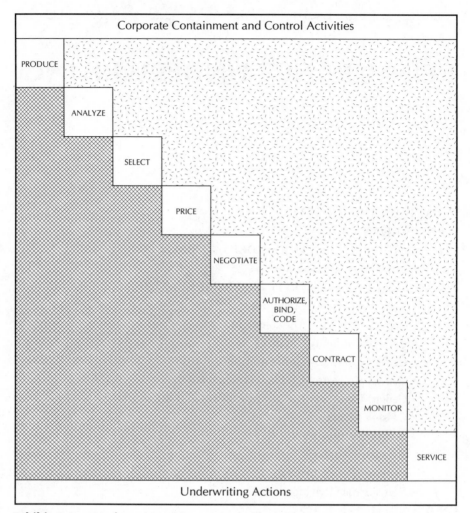

Exhibit 8.1.   Underwriting Management Flow Chart

with precision, it is not a science. Rather, one should think of underwriting as a business.

In this chapter we shall contrast the individual risk underwriting in primary and facultative situations with the bulk analysis that is characteristic of treaty underwriting.

Exhibit 8.1 displays underwriting components diagonally across the diagram. The upper right sector illustrates corporate containment and control activities. The lower left sector shows actions of the underwriter or underwriting department.

SHARED ACCOUNTABILITY

Underwriting is the process of selecting the specific accounts that will comprise a portfolio of business. The responsibility for the result or the developing portfolio rests with the corporate ownership and management. Management can delegate the accountability for the underwriting, but it always holds the responsibility. If, for example, management hires a third party to perform the daily underwriting function, that third party will hold some accountability for the result. When things go awry the blame shifts back and forth. The underwriting process is so fundamental to developing the business and to achieving the desired outcome that it is vital to set accountability and responsibility at the onset.

UNDERWRITING MANAGEMENT

First, let us briefly review the steps depicted in Exhibit 8.1.

1. *Production* Both facultative and treaty underwriters hold some production responsibility. Production may be led by an account executive for direct reinsurers or by an intermediary for the broker market. In either case, the underwriter is inextricably involved in the production process and thus holds some accountability. This includes meeting prospects, often travel, and performing other standard business practices involved in handling clients and building relationships.

2. *Analyze* The submission must be classified, measured, and tested against the company requirements and industry standards. The process varies by line and kind of business and at times is quite sophisticated in both the statistical treatment and decision hierarchy.

3. *Select* The account must be assigned a positive or negative perspective. This is a multistep process, linked throughout the remaining steps in the outline. It may fit the desired profile. One needs to further test its price capability and closely review the terms and conditions, all of which may change as the process moves forward. This step also includes modifying areas where the submission may fall short.

4. *Price* The steps of analysis and selection must be matched by a cost decision. This may be simple or complex and may involve other parties, such as actuaries.

5. *Negotiate* The negotiation process for treaty contract or facultative certificate includes give and take to arrive at the best possible coverage for the least cost. Often details are negotiated and compromised to set the final terms, cost, and payment schedule.

6. *Authorize, Bind, and Code*   Given a favorable outlook, the reinsurer authorizes or quotes the final terms, typically in writing, with an outline of the terms. Agreement is finalized in a formal binder, which is later replaced by the formal signing of the contract. The underwriter must then codify the terms so that the new business is appropriately entered into the data processing system, for accounting, claims, and cash tracking functions.

7. *Contract*   The formal contract, whether a treaty or certificate, is then written. The negotiating process usually follows industry standards, except for certain items that are negotiated. Thus the contract writing mixes "boiler plate" (i.e., standard) language, which is uniform for the reinsurer or intermediary, with the specifically negotiated terms. There may well be a second round of negotiations to get the contract wording to reflect the mutually understood concept and underwriting intent.

8. *Monitor*   The underwriter routinely monitors the account to be sure its development is as expected. There is assistance in this process by accountants, who track incoming reports and cash, and by claim handlers who process claims. All parties make sure each and every transaction meets the agreed terms. The underwriter also monitors developments against industry standards for the kind and class of business.

9. *Service*   This activity includes tasks accomplished by the accountants and claim handlers. The main function of the underwriter is to help with problems as they arise. Ultimately, problems become subject to considerations for renewal or additional business of the same kind or class. Other than price, this is a key area for reinsurers to distinguish themselves from the competition.

INTERACTION WITHIN THE UNDERWRITING PROCESS

A good interaction between management and underwriters is fundamental in the reinsurance industry; however, it does not always exist. The U.S. House of Representatives Report on Insurance Company Insolvencies, titled *Failed Promises,* and released in February 1990, describes one of the insolvent companies.

The management style . . . defies logic and general notions of how to run a business. Most important decisions were made according to how they felt at the time, rather than reasoned analysis and judgement . . . there were no written operating policies or guidelines . . . they considered it to be a subjective business which was not suited to such management controls.

This particular company is at one end of the spectrum. Most companies have systems and routines in place to control exposures accepted by their underwriters.

The corporate or management role is to define boundaries as well as to supply information and tools for underwriting. Boundaries contain and control the kind of business, limits afforded, and exposures accepted. They communicate, actually infuse, shared values about the types and amounts of risk the company is willing to consider. Amount is further defined in terms of limits on capacity as well as minimum rate levels needed for specific exposures.

Management can exert its control and containment on the underwriting process in many ways.

Production can be guided by management with clearly defined production targets and established corporate style preferences. The underwriter can be supplied with protocol designed to positively motivate additional business. There is usually uniformity among underwriters at the same company, reflecting the corporate style preference.

Analysis can be enhanced by supplying news, information, and research.

Selection is led by underwriting and line guides.

Price may be required to follow certain methodology and exceed specified minimums.

Negotiation may be limited and controlled by planning and set preferences. Management can also strongly support holding the line on certain terms and not second-guess the underwriter's prerogative to say "no."

Authorizing, Bind, and Code procedures can be clearly defined and the use of them required.

Contracts can be supported by standards and guides and a master file of clauses, such as that displayed in Chapter 15.

Monitoring can be enhanced with user-friendly electronic data processing. Cedents that are delinquent should be readily disclosed to underwriters. Also, the large claims, serious injuries, claim denials, catastrophic losses, and bad quarter reports should be highlighted for the underwriter's attention. The greatest hindrance to solving problems is ignorance about the existing problem.

Service is a team effort; thus, to be effective the staff in production, underwriting, claims, and accounting must communicate. This effort to communicate needs to be supported and fostered by management.

Underwriting Guidelines

In management's directions to the underwriter, substance is more important than style. The object is to relate a methodology that can be followed to permit a profitable segment of the business to be selected, while discouraging segments or parcels that might prove to be unprofitable.

It is a misconception that if business is written within the guidelines it will be profitable. Also, the author of the guideline does not hold accountability for the end result. Consider the following example:

CASE STUDY: WORKERS' COMPENSATION RATING GUIDELINE

Suppose that a guide is written for worker's compensation that restricts all classes with a high hazard rating or with a rate over $3. The median rate for all classes is perhaps $15 to $20, and truly difficult classes might have rates above $40 or $50. A roofing contractor, for example, might have a rate of $42. Workers with their feet on level ground would be rated lower. Those below $3 are seldom given tools, other than pencils and computers. Typically they work indoors. Even most storekeepers are rated higher. In sum, the supposed guideline is set to avoid all serious exposures.

Will it work? Will it guarantee a profit? Probably not. Such a guide has eliminated serious exposures but not serious claims. Admitting only low-rated classes of employees creates a situation where there are a great number of employees exposed to innocuous exposures. Slips and falls happen fortuitously. Some slips can result in very high claim settlements. While these occurrences are rare, having so many people exposed to the risk can create an imbalance. Imbalance, in turn, can lead to a poor result.

It might be better to include a few higher-rated, higher hazard classes which face a different frequency/severity potential. The worker's compensation rates tend to level the exposures, assuming the classes are priced to the appropriate level of credible measurement. If the rates are not understated some business in higher-rated classes might complement and thereby balance the lower-rated classes.

The guidelines must address more than exposures and specifically include pricing, composition, hazard level, portfolio balance, and complementary business with respect to cycles or complexity, exposure, source, etc.

There is a difference between the underwriting guide and the guidelines. Some companies versions prefer to put both within one document. The guide instructs the underwriter on how to do the job. The guidelines relate to boundaries for the business. Both are important.

In a company, the head underwriter is held accountable for interpreting the guide/guidelines to subordinates. The head is present and available to respond to questions, borderline situations, and gaps in the written version. With a capable leader as head underwriter, the guide/guidelines can be written in an abbreviated form.

The other end of the spectrum is delegated underwriting, where the insurance carrier transfers authority to a third-party administrator (TPA) or an MGA to perform the daily underwriting. While the TPA/MGA might have a very intelligent, broadly experienced underwriter, such an individual is not an officer of the insurance carrier, is distant and detached from the carrier, and often holds a different commercial objective. As such, they may not hold the same perspective. A more detailed guide/guideline is appropriate.

Company sponsorship of training is a corporate responsibility. A new underwriting student's individual effort in class and subsequent usage of the training is reflected in the lower portion of Exhibit 8.1, that reserved for underwriting. The diagram is intended to be dynamic. For example, production targets may be linked across and down to illustrate the impact of this one document on subsequent steps in analysis, selection, and pricing. However, the production targets have little impact further on down the chart or process. Exhibit 8.2 illustrates actions taken by an underwriter at the analysis step that contribute to the decision further along in the process.

Some classes of business require tighter controls, reduced flexibility, and restricted authority for the underwriter. And some kinds of business should have greater detail within the written guide/guidelines. That comment is valid across the underwriting chain, but perhaps is most evident in pricing. Setting rates, or pricing, is an area where there is wide diversity in method, sophistication, and style. Primary, excess, and reinsurance methods differ greatly. Some areas are suitable for actuarial methods, and the rate setting is delegated to another department. Pricing still remains part of the underwriting function. The dual departmental involvement is merely a matter of sophistication, one which necessitates coordination, cooperation, and teamwork. The pricing process may be accomplished by an individual in one situation or a team in another.

It is appropriate for the company to test its methodology; determine appropriate loadings, necessary conditions, and specificity of application; and set minimums. Control becomes more difficult when discounts or downward modifications are part of the flexibility within the underwriter's responsibility and decision.

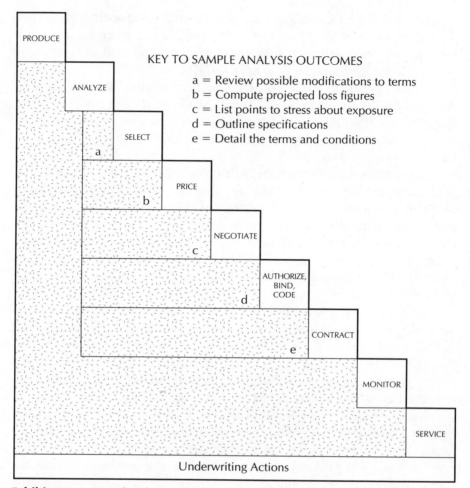

Exhibit 8.2.   Sample of an Underwriter's Action at the Analysis Step

No matter how finely structured or detailed the guidelines and methodology are, the decision of acceptance or rejection of the submission must be made by the underwriter. Does the deal make sense? The underwriter's decision is not made in a void. The submission may be rejected as offered, with a suggestion of variances in terms or conditions that would make the submission acceptable. The ultimate choice must be formulated within the authority granted by management and following its rules. Management also has responsibility to delegate authority appropriate to the level of the individual underwriter's skill and knowledge.

Unfortunately, it is not difficult to find examples of shortcomings where management has neglected its responsibilities to the extent that great gaps developed in its assertion of control. Perhaps the most common mistake is to have too much faith in the skills of the underwriter. Ill-advised management may assume levels of care and sophistication that frankly do not exist in practice. If the underwriter is allowed to act with little restriction, the chances for a miscue or blunder is enhanced.

Balance is critical. Management cannot create endless rules to assert its control. It must do so with understanding that the underwriter needs flexibility and cannot function efficiently if he is more concerned about following procedures than putting good business on the books. Thus the company must manage to build its systems and train its staff to work as a unit. The emphasis is on management's effort to ensure balance between efficient and effective productivity, with control.

An outside observer or auditor looks for the existence of procedures and controls. While they may make a mental note of the sophistication that is evident, the auditors focus on how the underwriting process is monitored by management. The monitoring system must be progressive if containment and concern for control exist in a real sense. "Progressive" here means routine testing and review over a variety of measured areas. Reassessment of the mode and manner of the delegation of authority to the underwriter should reflect a variety of criteria and goals. The monitoring process should not be limited to actions taken following a disaster. Most problems fester before rupturing. Many are news before crises. Management and, for that matter, the underwriter, should not be reactive to business trends; rather they should move to address potentials as part of the monitoring process.

Underwriters should never be in position to face or resolve a developing industrywide crisis on their own. As concern mounts, the underwriter should notify management. Likewise, management should not wait for the topic to be raised by those who might not comprehend its full impact. Bringing the matter forward is not a sign of weakness. Backed with a suggestion for addressing the matter, the underwriter can assert an appropriate attitude and a team orientation. The guide/guidelines, procedures, and delegation should also reflect change, adaptation, and progression.

Cases where underwriting authority is delegated to a TPA/MGA should merely add a second level to the process. Both insurance carrier management and TPA/MGA executives should function to monitor underwriting and address ongoing developments. Although the TPA/MGA situation represents a complex hierarchical structure, the scope of review should follow as described above. The detachment of the TPA/MGA calls for more control, certainly not less.

REINSURANCE UNDERWRITING CONSIDERATIONS

Treaties are accumulations of many policies. Homogeneity may or may not be prominent. At times complementary business may be a good idea. On the other hand, it is not suitable to cede particular policies that are incompatible, where there is so much variance that one definition cannot apply to all situations. Further, it is the perception of the exposure at the time of the cession that carries the decision, not the actual exposure that becomes evident after the term has passed. Reinsurers will list exclusions to eliminate many cessions by kind or class, but the ceding company must make decisions on permissible policies that happen to have unusual circumstances. Thus a treaty can apply to the entire span of business of a company, consisting of many kinds, classes, and types of exposure. This makes treaties far too complex to apply any of the site controls or policy-based considerations that are typical with facultative underwriting.

There are several considerations in treaty underwriting: cedent company structure, cedent company management, cedent company finances, cedent company underwriting, cedent company claims management, cedent company business practices and reputation, cession structure, treaty composition, exposure analysis, primary policy pricing, and reinsurance pricing.

The first six aspects are sometimes collectively tested against the thought, "Is this a company with whom our company should do business?" There is far more to the process than this single statement, however. Clearly, bundling the judgment can lead to overlooking shortcomings in one facet or another.

Remember also that treaty reinsurance is often a long-term relationship. Thus the selection process must consider the likelihood of problems and the cedent's abilities to resolve problems as they arise.

Cedent Company Structure

Obviously whether the company is a stock, mutual, reciprocal, or lloyd's has bearing on the selection process. Also, many cessions are designed for business developed through a particular agent or group of agents. If the cession is controlled by an MGA or if the processing is delegated to TPAs, the treaty underwriter must investigate and understand the dynamics of the structure, where the controls are set, and who is paid what.

The production source is one consideration. Are these independent agents or company employees? Are brokers involved? How much control does the company hold? Has the company developed a solid renewal history? While these structural considerations may seem remote to the actual exposure, they have direct bearing on both the cost of developing the business and the cedent's control over the business.

Cedent Company Management

The cedent's company management is a leadership consideration for the underwriter. Ethics are important. The management must be capable enough for the business, smart enough to build a good business, strong enough to keep a steady course, and must possess professional, ethical character. This is a subjective assessment. One can test these through references. If the corporate management is not personally known, it is critical to seek an independent perspective. Sources of information about management include Best's, Demotech, Duff & Phelps, Moody's, Standard & Poor's, and others.

Cedent Company Finances

Any weakness in the corporate finances can limit the choices of management in designing reparations to problems; shortcomings can also motivate decisions that are not in the collective best interests of cedent and reinsurer or best for the long term. Chapter 14 will address some tests for financial strength, liquidity, diversity, etc. A pronounced weakness could lead to poor results. Insolvency is a terrible situation; reinsurers are considered by liquidators or rehabilitators as potential assets they must maximize. Further, the process is one where reinsurers lose contact with the claim handling for lengthy periods; loss of contact relates to loss of control. Whatever the course, poor financial situations must be avoided for a healthy long-term contract. It is a serious matter for the underwriter to consider.

Earlier, we noted that most facultative carriers assess financials at the reinsurance management level and create a list of acceptable cedents for the underwriter. This permits the facultative underwriter to focus on the exposures. In treaty reinsurance, the type and structure of the deal has bearing upon the decision about financials. For example, property and short-term casualty business may be acceptable from a given cedent, while medical malpractice, director's and officer's, and errors and omissions policies may not be so acceptable. Management capabilities have bearing on this judgment, but the financials may not be sufficiently solid for the very long term. It may be a situation where certain kinds could be accepted while the company is in transition, with careful observation before other types are permitted.

If, for example, the company's financial rating is low, there may be concern whether they can build a sufficient amount of good business, since many insurance buyers use the financial ratings as a determinant in selecting their insurer. A low financial rating or a drop in financial rating may press the cedent to lower its prices to attract quality business. But the business may not be as attractive to the reinsurer at those depressed prices.

Cedent Company Underwriting

Often the head primary underwriter will be listed within the treaty offering. Treaty underwriters will be concerned about the capabilities of the head underwriter, who directs the development of the particular business subject to the treaty. The key factor is quality. How is the quality built? How is it maintained? How is spoilage kept out? There are many questions, and knowing something about who directs these important aspects is important.

Typically, reinsurers will obtain a copy of written underwriting guidelines, targets, and constraints upon individual underwriters. Inquiry into underwriting will give the reinsurers insight into how the business is controlled.

Cedent Company Claims Management

Claims are the crises to which reinsurance provide some remedy. Claims can get out of hand. The effort to contain the economic loss, provide assurance to the injured parties, and control the developing resolution of the event is quite important. Reinsurers want to measure their steadfastness, their talent, and their ability to rise to meet uncertainty in unusual, atypical, changing situations.

Reinsurers hold the right to participate in resolutions of underlying claims, bearing the additional cost of their participation. This is a seldom used right. It is intended for cases such as asbestosis, which are truly cataclysmic to the industry and where reinsurers want to have some say in the disposition. Generally, reinsurers prefer to do business with cedents that can handle most claims; thus they undertake the effort to measure the capabilities of each company.

Occasionally when truly difficult claims arise, reinsurers can have an impact. They may have been exposed to cases where certain techniques were employed that may have applicability in the case at hand. However, ultimate responsibility rests with the cedent. So even in situations where reinsurers participate or are asked for advice, the capabilities of the cedent are primary. So the reinsurer must be sure that the cedent can handle claims appropriately.

Cedent Company Business Practices and Reputation

This is often referred to as the moral or ethical quality behind the business arrangement. Trust is a key consideration in ceding business, and it is equally valued by assuming carriers. Often it is a value judgment of the person through whom the cession passed or was negotiated rather than an assessment on a corporate level. However, if trust is questionable or if past practices are thought to have been out of line, the consideration should be stopped. There are individuals and companies that skirt the bounds of ethics and fair dealing or who operate selfishly with respect to their net. Cheats, dolts, and rascals do not generally share exposures equitably nor do they produce sufficient profits for a comfortable relationship. Underwriters have long memories and will avoid doing business with such people, even if they switch positions or companies. Moral judgments are difficult to quantify and are not often stated as a reason for declination. However, this aspect is one of the major considerations in the reinsurance selection process.

Cession Structure

Insurance companies are composed of people. People make decisions that affect the outcome of the reinsurance partnership. A wise choice of people distinguishes good treaties from poor ones.

The cession structure must be appropriate for the intended use. The underwriter must understand the functions of the reinsurance and know if subject business is critical to the cedent or peripheral. Next, one must consider just how the treaty is constructed to respond to claims. Are the expected claims suited to the offered coverage? Is the layering, if any, appropriate? It is important to understand that the choice of structure is independent of price. It is always advisable to assess the structure for its own merits or disadvantages.

Treaty Composition

All the terms and conditions spelled out in the treaty are important. Each should be considered for its impact on cost. Often the terms are negotiated as part of the developing deal. One does not give away with one hand, hoping what has been taken with the other will be sufficient. Rather, one should measure the economic impact of each and build the combined cost.

Exposure Analysis

The most obvious consideration in treaty underwriting is the exposure covered by the treaty. This analysis may include considerations such as PML, which might be considered by some as artificial. Nonetheless, the underwriter should employ every technique to understand the exposure to which the treaty is subject.

Primary Policy Pricing

Some reinsurance pricing is dependent on the primary rate. The total insurance cost comprises the primary portion plus the reinsurance portion. For some coverages, total insurance cost is set. This is common for automobile coverages, where the total cost must pass through a stiff regulatory process and the rates and rate manual are fixed annually. In these situations, the reinsurance portion is a subportion. The portion allocated to reinsurance depends upon all the other facets.

Other coverages include the reinsurance cost as part of the insurance quote. Facultative reinsurance is one example. In building the total insurance cost of a huge structure or major single liability policy, the specifications are released to facultative reinsurers for quotations of their part. The total is the sum of all the parts.

Carriers negotiate most treaties annually and know the reinsurance portion to build into their total insurance cost. Reinsurers must understand these facts as they price their product. If their piece is not affordable, one of two things will happen: the coverage will be sold at a reduced limit or constrained composition, or another reinsurer will offer the same or similar coverage at the necessary price. If one cedent cannot secure reinsurance that makes the deal work at a given price, another cedent may hold better relationships and secure the support at the necessary price. Thus, reinsurance must be considered as a piece of a whole insurance package.

At times reinsurers' reluctance leads to higher overall insurance costs across the line of business or industry. At other times, reinsurers' aggressiveness leads to lower overall costs. Sometimes the blame or cause for failure to complete the deal is at the hands of the cedent. Thus, there is a delicate balance, often in negotiation, that must be compromised to make many deals work. It is important to keep the total concept in mind as one works and negotiates to determine appropriate charges.

Reinsurance Pricing

Reinsurance pricing is a key determinant in treaty underwriting and will be discussed in detail in Chapters 9, 10, and 11.

UNDERWRITING LOGIC

The underwriting process is necessarily complex and involves many steps. The underlying logic can be simplified into a few key questions:

1. Are we comfortable with the cedent?
2. Does the business fit within the guidelines and targets?
3. Do any exposure anomalies exist?
4. Is the price (for the primary and the reinsurance portion) right?
5. Should we undertake this deal?
6. If an intermediary is involved, are we comfortable with the firm?

There are cedents with whom a reinsurer has considerable business. The reinsurer is familiar with its management and financials and will seek additional business from this cedent. Good fit is a concept common to every business, and insurers and reinsurers work hard to build mutually profitable long-term relationships. So, at times the cedent source decision is easy.

The underwriter is so familiar with the applicable guidelines and so much of the business consists of familiar kinds and classes that the guideline test seems almost automatic. The underwriter knows when to go slow. So, fit is often a quick judgment. (A declination is often apparent before the first page of a presentation is read, yet the materials may be read and the decision made only after further consideration.)

The underwriter needs to check for anomalies in the exposure. If the offered business is personal lines business from a familiar carrier, the underwriter will know the forms, kinds, and types written. They need to consider concentrations and a few other points to be comfortable. If the offered business is accountant's professional liability, or the like, there should and will be many more questions.

We have appropriately approached pricing as a complex consideration. At times it is not so hard to accomplish. A profitable history will prove that the primary pricing is appropriate. Some commission schemes are fairly common, so some proportional reinsurance pricing can be done quickly. Again, if the composition of business is ordinary and the specifications standard, the price suggested within the initial offering may be acceptable. "Should we undertake this deal?" is always the bottom line. After all the other decisions have been made, this may seem perfunctory. Yet, it carries heavy responsibility.

Some underwriters defer decisions on the road. They do not wish to be in a position where their decision could be questioned as hasty, perhaps made during lunch, cocktails, or dinner where their faculties were not acute. Others prefer to complete deals face to face and agree on a handshake. Each company will have its protocol for decisions, such that each and every deal is formalized and checkpoints are met. This does not mean the entire process cannot be swift. For example, a facultative submission often consists of a single-page telex or facsimile. If the cedent and reinsurer have done dozens of similar deals, the acceptance may follow within minutes. Both know the current parameters. A treaty submission may be similarly comfortable, with a known cedent and class that is recognized to be the core business of the cedent's success. It also can be bound in a very short time.

Such a smooth transaction usually takes place when the cedent and reinsurer have a mutual relationship and seek to expand their business together. If the common business history is rocky, with some deals in loss, the process will not be so swift.

It is the underwriter's responsibility to slow the process down as complexities arise. If the kind of business has severe potentials, if pricing is constrained, or if the line is in crisis, the judgment must be carefully considered. The entire process is designed to proceed appropriately according to the kind, class, and type of business being offered and the existing business relationship.

While the decision time frame may be compressed, the list of inquiry points must always be complete. The speed should be directly related to the certainty that the deal meets all the criteria of a good business judgment, as outlined by the company in its guide and guidelines.

9

REINSURANCE PROPORTIONAL PRICING

There are many activities which precede pricing; defining guidelines, selecting the risks for acceptability, and ensuring the risk is conformable to or complementary to the existing portfolio of business written are just a few considerations. Another is collecting data about the exposures. These tasks must be completed in order to address the fundamentals of reinsurance pricing.

PRICING THEORY

What is the purpose of the reinsurance? This question should be kept in mind when assessing reinsurance pricing. The highest rate "the traffic will bear" is not often the best rate. Selfish negotiation, pressing hard, and only considering potential income from the deal is not a winning strategy for treaty reinsurance. Here, there is a difference between treaty and facultative considerations.

First, many treaties are long-term situations. The insurer must pass off or cede some important exposures for a relatively fixed cost over time. The price is "relatively" fixed since there are expected annual price negotiations. These take into consideration some market movement, as well as growth and change in the composition of the cedent's portfolio. For example, if the portfolio grows by 20 percent and the retention remains at the same level, the reinsurers can be expected to hold a larger portion of the exposure. Obviously, this assumes the policy limits profile either stays the same or increases with time. It is easy to simplify the discussion to such an extent that the complexity of the business is missed. The point in this example is that evolution within the portfolio itself causes change in the price. The business matures and grows throughout the year, all of which must be reconsidered in the renewal price.

Shifts in strategy of the cedent, significant changes in the production source, and dramatic changes in the portfolio profile can result in a broader change in price. For example, if an insurer of standard auto business decides to expand into long-haul trucking or taxi business, the new rate might not have any correlation to past pricing.

If the treaty reinsurer has had a poor record in the past, that is, more losses than ceded premium, it is said to be in a deficit position. The cedent may offer to adjust the rate to overcome that situation. Note the deliberate counterposition in negotiating. Likewise, if the reinsurer holds significant profit, often called a "bank," it will offer a price reduction as earnings for superior results. There is real pressure in both directions.

With reinsurers in deficit, can the cedent simply shift to new reinsurers and forget its past? This would be burning one's bridges. Since the number of reinsurers is finite, and they each have long memories, one might quickly run out of alternatives through repeated use of the dump-and-run strategy. Further, the new reinsurers will be cognizant of the situation, will surely realize the lack of continuity in the situation, and will not bid aggressively for such an account.

Reinsurers want profitable business. They do not press for just any business. However, this has not always been the case. During the Carter administration, from 1977 to 1981, there was a period of prolonged inflation, which climbed as high as 22 percent, well above the 6–8 percent historical average. That period inspired many new entrants to the reinsurance field, which in turn caused great pressure to lower rates. The new entrants were not considered to be as knowledgeable by long-term players in the reinsurance market. That perspective is not altogether true. Many old and new companies appeared to adopt the strategy that any long-term liability business could be written at current terms, when the loss payout would fall several years later, after earning considerable interest on the invested premiums for that year. Let us digress to discuss how this process works.

Including an interest consideration in the pricing scheme is not an error; however, experiences in the past 20 years have demonstrated just how

CASE STUDY: INTEREST INCOME

Suppose a reinsurer takes in $1 million in premium with an expected loss ratio of 62 percent. Let us assume that the past claims have been paid out at a rate of 20 percent each year. Note we have not assumed how these might have become known or been incurred. Let us say the claims were set at $620,000 from the very start. With 20 percent paid each year, the tail or payout should be finished in five years, at a pay-out pace of $124,000 per year.

With 8 percent interest, a bank account would double in a little more than eight years. With 16 percent interest, a bank account would double in less than five years, so there is a considerable advantage with a high rate of insurance. Due to the inflow of premium and out-flow of loss payments, the real-life situation for reinsurance funds does not parallel savings funds, which tend to remain in the bank undiminished for the full term. Exhibit 9.1 is a somewhat simplistic il-lustration of interest income. The precision or calculation scheme need not be investigated by the reader, other than to note that interest has been calculated on the unpaid claim amount rather than the full premium on the account.

Year	Claim Payout	Interest @ 8%	Interest @ 16%
1	$620,000	$44,640	$89,280
2	$496,000	$38,291	$83,725
3	$372,000	$27,863	$62,996
4	$248,000	$17,109	$39,839
5	$124,000	$ 6,329	$16,294
6	$ 0		
Total Interest		$134,232	$292,134

Note: Interest applied midyear assuming half that year's payout has been spent. Also, interest is compounded.

Exhibit 9.1. Reserve Interest

If the reinsurer is confident about a return such as 16 percent, it could afford a lower premium for the business. Perhaps it might per-mit a 33 percent commission, thinking it would pay 62 percent in claims and still have 5 percent for profit or as a margin for error. The high investment income would permit an attractive profit potential, even if it was not guaranteed. Clearly the willingness to offer high commissions or low rates would be increased by such high interest levels.

unpredictable the call for claim payouts can be, regardless of the class of business. The several years after the atypically high inflation period that occurred during the end of the Carter administration produced some of the industry's worst composite results. Assumptions about the claim payout rate were inaccurate. Premium inflow assumptions also may not have been realistic. In addition, the combination of assumptions led to negotiations that did not adequately consider the exposures. Asbestoses, toxic shock syndrome, environmental problems, and urea formaldehyde foam installation claims were characteristic of happenings that were not adequately considered by many in the insurance/reinsurance industry. More claims went to trial, more trials were presented before juries, and many insurers faced a flood of litigation in an expanding environment in the United States. The years 1979, 1980, 1982, 1983, 1984, and 1985 were each above the norm for property catastrophic losses. All of these adverse trends combined to overcome the perceived interest advantage. Reinsurers who cut prices to build volume were adversely affected, many seriously so.

Of course, practice often defies theory. While the illustrated benefits can be estimated, the cause can result in other changes to the industry. When the rate of interest skyrocketed from 1979–1981, insurers sought to maximize their returns and delayed premium payments. In retribution or perhaps consequent to the same trend, reinsurers delayed loss payments. Each party endeavored to hold on to the money, and some long-term proportional reinsurance relationships floundered during this period. An expression of the time, was that "money was flowing like glue."

Accordingly, the interest factor should be understood within the pricing scheme as should the long-term nature of treaty reinsurance. The test of mutual reasonableness applies. If the reinsurer in deficit presses too hard to get it all back in one short year, price negotiations might break down. Likewise, reinsurers holding a large bank or profit who appear reluctant to relax pricing might face discontinuity. Each party must feel comfortable with the progress, the upcoming year, and the statements and reactions of the other party to significant happenstances. Thus the long-term relationship is built on mutual trust and support in times of trouble, as well as on empathy and understanding for common benefit.

There are many striking examples of mutual support and interest in perpetuating longevity of the relationship. The author recalls participating on a treaty with 17 consecutive years of healthy profits, such that a $2.2 million profit sharing was due. This occurred when the cedent experienced a quite difficult first quarter, which was likely to produce a loss for the full year. This carrier unilaterally waived $2 million of the profit commission, not wishing to further aggravate the adverse cash flow of its reinsurance partners. The surprising fact is that the reinsurers were holding over $35 million in accumulated profit over the period of the contract. Why? Continuity was important to the cedent. It realized the difficulty of the times and chose a course of action that would foster continuity. This contract was positioned at the heart of the cedent's program, which made its results most critical to the cedent, and obviously prompted its actions.

The benefits of long-term relationships are not the exclusive preserve of treaty reinsurance. Facultative reinsurers have some accounts that they hope to renew for many years. Like insurance, renewal business is more profitable than most new business. Ongoing relationships generate familiarity, and often, expectancy is rewarded by fulfillment. That confidence is lacking with new business due to the absence of frequent interactions to foster comfort in the relationship. Thus it is a misconception to believe all facultative business lacks the benefit of long-term relationships. Much of the facultative business is generated from core accounts, arising from familiar cedents, ceding directly, or indirectly through intermediaries.

We have characterized facultative accounts as complex or unusual exposures. Once the account has been developed and the reinsurance secured, it is natural that the cedent would wish to renew the account and maintain its facultative structure and reinsurers, obviously updated for renewal conditions. However, while treaties are composed of a group of accounts, where successful renewal coupled with new business of a similar nature might lead to renewal "as is", facultative business is ceded on an "each risk" basis, with some certificates renewed and others not. Given the same turnover rate, a portfolio of facultative business will have more certificates held for just one or two years than will most treaty portfolios. Perhaps more importantly, the facultative pricing depends more on the individual characteristics of the account than on the longevity of the account. Turnover is a fact of life, yet there are pressures in both treaty and facultative cessions for continuance by both parties to the reinsurance agreement. Both facultative and treaty reinsurers tend to maintain longstanding relationships with particular ceding companies.

In very simple terms, pricing is the activity of cost determination. Cost must cover the claim activity that arises from the exposure, so one most measure exposure carefully and understand where potential claims lie. Is the reinsurance exposed to frequency of loss or to severity? Are multiple claimants from the same event a real possibility? Are unusual circumstances or conditions present or possible? Those are hard questions to quantify, but the pricing activity must do so. To arrive at a viable price, the basic claims must be covered and expenses must also be considered and included. Some must be contained to make the reinsurance cost-effective. The pricing may include acquisition and handling costs of the cedent. It may include brokerage for the expenses of a reinsurance intermediary and it must include expenses of the reinsurer itself. There are so many expense items to consider it is easy to come up short in this regard. In proportional reinsurance, expenses run about one third of all costs, more or less depending on the nature of the business.

Profit must be considered. Profit is the motivation for taking the business. If there is little or no profit potential, the deal will not work and the submission should be passed. Note use of the word "passed" rather than "declined." If the submission is otherwise permissible, an unattractive price should be "passed" with an indication of just how much additional premium would be necessary for the business to be attractive, that is, a counter quote or offer.

While most personal lines business has preset, preapproved pricing published in rate manuals, reinsurance pricing is negotiated on each and every treaty or facultative certificate. There are substantial differences in the composition, characteristics, and profiles of each reinsurance agreement which demand careful and special consideration of the price. Often the reinsurer will employ its broad-based knowledge of the class, kind, or sector, in addition to the qualification of the cedent itself.

Reinsurance pricing is not easy to understand, nor are the techniques applied in the process simple. The cedent may be passing off a component of its business with which it is uncomfortable or unfamiliar, or which is unusual, volatile, or troublesome. While the reinsurer may have some advice on the problematic aspect, their speciality is quantifying or estimating the economic impact and expense of that cession and working up a suitable price. When that price is mutually attractive to both the cedent and assuming reinsurer, then the transfer of exposures can be accomplished.

Note that if both parties are not comfortable with the price, the deal will likely not happen. Thus it is always a negotiated acceptance. Also, there are other bidders. A price that is not acceptable to one reinsurer may be acceptable to another. It is negotiation with competition.

The cedent has the option of moving the account to another reinsurer for a lower price. In shifting it may lose the familiarity of a long-term relationship. It may lose the security of a reinsurer holding profits from prior years. And it may lose the special expertise provided by the existing reinsurer who may have helped develop the business along the way. Thus continuity is a major consideration in pricing.

TYPES OF REINSURANCE PRICING

The two types of reinsurance pricing are "proportional" and "excess" pricing. These can also be called "commissions" and "rates." Commissions can be applied to either proportional or excess business. Typically, however, proportional reinsurance has a commission scheme and excess of loss is rated. Reinsurance excess pricing will be discussed in Chapter 10.

COMMISSIONS

This is the simplest form of reinsurance pricing. Yet, there is no industry-wide agreement as to just how commissions should be set. Our emphasis here shall be to show how they work, with just a modest amount of discussion on price setting consideration.

Flat Commission

A commission can be preset and fixed. Suppose the producing agent requires 18 percent, and the Mythical Insurance Company's expense is another 9 percent. A reinsurer might agree to a flat commission of 27 percent to cover those underlying costs.

This type of pricing would generally apply to proportional reinsurance, with a homogeneous base of business, such as private passenger auto or homeowner's. These lines tend to have similar types of exposure and consistent costs. It does not take much more time to underwrite a $250,000 home than a $150,000 home, so the business acquisition/developmental cost is consistent from one submission to the next.

This type of commission does not reward the cedent for profitable business or penalize the company for poor results. It may be paired with a secondary calculation that accomplishes these results.

Contingent Commission

A flat commission can be combined with a profit commission to motivate better business. Typically such commissions are contingent upon the existence and size of profit that is developed; thus, it is often called a contingent commission. If the flat commission just matches or is just short of the acquisition cost, the existence of a contingent commission can be a strong motivator of the quality of business written in a particular program.

The formula may be designed to promote both the desired quality and quantity of business by its structure as well as the amount of reward that is offered as additional commission earned with good results. If the cedent is offered a flat commission above its acquisition cost, it should be motivated to produce and underwrite a large quantity of business. If the reward for good results is significant, the cedent may work hard at selecting better quality business.

The typical setup is a flat commission of something like 27.5 percent with a contingent commission of 30 percent of any profit that exceeds an initial

10 points of a reinsurer's expense allotment. This formula would award the cedent 30 percent of each point where the loss ratio falls below 62.5 (e.g. 100 − 27.5 − 10). For example, a loss ratio of 52.5 percent would be 10 points of excess profit, thus generating 30 percent of 10 percent, or 3 percent additional commission. The total commission would be 27.5 + 3.0 = 30.5 percent.

The structure of this commission is relatively simple and straightforward. The flat commission is intended to cover cedent acquisition costs, while the allotment is intended to cover the reinsurer's expenses. Thereafter, any profit would be split according to the agreed formula.

The profits do not have to be split 50/50. The reinsurers must amass profits in good times for the inevitable bad times when loss exceeds premium and investment income. Once the profit bank becomes too large, the negotiations tilt in favor of the cedent, just as large losses will promote tighter terms and reduced commissions.

Sliding Scale Commission

The commission can be designed to float with the results, rewarding overall profit and penalizing poor results. Most often such commissions are tied to the developing loss ratio. For example:

Provisional commission = 30%
Maximum commission   = 35.0% at 45% loss ratio,
Minimum commission   = 25.0% at 65% loss ratio
Slide   = 1/2 for 1
Terms   = To be calculated quarterly, after 6 months on
                       the year-to-date loss ratio
                       Payable in 30 days

Here, the cedent can earn 0.5 percent for each full point drop in loss ratio. The cedent and reinsurer are splitting the profit after the first 5 percent has been recorded, through the next 20 percent of profit. Beyond 35 percent, the reinsurer retains full benefit.

The scale is structured with 10 points of additional commission to be earned over 20 points in the loss ratio, that is, a 1/2 for 1 scale. Normally commissions are described in terms of the portion of additional commission earned for each full point reduction in loss ratio.

The advantage of a sliding scale is that it addresses both quantity and quality of the business written. The higher the loss ratio, the lower the commission. The lower the loss ratio, the greater the commission. It is always such an inverse relationship. It is the maximum and minimum that determine the scope of penalty for poor business or reward for good business.

Loss ratio	Commission	Total	Reinsurer's margin	Cedent's margin
75.0%	27.0%	102.0%	−2.0%	1.0%
70.0%	27.0%	97.0%	3.0%	1.0%
65.0%	27.0%	92.0%	8.0%	1.0%
60.0%	27.0%	87.0%	13.0%	1.0%
55.0%	27.0%	82.0%	18.0%	1.0%

Exhibit 9.2. Margin Chart: Flat Commission

Margins

The choice and amount of commission depends on competition. The lack of competitive bidding permits the reinsurer to keep more in its margin. Viable competition may have a direct impact on reducing that margin.

In defining the above commissions, the margin was purposely not addressed because the margin or projected margin must be measured against a loss ratio. Margin is the difference between the sum of commission offered plus the actual or developing loss ratio and 100 percent. The margin covers the reinsurer's expenses, profit, and some measure for adverse development.

The cedent may also have a margin. We calculate that as the difference between the total commission earned and the cost. The cost includes both acquisition costs and insurer expenses.

The margin calculation is simple for flat commissions and somewhat more complex for sliding scales and contingent commissions. In the case of a flat commission the margin is readily apparent. In these examples let us assume the cedent's cost is 26 percent.

In the above example, the underlying facts would seem to indicate that a loss ratio as high as 65 percent was not likely, because the reinsurer accepts a thin margin above that point. Note also that the cedent does not benefit in the results of that portion ceded, but that it is likely that the cedent retains a significant amount of the quota or surplus share of the business, net for its own account. Thus this scheme is a straight cession, for a fixed commission.

When the flat commission is tied to a contingent commission the entire calculation must be considered when determining the amount of margin. The cedent's cost is still assumed to be 26 percent. Here the 27.5 percent preliminary or flat commission is augmented by a 30 percent contingent after a 10 percent reinsurer's expense allotment.

Clearly, the requirements of a 27.5 percent provisional commission plus 10 percent for reinsurer's expenses cannot be met in full with a loss ratio above 62.5 percent in this formula. However, when the ratio falls below that point the cedent is rewarded with additional commissions.

Loss ratio	Flat commission	Sub-total	Expense allotment	Contingent commission	Total	Reinsurer's margin	Cedent's margin
75.0%	27.5%	102.5%	−2.5%	Nil	102.5%	−2.5%	1.5%
70.0%	27.5%	97.5%	2.5%	Nil	97.5%	2.5%	1.5%
65.0%	27.5%	92.5%	7.5%	Nil	92.5%	7.5%	1.5%
60.0%	27.5%	87.5%	12.5%	0.8%	88.3%	11.7%	2.3%
55.0%	27.5%	82.5%	17.5%	2.3%	84.8%	15.2%	3.8%

Exhibit 9.3. Margin Chart: Flat Commission with Contingent

In the above example, at a 55 percent loss ratio, the cedent gets 27.5 percent as a provisional commission and another 2.3 percent later when the profit is determined, totaling 29.8 percent. With the cedent's cost at 26 percent, the cedent's margin is 3.8 percent. The reinsurer's margin at that point is 15.2 percent. This margin includes an allotment for reinsurer expenses of securing the business, brokerage, running the accounts, auditing, etc. There should also be something included in the allotment each good year to cover the eventual year when the loss ratio rides above the necessary break-even point. Reinsurers will propose more savings for the future from an extraordinarily fine year than from an average year to build for the eventual bad year when the law of large numbers balances the score.

The sliding scale formula typically sets a provisional commission that applies until the initial loss ratio calculation. Thereafter, a running calculation sets the commission on a developing basis. Again, the cedent's cost is assumed to be 26 percent.

Unlike the other examples, many sliding scale formulae carry a penalty on the cedent for poor results, obviously subject to the minimum commission. The other types afford a guaranteed commission. As a result, only the sliding

Loss ratio	Sliding scale	Total	Reinsurer's margin	Cedent's margin
75.0%	25.0%	100.0%	0.0%	−1.0%
70.0%	25.0%	95.0%	5.0%	−1.0%
65.0%	25.0%	90.0%	10.0%	−1.0%
60.0%	27.5%	87.5%	12.5%	1.5%
55.0%	30.0%	85.0%	15.0%	4.0%
50.0%	32.5%	82.5%	17.5%	6.5%
45.0%	35.0%	80.0%	20.0%	9.0%

Exhibit 9.4. Margin Chart: Sliding Scale

scale affects the production volume and the quality of business written. A contingent commission can be structured to affect the volume, only if the provisional or flat commission does not fully cover the acquisition costs of the cedent. In such a case, the cedent must rely on profit to gain from writing the business.

The preceding sections are intended to introduce the types of commissions offered with simple calculations. As examples, they may not seem realistic, but remember that each would be designed for a specific cedent. Reality or acceptability would largely be determined by the particular history and exposures of the business. Since the examples lacked such accompanying detail one should not make judgments about the realism.

Consider the following example, which contains some considerations about the choice of type of commission and the development of the formula.

One must always be careful when most of the available years fall above the average. Here too, the premium growth was greater after the one excellent year and appears to have been controlled once the loss ratio moved to the higher level. There are obvious questions to be asked about the cause of the higher loss ratio and about controls over the business. We shall not answer these questions here, but these are the types of questions that should arise in analysis of the past history.

Note that the loss ratio has been fairly stable, ranging from the low of 45 percent to a high of 59 percent. However it has been at or near that high point for the past four years. The volume is sufficient to give credibility to the data. Nonetheless, the data should be considered in light of the industry trends for the business segment. The lower the volume the more weight should be assigned to industrywide trends and averages.

The cedent contracts with its agency at 18 percent, plus contingent commissions for the larger, preapproved premier agents. The average has been around 20.7 percent for the past several years. The cedent routinely checks agency records but does not inspect or engineer new business. It estimates its costs to be 7.5 percent.

Year	Premium	Loss	Loss ratio
1	$ 35,111,111	$ 15,799,999	45%
2	$ 39,222,222	$ 23,356,667	57%
3	$ 42,333,333	$ 23,706,666	56%
4	$ 44,444,444	$ 26,222,222	59%
5	$ 45,555,555	$ 26,422,222	58%
Total	$206,666,665	$115,507,776	55.4%

Exhibit 9.5.   Commission Case Study

This is a new prospect; the producer was lucky with timing. A principal at the cedent company mentioned that it was concerned about the volume of business written in relation to some of its financial measurements. The producer suggested a new 25 percent quota share to drop volume for a few years, while the financials grew. What should the underwriter quote?

In this case, a declination is in order. Treaty reinsurance is a long-term business, and one should not enter such a contract with scant information. Here we know just the short story, which should never satisfy an underwriter; he or she should seek additional information to reveal exposures, address procedures, satisfy strengths in management and staffing, etc. However, for the sake of this example, let us assume that the detail was provided and acceptable.

One should begin by considering the purpose of the reinsurance. Here it is given as a financial concern. One needs to know more:

1. What is it about the financials that raises the concern?
2. Are there implications within that concern which make the cedent company unacceptable?
3. Is the quota share the best solution?

Assuming these questions are answered adequately, let us proceed.

Each cedent must be measured for expertise, management insight, underwriting and pricing ability, administration, and claims handling. Here we sweep all that into a judgment that some additional motivation seems necessary. Obviously, such considerations are always easier in a hypothetical situation.

The next consideration is the cedent's costs. In this case it is 20.7 percent for acquisition of the business and is estimated to be 7.5 percent for the cedent's operations. Thus totals 28.2 percent. Is this correct? Is it typical? Can it be sustained by the results?

These are questions that arise immediately. The reinsurer should track such costs by line of business and type of exposure so that it can respond to the concerns by supplying industry sector knowledge. The reinsurer needs to have ready comparisons in order to make a proper judgment. That is part of their expertise and corporate knowledge base. If the concept is not acceptable or economically sustainable, this process should stop with a declination. In this case, the loss ratio is less than 60 percent and thus appears to sustain the requested amount of commission.

One should decide the type of formula to use for commissions. Whether this is a quota share or surplus share cession does have an impact on this decision, as does the proportion of each risk that the cedent retains. Generally speaking, the greater the portion retained by the cedent the less one needs to motivate quality within the cessions. This means a flat commission or contingent commission may work best where the cedent is retaining a very large portion of each risk. A sliding scale may add motivation for quality when the proportion retained is not sufficient by its own weight.

Competitive considerations also must be considered. Here we seem not to have competition, but the cedent might be entertaining other quotes or even alternate proposals. This is a point about which one should inquire. There *will* generally be competitors or a competitive option.

Although the cedent is retaining 75 percent, let us say we are concerned enough that the experience might be deteriorating to require a sliding scale. This appears to be a simple judgment; it never is straightforward or easy. If the loss ratio continues to rise, the cedent's acquisition formulae will squeeze the agency force. Thus the agents will be motivated to press for better quality. Also, it is likely that the cedent will raise prices. These are just two of many possibilities. The cedent has many options when faced with deteriorating results; some causes can be controlled, others seem beyond the reach of an individual carrier. The commission scale cannot rectify everything; it should only be considered a motivator. Cutting the cedent's margin or creating a situation where the acquisition costs are not covered are harsh steps that should inspire corrective actions by the cedent.

Let us now attempt to design a sliding scale appropriate to this case. Exhibit 9.6 spreads the known cedent's known costs, or costs evident in the past history, over a range of possible loss ratios.

Theoretical loss ratio	Cedent's cost	Subtotal	Preliminary margin
75.0%	28.2%	103.2%	−3.2%
72.5%	28.2%	100.7%	−0.7%
70.0%	28.2%	98.2%	1.8%
67.5%	28.2%	95.7%	4.3%
65.0%	28.2%	93.2%	6.8%
62.5%	28.2%	90.7%	9.3%
60.0%	28.2%	88.2%	11.8%
57.5%	28.2%	85.7%	14.3%
55.0%	28.2%	83.2%	16.8%
52.5%	28.2%	80.7%	19.3%
50.0%	28.2%	78.2%	21.8%
47.5%	28.2%	75.7%	24.3%
45.0%	28.2%	73.2%	26.8%
42.5%	28.2%	70.7%	29.3%

Exhibit 9.6. Margin Chart: Case Study Preliminary

With the existing five-year average loss ratio of 55 percent, the margin appears to be nearly 16.8 percent. However, in this case, the four more recent years have been working at about a 57.5 percent average. There the margin is 14.3 percent. A jump to 62.5 percent in the coming year is an increase of 5 points and represents an 8.7 percent variation from the four-year average. Analysis of the probability of that sort of happenstance can be measured against industrywide data for a similar sector of exposures. Some might feel it more likely to jump up 5 points from 57.5 percent than to drop 5. One should not neglect the fact that the five-year average is 2.5 points lower at 55 percent and the longer term center point may prevail. Analysis of this sort may permit some comfort on the part of the reinsurer that it can fully cover its own costs and accumulate funds for the future.

One possible choice is shown in Exhibit 9.7. Here the cedent is additionally rewarded by 40 percent of each reduction in loss ratio over the range, as the slide is 2 points for each 5-point improvement in loss ratio. Forty percent is an attractive benefit. Note, however, that while the cedent receives additional commissions below the latest four-year average loss ratio, a penalty is immediately imposed if the loss ratio worsens. This is rather severe. The cedent may well prefer to take a lower percentage of the profit in return for some lee-

Theoretical loss ratio	Sliding scale	Subtotal	Reinsurer's margin	Cedent's margin
75.0%	27.0%	102.0%	−2.0%	−1.2%
72.0%	27.0%	99.0%	1.0%	−1.2%
69.0%	27.0%	96.0%	4.0%	−1.2%
66.0%	27.0%	93.0%	7.0%	−1.2%
63.0%	27.0%	90.0%	10.0%	−1.2%
60.0%	28.0%	88.0%	12.0%	−0.2%
57.0%	29.0%	86.0%	14.0%	0.8%
54.0%	30.0%	84.0%	16.0%	1.8%
51.0%	31.0%	82.0%	18.0%	2.8%
48.0%	32.0%	80.0%	20.0%	3.8%
45.0%	33.0%	78.0%	22.1%	4.8%
42.0%	33.3%	75.3%	24.7%	5.1%

Terms: Minimum 27% at 63% loss ratio or higher; provisional
28.2%; maximum 33.3% at 43% loss ratio or lower.
Slide: Two additional points for each 5 points in reduced loss ratio;
to be calculated quarterly, commencing after the first six
months.

Exhibit 9.7.   Margin Chart: Case Study Sliding Scale A

Theoretical loss ratio	Sliding scale	Subtotal	Reinsurer's margin	Cedent's margin
75.0%	27.5%	102.5%	−2.5%	−0.7%
72.5%	27.5%	100.0%	0.0%	−0.7%
70.0%	27.5%	97.5%	2.5%	−0.7%
67.5%	27.5%	95.0%	5.0%	−0.7%
65.0%	27.5%	92.5%	7.5%	−0.7%
62.5%	28.1%	90.6%	9.4%	−0.1%
60.0%	28.8%	88.8%	11.3%	0.6%
57.5%	29.4%	86.9%	13.1%	1.2%
55.0%	30.0%	85.0%	15.0%	1.8%
52.5%	30.6%	83.1%	16.9%	2.4%
50.0%	31.3%	81.3%	18.8%	3.1%
47.5%	31.9%	79.4%	20.6%	3.7%
45.0%	32.5%	77.5%	22.5%	4.3%
42.5%	32.5%	75.0%	25.0%	4.3%

Terms: Minimum 27% at 63% loss ratio or higher; Provisional
28.2%; maximum 33.3% at 43% loss ratio or lower.
Slide: Two additional points for each 5 points in reduced loss ratio; to
be calculated quarterly, commencing after the first six months.

Exhibit 9.8. Margin Chart: Case Study Sliding Scale B

way before the penalties begin. An alternative might be a 25 percent sharing for each point drop in loss ratio over the range, as shown in Exhibit 9.8.

This scale allows the cedent a small margin over its costs when the loss ratio is 60 percent or lower. Note the reinsurer's margin at 60 percent is 11.3 percent versus 12 percent in the previous example. Thus there is some giving and taking in each change.

There are several terms in the formula and each is critical to the outcome.

Range
The range is the difference between the loss ratios where the maximum and minimum apply. In the first 2/5 commission example, the slide range was from 43 to 63, while in the 1/4 example it was from 45 to 65.

Slide
Slide refers to the arithmetic formula. In these examples, a single formula holds over the entire range. This need not be the case, as the range can be split into subranges, each with a separate formula or slide. Obviously, there can be only one commission for a given loss ratio. The point is that it need not be a simple algebraic formula.

Provisional Commission

This is the up-front commission that applies up to the time when the first calculation is made.

Maximum and Minimum

These are merely end points in the formula. However, they have obvious impact as they limit the range over which the formulae apply. They serve to cap or contain the amount of commission.

SUMMARY

In addition to pricing theory, this chapter deals with commissions and concepts that are or can be part of the pricing analysis for other rating schemes. One must be concerned about acquisition cost under all types. Margin is another concept that has merit in all pricing. In reinsurance pricing, a few key questions must be addressed. How much does the business cost to acquire and administer? What portion is available for claims? What are the reinsurance expenses? How much margin is left over after all the rest is spent?

10

FACULTATIVE EXCESS PRICING

FACULTATIVE TECHNIQUES
- **First Layer Excess Pricing**
- **Higher Layer Excess Pricing**
- **Prequote Checks by Facultative Underwriters**

FACULTATIVE TECHNIQUES

Proportional facultative business is priced on a commission basis similar to that related in Chapter 9. This chapter focuses on excess facultative, which is the more common type of coverage. Since facultative reinsurance involves individual risk analysis, the technique has more similarities to primary pricing for commercial business than treaty pricing.

This section will relate facultative methodology that is derived from the primary pricing. However, one should understand that pricing specific to the cession or layer is also common but beyond the scope of this text.

Treaty pricing involves analysis of the management and claim handling strengths of the cedent as well as the financial capabilities of carrying the business and sustaining growth. This analysis is a part of the underwriter's selection criteria and pricing methodology. On the other hand, facultative management preselects the carriers and production sources for facultative underwriters. The underwriter must only check to see that the cedent (and intermediary if used) is on the acceptable list. This does not mean that facultative pricing is easier than treaty pricing.

Reinsurance company management has the obligation to provide guidelines about pricing methodologies as well as selection criteria. The process of collecting data, working it through standard methodologies to gain perspective about exposures and potentialities, and calculating the necessary price are routines that should be part of the guidelines provided to underwriters. Management should provide the tools, outline the standard analysis techniques, and provide selection criteria and other methodologies that are part of the underwriting process. The hard work of putting it all into perspective remains to be done. It is important to realize that good business sense and instinct are key components of the underwriting methodology. In the end the acceptance decision is the crucial item in the process.

First Layer Excess Pricing

In facultative pricing, the first layer is critical. In most instances it alone has exposure to ordinary loss and loss frequency. Often property business is considered to be a single loss situation—if it burns, it burns to the ground. That is not the case in most situations. Thus for property and liability alike, the primary and first layer may be exposed to claim frequency. Higher layers are really exposed to only large claims, which are not repetitive or frequent.

Typically, the first excess layer attaches under $1 million. In higher attachment situations, one finds the business bigger, the exposures greater, and the pricing more complex.

Often, the first layer is priced as a portion of the primary price. Since it is excess it is elevated and attaches once the claims reach a specified size. This retention eliminates some of the small claims, which tend to occur with frequency. Eliminating this potential is similar to applying a deductible to a primary rate. The greater the deductible, the larger the reduction in rate. Likewise, the greater the retention level, the lower the price, given the same amount of capacity.

Essentially that means the first layer rate is the primary rate times a factor. This does not seem complex; however, choosing the factor is difficult. Both retention and limit are determining criteria. As the retention level increases, the rate drops, but as the limit increases the rate increases. Low attachment with a high limit should be expensive. High attachment with a low limit should be relatively inexpensive.

Obviously, the kind of business bears significantly in setting the rate. Since some lines are substantially more complex, the pricing varies greatly by kind of business. Kind of business is related to the line, class, and type of coverage.

If the facultative reinsurer sets the rate at 35 percent of primary, many considerations may have been undertaken to reach that figure.

Property
Once a base rate is calculated based on the kind of coverage, plus the limit and retention as related to property value, that base rate may be adjusted for

the geographical area, the quality of the local fire protection, the distance from the fire department, the presence of sprinklers, the contents, type of construction, and business occupancy class.

Casualty

Generally the base rate will be calculated for the type of insurance coverage, plus limit and retention related to receipts or payroll or other size criteria. Casualty adjustments typically relate to coverage features which may be included within the coverage.

Since the coverage features are generally the same for the primary and first layer, the final rate will generally be a portion of the primary rate of price. It may take a lot of calculating to determine which factor is appropriate to use for the specific policy, but the rate itself will be a simple factor, like 15 percent or 24 percent of the primary cost. The size of the factor depends on the several considerations previously discussed and can be a multiple of the primary rate if the capacity of the layer is large in comparison to the amount retained by the primary carrier.

Higher Layer Excess Pricing

As one moves above the primary coverage in successive layers, the exposure changes. In most situations, the risks consist of or generate a great many small claims, a moderate number of medium-sized claims, and rare but severe large claims. The primary retention cuts off that very large claim potential. Our perspective in the previous section was that the first layer approximates the primary exposure. Thus subsequent or higher layers relate more to that large claim exposure than to the exposure that generates the small but frequent type of claims.

One must understand, however, that the monetary impact from frequent small claims can be quite significant. Also, a very large claim can be financially significant. Each is a concern in pricing.

CASE STUDY: UNION CARBIDE GAS LEAK

Union Carbide Corporation had no prior large loss history before the gas leak in India. The previous largest event had been an auto accident, amounting to less than $5 million. Yet the company was an industry giant, handling chemicals around the world. It needed insurance protection and purchased several hundred millions of dollars in coverage.

These several layers of liability excess of loss reinsurance were priced on a consensus basis where the reinsurers agreed on the rate applicable for each layer. The potential was relatively unknown, because an event had not occurred in the past. Also a great many of the chemicals were not explosive, not flammable, or not considered harmful to humans. Cessions of this individual policy were mainly facultative excess cessions, where the ceding company lined up the necessary capacity while it was quoting the business.

CASE STUDY: EXCESS OF LOSS LAYERING

A 20-story building worth $120 million must be insured against fire. Most fires would be contained in a closet, room, or floor. Roughly speaking, a single floor would be worth $120 million/20 = $6 million. Here we ignore the fact that the ground floor may have greater value or that a particular floor would contain special features. Most fires would have damages less than $6 million. Given that rising smoke might damage the floor above and water from sprinklers the floor below, three floors might be considered a probable maximum loss (PML). Probable maximum loss is defined in many ways. Some companies ignore the features illustrated above, while some expand the PML figure based on features. Some calculate the number with fire protection in place, others assume the fire protection fails. The definition must be held to the specific context of the type of building. A PML of three to five stories has little meaning for residential structures or for manufacturing plants that typically are single-story structures. The reader is encouraged to learn the specific definition that applies to their company or division. The important point here is the technique of assessing loss potentials. Thus the PML in this example might be three stories or $18 million in value.

Losses above the PML could occur but would be very rare events. For example, a glass building would be unlikely to have a fire spread upward to successive floors, unless the event also causes windows to break. Thus, an explosion with a subsequent fire might result in far greater damage. Structural damage might make the building uninhabitable, resulting in a total loss.

Thus insuring high-rise buildings against fire is a case where the values are quite high, motivating the insurer to take precautions by lay-

ing off much of the exposure. The situation is very suitable for layering. Let us assume the primary carrier writes the $120 million policy
(gross capacity) and intends to keep 7.5 percent net for its own account
being $9 million.

Ceding the reinsurance on an excess basis means the cedent intends
to retain all claims smaller than $9 million each loss. That usually im-
plies that they also keep a very large portion of the total premium, that
is, a big retention. Let us further assume that the first layer is set at $9
million excess of $9 million. In this example, this means that all claims
within the PML would fall into the net and first layer.

	$120,000,000
5th excess 30 million × 90 million	
	$90,000,000
4th excess 30 million × 60 million	
	$60,000,000
3rd excess 30 million × 30 million	
2nd excess 12 million × 18 million	$30,000,000
1st excess 9 million × 9 million	$18,000,000
Primary net $9 million	$9,000,000

Exhibit 10.1. Layoff Chart: Facultative Excess of Loss

The third, fourth, and fifth layers in this example each have $30 million in capacity and are successively higher layers. There is a rule of thumb that says each successive layer should be priced at half the rate of the lower layer. However, this business is far too complex for such simplistic rules to hold with effectiveness.

Being more remote means the exposure is reduced. Being above the PML in a property coverage or above past claim history in a casualty coverage places these layers into a remote likelihood situation. In this situation there is very little exposure charge within the rate. There is always some such consideration that makes the lower layer cost more than the next layer. While it is somewhat difficult to visualize the exposures to these remote layers, companies do develop a consistent methodology for their pricing.

Whether the method is an amortization concept or a more sophisticated method applied by class or kind of business, there are some relativities that are important:

1. Attachment point to PML or largest past claim
2. Largest past claim limit from the ground up, FGU to PML
3. Attachment point to property value or to receipts
4. Attachment point to a past industry high standard claim for the type of coverage

These relativities help the underwriter relate the actual or perceived exposure to a standard that they might have used to rate previous policies. In this example, we have not set receipts or past claim amounts so the only available relativity is that to the PML, which is $18 million.

The second layer attaches at the probable maximum loss estimate. It is exposed to a "blown PML," or to an inadequate PML formula. It is important to understand that PML is only an estimate and the purpose is to set a loss estimate based on a given and consistently applied set of conditions. It is better than the total value for assessing losses, since it permits the underwriter to assess layering within the total value of the property or amount of liability coverage that has been purchased.

The third layer attaches at $1.667 \times$ PML and provides capacity up to the $3.333 \times$ PML level. That is a layer width of $1.667 \times$ PML.

Underwriters should have at their disposal a preferred rate for the next PML, or the layer from $1.000 \times$ PML up to $2.000 \times$ PML, and $2.000 \times$ PML to $3.000 \times$ PML, etc. They may have rating determi-

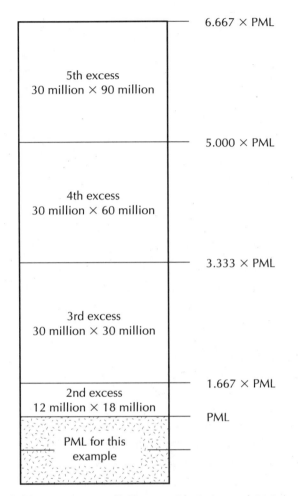

6.667 × PML

5th excess
30 million × 90 million

5.000 × PML

4th excess
30 million × 60 million

3.333 × PML

3rd excess
30 million × 30 million

1.667 × PML

2nd excess
12 million × 18 million

PML

PML for this
example

Exhibit 10.2. Layoff Chart: With Estimated PML

nants for types of buildings, types of occupancy, etc., and a similar setup for casualty coverages. The relativity concept permits the underwriter to relate the exposure on the given layer to some kind of standard. Let us assume the rate used as a standard by this company is as follows:

1 to 2 × PML layers: rate = \$12,000 per million of coverage
and 2 to 3 × PML next higher layer: rate = \$7500 per million
and 3 to 4 × PML layer: rate × \$5000 per million

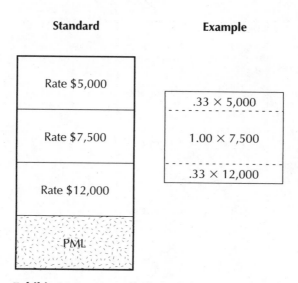

Exhibit 10.3.   Layoff Chart: Pricing Illustration

This type of analysis permits a rate calculation. The above method generates $13,165. The underwriter still must apply tests of reasonableness and perhaps some discount considerations. The point of this example has been to illustrate a type of analysis which might generate a base rate, one developed with the company's accumulated past experience and calculated with consideration of the specifications and exposure characteristics of the prospective policy.

There are any number of formulae that can be applied. The above example is simplistic and probably not used by any particular facultative reinsurer. It has been devised to illustrate the relationship of one layer to the next, coupled with a mechanism that relates to the exposure, PML in this example. Obviously, many reinsurers would have more sophisticated methods. Also, it is necessary to have a different methodology for property and for casualty coverages, because the underlying exposures would be measured or quantified in different ways.

The ceding company may in turn test the price against other quotes or, by using an intermediary, compile a consensus rate. The lowest rate may not be the best rate. One must consider the financial security behind the reinsurance offer and long-term considerations. A higher rate may include loss prevention services which may ultimately prove to be cost-effective.

Prequote Checks by Facultative Underwriters

It is vital that facultative underwriters pass each and every submission against measures of its portfolio. Given that most reinsurers have many facultative underwriters, typically distributed across the country, the business typically arises through local company contacts, but may be located anywhere. Thus the underwriter must test the submission against existing accounts to see if it is already written.

First, the company might be committed with its full capacity at some other layer. Alternatively, there might be an outstanding quote through a competing carrier: one never wants to be in the position of competing against oneself. That is a no-win situation which also creates relationship problems with ceding carriers and intermediaries.

Further, property accounts must be tested for concentration that could accumulate an uncomfortable catastrophic exposure to storms or conflagration. Many reinsurers record property business by address, town, and zip code. They want to fix the site. Multiple location property schedules present record keeping problems. Typically only the large sites are recorded; some carriers do their best to record the schedule as completely as possible.

Thus, although there are several considerations, the facultative underwriter undertakes a precise effort to maintain control over the account and site of each submission.

Facultative reinsurers also develop records about type, kind, and class of business, as well as layer and capacity. These allow assessment of concentrations as well as spread and balance within their portfolio. Thus they consider each submission on its own merits and then how it contributes to the development of the business as a whole.

11

TREATY EXCESS PRICING

EXCESS OF LOSS TREATY TECHNIQUES
MEASURING TREATY REINSURANCE EXPOSURES FOR PRICING
MYTHICAL INSURANCE COMPANY CASE STUDY
- **Burning Cost**
- **Measurement of Retention Effectiveness**
- **Limit Profile: Exposure Analysis**
- **Measure of Coverage Changes: Premium Analysis**
- **Assessment of Trends: Premium Analysis**
- **Calculating the Developmental Potential**
- **Unused Capacity**
- **Size Relativity**

INDICATED RATE: LOSS LOADING METHOD
- **Perspective and Negotiation**

LIMITS EXPOSING METHOD

This chapter will offer a single example of pricing excess reinsurance. The reader must appreciate that there are significant variances for property as opposed to casualty business and for high layers as opposed to low layers. Pricing also varies with line type and class of business.

In the case of many property claims, the cause of loss can be readily determined. Generally one can tell if careless use of smoking materials, spontaneous combustion, wind, hail, or some other force was the cause. Further, the property damage can be estimated with close approximation.

While property claims can be evaluated accurately and swiftly, casualty claims are another story. It happens to be very difficult to place blame for many incidents and to assess damages, even with known injuries. A broken leg to one person may be a debilitating handicap to another. So casualty claims are characterized by slow settlement and escalating values as the situation unfolds.

Why do cases take so long to settle? In an automobile accident, for example, there are some obvious reasons. Since blame may be a disputed point, one party may gain by delay. Witnesses may be lost or rendered less effective with delay. Also, the injured party may have other sources for medical treatment and thus may not press the case until the full damages are known. If a child is injured, the case may be held until the child reaches maturity and can press his or her own case.

While many auto cases do settle quickly, there are some difficult cases that carry on for several years.

Worker's compensation is a line where the claims are filed swiftly, but in which the evaluation and settlement may take more than 20 years. General liability is a line with moderate developmental potential, perhaps 6–12 years. Medical malpractice takes longer, on average. Director's and officers' errors and omissions and professional liability cases may take longer than 24 years to work out. Accountants' legal liability and architects' and engineers' liability may take even longer to resolve.

EXCESS OF LOSS TREATY TECHNIQUES

It is important to restate the fact that treaties are accumulations of many policies. Homogeneity may or may not be prominent. At times complementary business may be a good idea. On the other hand, it is not suitable to cede particular policies that are incompatible or nonconformable. These are subjective qualities, so one definition cannot apply to all situations. Further, it is the perception of the exposure at the time of the cession that carries the decision, not the exposure that becomes evident after the term has passed or after losses have arisen. Reinsurers will list exclusions to eliminate many kind or class cessions, but the ceding company must make decisions on permissible policies that happen to have unusual circumstances. A treaty can apply to the entire span of business of a company and thus consist of many kinds, classes, and types of exposure. This makes treaties far too complex to apply any of the site controls or policy-based considerations that are typical of facultative underwriting. There is pressure on the cedent to keep out individually difficult policies, which by their very nature could skew the results of the treaty. Poor decisions in collecting the cessions can lead to nonrenewal or higher rates.

MEASURING TREATY REINSURANCE EXPOSURES
FOR PRICING

There are a number of measures that reinsurers can take for selection and underwriting purposes. Remember that most proportional treaties are priced with a commission while most excess of loss treaties have a rate. A commission scheme accepts a *pro rata* portion of the subject premium while permitting an offset for acquisition costs and processing. Thus, a commission implies the primary pricing is being shared by the reinsurer. It has greatest applicability for quota share and surplus treaties, which are contracts that share in the primary exposure.

A rating scheme applies a rate to the subject business to generate income for the reinsurance. The theory is that small losses will greatly outnumber large losses. When small claims are combined with the net portion of the large claims, the entire net presents a significant portion of the loss total.

Some policy limits might not expose the layers, simply because they fall entirely within the net retained limit. However, excess layers normally are rated using the total subject premium as a base. Subject premium has been defined as the premium of all policies to which the treaty applies. It may be either written or earned.

It is also possible to price proportional business on a rated basis and excess of loss on a commission basis. This text shall not delve further into this issue other than stating that there is great flexibility in reinsurance.

MYTHICAL INSURANCE COMPANY CASE STUDY

This chapter illustrates excess pricing technique through the analysis of one sample case study, that of Mythical Insurance Company. This is a casualty excess example, based on "other" liability policies. Our intent is not to be specific about the kind or class. However, the developmental tail illustrated in this case study is short for the "other" liability expectations, and is perhaps closer to that which might be normal for auto liability. On the other hand, the premiums are low for auto liability. The illustration is intended to be nonspecific, thus we have classified it as "other" liability.

CASE STUDY: MYTHICAL INSURANCE COMPANY— BURNING COST RATING

Mythical Insurance Company has supplied ten years of data for analysis. With a fewer number of years, the reinsurer should expand its loading for contingencies. Price should be lowered with knowledge and raised in situations where there are few available facts.

The company writes policies with a variety of limits, with a maximum limit of $500,000. Next year, it anticipates writing $12 million in premium volume. The average premium per policy is $301; thus, they expect to write about 36,428 policies.

Mythical Insurance Company

Year	Claim reference	Incurred loss + LAE	Excess over $100,000	Subtotals	Excess over $125,000	Subtotals
1	A	130,000	30,000		5,000	
1	B	122,250	22,250			
1	C	121,738	21,738			
1	D	88,250		73,988		5,000
2	A	135,000	35,000		10,000	
2	B	82,500				
2	C	77,000		35,000		10,000
3	A	160,000	60,000		35,000	
3	B	117,250	17,250			
3	C	110,000	10,000			
3	D	99,100				
3	E	72,850		87,250		35,000
4	A	200,000	100,000		75,000	
4	B	162,500	62,500		37,500	
4	C	72,500		162,500		112,500
5	A	125,000	25,000		1	
5	B	125,000	25,000		1	
5	C	107,500	7,500			
5	D	100,000	1			
5	E	86,250				
5	F	75,000				
5	G	75,000		57,501		2
6	A	225,000	125,000		100,000	
6	B	137,500	37,500		12,500	
6	C	108,000	8,000			
6	D	87,500		170,500		112,500
7	A	172,500	72,500		47,500	
7	B	167,500	67,500		42,500	
7	C	105,000	5,000			
7	D	103,200	3,200	148,200		90,000
8	A	99,250				
8	B	97,500				
8	C	95,000				
8	D	90,000				
8	E	72,750		0		
9	A	110,000	10,000			
9	B	107,250	7,250			
9	C	92,500				
9	D	72,250				
9	E	66,000		17,250		
10	A	125,000	25,000		1	
10	B	121,250	21,250			
10	C	102,750	2,750			
10	D	90,000				
10	E	75,000				
10	F	70,000		49,000		1
Claim Count		46		25		12
Totals		4,965,138		801,189		365,003

Note: All claims at 50% of $100,000 or greater.

Exhibit 11.1.   Large Claim History

For the past few years, Mythical has purchased a single layer of reinsurance attaching at $100,000, with a limit of $400,000. It purchases a separate treaty that includes events where multiple policies are involved in the same event, including other aggregate exposures. Thus the excess of loss cover has a focus on single claim situations.

Exhibit 11.1 is a display of losses at $50,000 and above. This list includes claims at half the current attachment point. We shall illustrate techniques that apply to those claims greater than $100,000. However, those claims above $50,000 but below $100,000 are also considered by an adaptation in the pricing methodology. These smaller claims could develop into claims incurred within the layer if the situation or view of the claim deteriorates.

Note that we have illustrated the situation with the existing retention of $100,000 and a higher option at $125,000. With this example as a basis, we will discuss several measures of exposure as well as pricing.

Burning Cost

Burning cost is the simple ratio of losses to subject premium. It is calculated from the perspective of the reinsurer and includes all losses to the layer (or cover), divided by the appropriate subject premium. Actuaries commonly refer to this ratio as "pure premium," or that portion of the premium which is returned to the policyholder or cedent as reimbursement for claims incurred during the term. It typically includes loss adjustment expense. However, it does not include commission, brokerage, override, or profit.

The simplest pricing method is to apply a loading factor to the burning cost. For example, some reinsurers may double the burning cost to arrive at a base rate:

Next year subject premium = $12,000,000
Average incurred loss   = $ 70,596
Average LAE   = $ 9,523
Average incurred   = $ 80,119
Burning cost   = 0.67% (80,119/12,000,000)
Base rate   = 1.34% (.67% × 2 or 200%)

The obvious question is, Why 200 percent? Proponents of this method point to its simplicity and believe that if they carry a healthy margin for expenses and profit, this will generate profits over time.

The problem arises when competition and negotiation enter the picture. With the question of Why 200 percent in mind, the cedent can say, "Ours is a good deal, let's apply a 1.75 percent loading." Just how does the reinsurer counter that response?

Another perspective is that the claim history amounts to $801,188 over ten years. That is an average of $80,119 each year. Yet the 1.34 percent rate on $12 million in volume generates $160,800 in reinsurance premium. The cedent always wonders just what all that extra is all about. The methodology offers no explanation.

The concept involves a magic factor. There is no basis to the 200 percent. Should every contract have the same loading? Or would it not be appropriate to load some exposures higher than others? Is 200 percent fair? How can the cedent be sure that this calculation does not put it at a disadvantage? If the loading is reduced one year due to outside competitive pressure, why should it revert to 200 percent at renewal? How does the reinsurer respond to the observation that the cedent's business has changed considerably over the years within the burning cost calculation? There are many similar questions that can arise. There are few adequate answers. The term "magic factor" is appropriate since the loading cannot be statistically supported.

Burning cost is an appropriate statistical measure. It is the loss ratio for the layer. That is valuable information to know. It just happens that there are better ways to calculate the rate.

Another criticism is that this calculation applies an average of losses in past years to next year's premium. Is that an apples-to-oranges comparison? The answer is yes. The remainder of this chapter addresses several aspects that should be considered in making this calculation.

Measurement of Retention Effectiveness

Retention level is the attachment point. It is the point above which losses will be recovered from the excess reinsurance layer. In our society, inflation is variable, yet positive. The cost of bread today is lower than what it will be tomorrow. Wages grow to compensate, but in spite of hard work, one is never sure one is staying ahead of inflation.

Inflation has impact on claims as well. Suppose inflation is 5 percent. If a layer has averaged $120,000 in claims this year, and all else is equal, the claims next year should be $126,000. Reality brings another perspective, however. A really bad year might triple the claim total. A really good year might cut claims to zero. So while happenstance has a dominating effect, inflation can and should be measured.

Consider the following measure of a retention increase on the number of claims.

Mythical Insurance Company

Year	Claim count in excess of $100,000	Claim count in excess of $125,000	Percent reduction in count
1	3	1	−66.7%
2	1	1	0.0%
3	3	1	−66.7%
4	2	2	0.0%
5	4	2	−50.0%
6	3	2	−33.3%
7	4	2	−50.0%
8	0	0	0.0%
9	2	0	−100.0%
10	3	1	−66.7%
Total	25	12	−52.0%

Exhibit 11.2.   Effect of Retention Increase on Claim Count

Note, this calculation does give a measurement, but it seems to have short-comings. Three of the years have no reduction in count, even though the retention is lifted $25,000. So count is not always the telling statistic. Note also that there has been a greater reduction in claim count during the last five years than in the first five. The earlier period dropped from 13 to 7 claims, while the later period dropped from 12 to 5 claims. Since these are casualty claims, the earlier period is likely to be reserved closer to the ultimate settlement amount than the later period; thus the perspective in counts as well as amounts should be viewed with development in mind. That consideration implies that the drop illustrated here in the later years should not be given credibility.

One would expect that with general inflation, more higher limits would be sold in recent years and that the average claim would be larger. While that logic may be statistically correct, it may not be evident when looking at just the very large claims. And the change in claim counts may not be as telling as the change in amount. Let us next see how the shift in retention affects the loss amounts.

First, this is not a fully credible portfolio. It lacks size, and the case study has not supplied data on diversity or geographic spread. (This has implications for liability as well as property.) Having a a ten-year history helps. Less data and a smaller size would imply less credibility, which in turn means that an analyst should not give as much credence to a result based on such information.

Mythical Insurance Company

Year	Subject matter premium	Portion of loss excess of $75,000	Burning cost	Portion of loss excess of $100,000	Burning cost	Percent reduction in B/C
1	4,900,330	73,988	1.51%	5,000	0.10%	−93.2%
2	5,450,960	35,000	0.64%	10,000	0.18%	−71.4%
3	6,355,461	87,250	1.37%	35,000	0.55%	−59.9%
4	7,037,056	162,500	2.31%	112,500	1.60%	−30.8%
5	7,809,634	57,501	0.74%	2	0.00%	−100.0%
6	8,177,232	170,500	2.09%	112,500	1.38%	−34.0%
7	9,838,112	148,200	1.51%	90,000	0.91%	−39.3%
8	9,235,145	0	0.00%	0	0.00%	0.0%
9	10,595,256	17,250	0.16%	0	0.00%	−100.0%
10	10,960,000	49,000	0.45%	1	0.00%	−100.0%
Total	80,359,186	801,189	1.00%	365,003	0.45%	−54.4%

Exhibit 11.3. Effect of Retention Increase on Burning Cost

In this example, our reinsurer assumes that $50 million in premium volume is sufficient for full credibility. With $12 million in estimated subject premium, the credibility can be measured against this reinsurer standard. (The standard happens to be fictitious; however, the reinsurer could develop this kind of standard by assessing data over many years and many compositions in its portfolio.) The calculation is straightforward, $12 million/ $50 million = 24 percent. This statistic will be used later in this chapter. Further, this "standard" is a simplistic approach and surely not the only method used for quantifying credibility. More sophisticated methods exist, but they are not within the scope of this text.

Secondly, the size of claim may affect this measurement. Averages are statistically affected by single large items. The object here is to test the retention. Thus, the analyst should make sure there is no single very large claim that distorts the calculation.

This particular calculation measures the change from one retention to another. In order to assess the effectiveness the first time it is necessary to have claim values below the attachment point. This is one reason reinsurers request claim reports at half the attachment level and also request any claims relating to death, serious injury, or highly unusual circumstances.

One must measure what kind of frequency can be expected to penetrate the layer, as well as the economic impact of those claims. If it is a first calculation, one should measure the difference between half the retention and the retention itself. The purpose is to understand the value of the retention and the impact of inflation on the claims. We suggest that alternative retention levels be considered each and every year; the perspective over time can be beneficial in making decisions.

Note, the change in retention dropped claim counts by 52.0 percent and cut the total claim amount by 54.4 percent. It also dropped the ten-year claim total from $801,188 to $365,000. (The calculation of the drop in claim amounts will match that of the burning cost drop, because both burning cost ratios have $80,359,186 as a denominator.) It is best to consider more than a single measure to give credibility to the perspective to be gained in the effort.

Note that when the ten-year total loss amount is compared to the ten-year subject premium, the burning cost is 1.00 percent rather than the 0.67 percent calculated previously. That is an improved perspective, but not yet the best one can calculate.

Limit Profile: Exposure Analysis

The limits profile is a prime measure of exposure. A claim may have some-what equal probability for any policy. The average should be greater for poli-cies with higher limits, simply because the lower limit policies cannot incur claims with the same severity. The premium is greater for policies with higher limits, so theoretically from a loss to premium perspective, all the limit bands are roughly equal.

Given the equality within the bands, the underwriter still wants to assess the limits profile to obtain a likelihood of loss to a given layer.

In Exhibit 11.4, 60.1 percent of the policies have limits below the $100,000 attachment point. That means 39.9 percent expose the layer. Like-wise, 68.9 percent of the limits are below the $125,000 alternate attachment point, and 31.1 percent expose that layer. Note, 31.1 percent/39.9 percent = 77.9, which implies the number of policies exposing the higher layer is 22.1 percent less. We now have three measures of the exposure difference be-tween these two layers: −52.0 percent of losses, −54.4 percent of burning cost, and −22.1 percent of limits. Those are not discordant measurements. These are separate measures of similar concepts. Together, they show that the difference is probably less than 50 percent. Therefore, it is better to dis-count the price by a smaller factor than to assume the increase in retention will generate a true cost savings of close to 55 percent.

We have displayed policy limits by count. Very likely you may see the profile on a premium basis instead of policy count. Both have value for analysis. The underwriter must learn to appreciate the nuances of each basis. The volume display follows later in this chapter.

We also know that there is $12 million in estimated premium for the year. With 36,428 policies, the average premium is $301. Higher premiums usu-

Mythical Insurance Company

Range boundaries		Policy	Percentile	Cumulative	
Lower	Higher	count	distribution	percentage	
0	24,999	0	0.0%	0.0%	Limits that
25,000	49,999	6,136	16.8%	16.8%	do not
50,000	74,999	11250	30.9%	47.7%	expose the excess
75,000	99,999	4,493	12.3%	60.1%	treaty
100,000	124,999	3,234	8.9%	68.9%	
125,000	149,999	0	0.0%	68.9%	
150,000	174,999	2,155	5.9%	74.9%	
175,000	199,999	0	0.0%	74.9%	
200,000	224,999	1,899	5.2%	80.1%	
225,000	249,999	0	0.0%	80.1%	Limits that
250,000	274,999	1,644	4.5%	84.6%	have
275,000	299,999	0	0.0%	84.6%	some net
300,000	324,999	1,571	4.3%	88.9%	and some
325,000	349,999	2	0.0%	88.9%	ceded
350,000	374,999	0	0.0%	88.9%	portion to
375,000	399,999	0	0.0%	88.9%	the excess
400,000	424,999	1,826	5.0%	93.9%	treaty
425,000	449,999	0	0.0%	93.9%	
450,000	474,999	26	0.1%	94.0%	
475,000	499,999	0	0.0%	94.0%	
500,000	524,999	2,192	6.0%	100.0%	
525,000	and over	0	0.0%	100.0%	
Total Count		**36,428**			Unused

Note: It is vital to display extremes even if unused as well as gaps where the cessions are rare or not made. "Where not" helps define "where used."

Exhibit 11.4. Increased Limits Profile: Loss Loading Method

ally mean greater exposure, so $301 per policy should have some kind of implication to the underwriter, who is familiar with the line and class of business. Here we have not specifically mentioned the kind or class of business, so it means very little in our sample case study.

Remember also that if the excess of loss reinsurance treaty is $400,000 excess $100,000 the internal limits have meaning as well. How many exceed $250,000, which is about half the layer, is also of interest.

If possible, one should secure a limits profile for the last couple of years. Is the company pressing higher limits as part of its marketing effort? Is this changing at a greater pace than inflation? If the pace is faster, the excess layer's exposure is growing and that fact should be reflected in the rate. The purpose is to get comfortable with the exposure, to understand how the norms work, and to assess the prospects of the deal.

Measure of Coverage Changes: Premium Analysis

Another step is to measure the economic impact of the changes in coverage or the policy language and to increase the price by taking such changes into consideration. How to measure the changes is beyond the scope of this text. It is information that should be assessed and incorporated into the pricing process. Generally, the change will be measured in a relativity that would indicate a positive change or growth in the exposure. Adding benefits to make the policy more attractive to the public would be a positive change in coverage.

For the purpose of the case study, let us assume that the policy terms were expanded in year 5 by 7.5 percent and again in year 9 by 2 percent. In order to use this information it is best to turn the percentages into relativities. A 2 percent increase is a factor of 1.020, while a 7.5 percent increase is a factor of 1.075.

The older years have a smaller exposure because of more constrictive policy terms. Therefore if those losses were to occur in the coming year, they would be expected to be greater by the amount of the relativity factor.

Mythical Insurance Company

Year	Change	Calculation	Relativity
1		1.020 × 1.075	1.097
2		1.020 × 1.075	1.097
3		1.020 × 1.075	1.097
4		1.020 × 1.075	1.097
5	7.5%	1.000 × 1.020	1.020
6		1.000 × 1.020	1.020
7		1.000 × 1.020	1.020
8		1.000 × 1.020	1.020
9	2.0%	1.000	1.000
10		1.000	1.000

Exhibit 11.5.   Change in Policy Terms

Exhibit 11.5 indicates that the older year losses need to be expanded by a factor of 1.097 in order to match the situation perceived for the upcoming year. The object is to restate the actual losses as they might be expected for the coming year.

Assessment of Trends: Premium Analysis

Property and casualty policies are exposed to trends in different ways. Because most property losses are fully paid within five years, the property line is affected by short-term trends. Also, in five years, most property changes very little. For perspective, in some parts of the country, houses are painted twice in five years, others once. The aging process has very little effect on property; rather, most properties increase in value each year.

Casualty losses, however, may take many years to conclude. In the case of professional liability, libel and slander, medical malpractice, errors and omissions, etc., claims may remain open for long periods. This permits all sorts of trends to affect the situation.

Property and casualty alike are exposed to inflationary trends. They may be measured differently.

Property damages are generally not difficult to assess. One can take count of the numbers and kind of items that need to be replaced and assess the amount of labor involved in repairing or replacing the damaged property.

Realtors publish average sales figures from which one can assess the inflationary impact on residential housing and commercial real estate. American Appraisal Company, Milwaukee, Wisconsin, publishes a construction index. The federal government publishes similar indexes. The BOECHK Index calculates the cost of a fixed amount of supplies necessary to build a typical residence. It adds labor costs, keyed to the going union rate by city. As the cost of nails, wallboard, and wood escalate, the BOECHK Index mirrors that cost, relative to its impact on the cost of a home. Thus there are very good statistics one can use in relation to property insurance.

The consumer price index is often used for casualty pricing. Inflation is an elusive matter. Remember that casualty claims are difficult to assess and are subject to long-term development. Inflation cannot simply be applied to medical costs. More liability cases are being tried in court and argued before juries; awards are more generous. All these observations illustrate the complexity of measuring inflation in liability cases.

Trends other than inflation should also be measured. Again, the measurement methods are not the subject of this text; we only emphasize that these matters should be considered in reinsurance pricing. The intricacies of the calculations must be learned over time.

Mythical Insurance Company

Year	Inflation	Relativity	Cumulative
1	6.4%	1.064	1.598
2	6.6%	1.066	1.502
3	6.1%	1.061	1.409
4	5.7%	1.057	1.328
5	5.2%	1.052	1.256
6	5.5%	1.055	1.194
7	4.5%	1.045	1.132
8	3.1%	1.031	1.083
9	2.0%	1.020	1.051
10	3.0%	1.030	1.030

Exhibit 11.6.   Measure of Inflation

It should also be understood that the above change in policy terms is independent of inflation and other trends. One consideration is that the terms have expanded, the other is that inflation would make the claims arising under those terms greater over time.

Calculating the Developmental Potential

Property claims tend to be measured swiftly and fairly accurately. Typically, any current or recently completed year will have some moderate development. Often this aspect is ignored. However, in a growing portfolio, it is best to expect some development in the recently completed year.

Redundancy exists if reserves are sufficient to cover all costs with a little extra. It exists on a case-by-case basis. Claims professionals are quite good at assessing potentials. The problem arises in having four claims of a type that may mushroom in one out of ten cases. If the potential is $100,000 should a company put up $10,000 on each case? With this strategy, the company would put up $40,000 in reserves. If one of these four cases develops adversely to $100,000, the company is underreserved. Normally the reserves are set on an individual case basis, which may or may not be at the $10,000 level illustrated here.

Most primary carriers can demonstrate fairly accurate overall claim reserving. For example, worker's compensation claims are typically reported by the employer to the insurer swiftly. Employers are required to post all injury situations on an OSHA log and typically report to the carrier at the same time. The injury potentials are often hard to assess, particularly when subsequent deterioration of the injury may increase the costs for the claim.

A bodily injury may require ongoing treatment. That treatment may cost a certain amount now and could escalate over the years. For example, the injured party may need brief daily nursing today, but as the situation develops, the party may require full-time, perhaps around-the-clock, or even specialized nursing care. Each of these stages adds to the cost. Since the injury may affect the person's life for the rest of his or her days, that cost and the developmental aspects may be very hard to calculate. The curiosity in this situation is that while worker's compensation claims are reported swiftly, the line has one of the longer developmental tail profiles.

Exhibit 11.7 shows the incurred total on each of the claims of Mythical Insurance Company over the past ten years. In Exhibit 11.8, the information has been condensed into relativities. Each factor is the subsequent year divided by the prior year, which results in a year-to-year developmental factor. "No change" is represented by 1.000. A 2 percent reduction is represented by the factor .980. Note the incurred amounts are often adjusted by sizeable amounts during the initial few years and by smaller adjustments in later years.

Exhibit 11.8 illustrates the tendency for Mythical's claims to almost double from the reserve at the end of the first year to its ultimate conclusion. Remember that this is the tendency for very large claims and certainly may not reflect the all-claim average for Mythical.

Several sources compile developmental data for the U.S. insurance industry and for significant subgroups. Exhibit 11.9 is an illustration of the data, beginning with the year-to-year relativities calculated as above for "other liability," line 17, of the annual report. Note, the industry data has been compiled for many years. It shows there is reserve activity to 20 years (and beyond in some cases) in this line of business.

To simplify our calculations, the calculation has been split into the initial ten years and the remaining development beyond that point. The factor 1.113 indicates that the line has 11.3 percent development beyond ten years. The data from Mythical Insurance should be compared to that of the industry in general. There may be very valid reasons why Mythical's pattern is different from that of the industry as a whole. The composition of its business is a major consideration. There may be secondary considerations, such as ethnic or cultural restrictions, kind, class, quantity, etc.

Typically, the data from an individual company is not considered to be fully credible. Mythical Insurance has just 46 claims in the ten-year period. That is not a sufficient number for full credibility. Reinsurers develop ways to assess credibility of the data so that they can effectively merge the statistics. Here we shall apply the simple, straightforward credibility measure related in the section on measurement of retention effectiveness. The 24 percent

Mythical Insurance Company

Evaluation Period Year	Claim #	At 12 mo.	At 24 mo.	At 36 mo.	At 48 mo.	At 60 mo.
1	A	0	125,000	125,000	125,000	125,000
1	B	75,000	75,000	75,000	90,000	90,000
1	C	75,000	100,000	100,000	121,738	121,738
1	D	−5,000	45,000	75,000	75,000	75,000
Year Totals		145,000	345,000	375,000	411,738	411,738
2	A	50,000	95,000	100,000	120,000	125,000
2	B	50,000	50,000	50,000	55,000	55,000
2	C	60,000	60,000	75,000	75,000	75,000
Year Totals		160,000	205,000	225,000	250,000	255,000
3	A	55,000	105,000	125,000	145,000	145,000
3	B	82,500	97,500	112,500	112,500	112,500
3	C	25,000	95,000	110,000	110,000	110,000
3	D	50,000	75,000	100,000	100,000	100,000
3	E	40,000	40,000	40,000	65,000	72,850
Year Totals		252,500	412,500	487,500	532,500	540,350
4	A	125,000	125,000	175,000	175,000	200,000
4	B	60,000	120,000	135,000	160,000	160,000
4	C	35,000	65,000	65,000	65,000	65,000
Year Totals		220,000	310,000	375,000	400,000	425,000
5	A	60,000	60,000	125,000	125,000	125,000
5	B	75,000	100,000	100,000	100,000	100,000
5	C	60,500	70,000	84,500	95,000	107,500
5	D	55,000	80,000	85,000	95,000	95,000
5	E	25,000	75,000	75,000	85,000	86,250
5	F	50,500	75,000	75,000	75,000	75,000
5	G	50,000	50,000	50,000	75,000	75,000
Year Totals		376,000	510,000	594,500	650,000	663,750
6	A	95,000	160,000	175,000	225,000	225,000
6	B	75,000	100,000	125,000	137,500	137,500
6	C	85,000	110,000	108,000	108,000	108,000
6	D	55,000	85,000	87,500	87,500	87,500
Year Totals		310,000	455,000	495,500	558,000	558,000
7	A	75,000	125,000	152,500	172,500	
7	B	150,000	150,000	147,500	167,500	
7	C	54,250	92,250	105,000	105,000	
7	D	75,000	85,000	103,200	103,200	
Year Totals		359,250	452,250	508,200	548,200	
8	A	55,000	95,000	99,250		
8	B	50,000	75,000	97,500		
8	C	50,000	75,000	95,000		
8	D	25,000	65,000	90,000		
8	E	32,750	32,750	72,750		
Year Totals		212,750	342,750	454,500		
9	A	75,000	110,000			
9	B	64,750	107,250			
9	C	52,500	92,500			
9	D	25,000	72,250			
9	E	25,000	66,000			
Year Totals		242,250	448,000			
10	A	125,000				
10	B	121,250				
10	C	102,750				
10	D	90,000				
10	E	75,000				
109	F	70,000				
Year Totals		584,000				

Exhibit 11.7. Loss Reserving History

At 72 mo.	At 84 mo.	At 96 mo.	At 108 mo.	At 120 mo.	Current
125,000	125,000	125,000	125,000	130,000	130,000
90,000	90,000	115,000	115,000	119,750	122,250
121,738	121,738	121,738	121,738	121,738	121,738
87,500	87,500	87,500	88,250	88,250	88,250
424,238	424,238	449,238	449,988	459,738	462,238
125,000	125,000	125,000	135,000		135,000
80,000	80,000	82,500	82,500		82,500
75,000	77,000	77,000	77,000		77,000
280,000	282,000	284,500	294,500		294,500
145,000	160,000	160,000			160,000
114,750	114,750	117,250			117,250
110,000	110,000	110,000			110,000
99,100	99,100	99,100			99,100
72,850	72,850	72,850			72,850
541,700	556,700	559,200			559,200
200,000	200,000				200,000
160,000	162,500				162,500
72,500	72,500				72,500
432,500	435,000				435,000
125,000					125,000
125,000					125,000
107,500					107,500
100,000					100,000
86,250					86,250
75,000					75,000
75,000					75,000
693,750					693,750
					225,000
					137,500
					108,000
					87,500
					558,000
					172,500
					167,500
					105,000
					103,200
					548,200
					99,250
					97,500
					95,000
					90,000
					72,750
					454,500
					110,000
					107,250
					92,500
					72,250
					66,000
					448,000
					125,000
					121,250
					102,750
					90,000
					75,000
					70,000
					584,000

Exhibit 11.7. (continued)

Mythical Insurance Company

Year to year	1 to 2	2 to 3	3 to 4	4 to 5	5 to 6	6 to 7	7 to 8	8 to 9	9 to 10
Year 1	2.379	1.087	1.098	1.000	1.030	1.000	1.059	1.002	1.022
Year 2	1.281	1.098	1.111	1.020	1.098	1.007	1.009	1.035	
Year 3	1.634	1.182	1.092	1.015	1.002	1.028	1.004		
Year 4	1.409	1.210	1.067	1.063	1.018	1.006			
Year 5	1.356	1.166	1.093	1.021	1.045				
Year 6	1.468	1.089	1.126	1.000					
Year 7	1.259	1.124	1.079						
Year 8	1.611	1.326							
Year 9	1.849								
Year 10	n/a								
Average Year to year	a 1.377	b 1.160	c 0.941	d 1.020	e 1.039	f 1.010	g 1.024	h 1.018	i 1.022
Cumulative year to 10th year	$r = a \times q$ 1.598	$q = b \times p$ 1.092	$p = c \times 0$ 0.960	$o = d \times n$ 1.059	$n = e \times m$ 1.049	$m = f \times l$ 1.034	$l = g \times k$ 1.043	$k = h \times j$ 1.040	$j = i$ 1.028

Exhibit 11.8. Loss Development Index

"Other" Liability Development

Year-to-year	1 to 2	2 to 3	3 to 4	4 to 5
Year a				
Year b				
Year c				
Year d				
Year e				
Year f				1.098
Year g			1.117	1.097
Year h		1.156	1.075	1.090
Year i	1.776	1.202	1.083	1.013
Year j	1.819	1.225	1.095	1.095
Year k	1.976	1.281	1.092	1.129
Year l	2.223	1.192	1.193	1.012
Year m	2.008	1.280	1.147	1.083
Year n	2.296	1.384	1.161	1.049
Year o	2.341	1.210	1.137	1.057
Year p	1.853	1.232	1.124	
Year q	1.824	1.145		
Year r	2.100			
Average year-to-year	a 2.022	b 1.231	c 1.122	d 1.072
Cumulative year-to-10th year	$r = a \times q$ 2.488	$q = b \times p$ 1.381	$p = c \times o$ 1.204	$o = d \times n$ 1.117
year-to-year	**10 to 11**	**11 to 12**	**12 to 13**	**13 to 14**
Average year-to-year	a 1.016	b 1.016	c 1.016	d 1.022
Cumulative year-to-ultimate	$s = a \times r$ 1.113	$r = b \times q$ 1.096	$q = c \times p$ 1.078	$p = d \times o$ 1.061

Exhibit 11.9. Industry Data: Year To Next Year Factors

credibility factor is used as a weighting factor in merging the Mythical Insurance Company data with industry developmental trends.

Notice, the Mythical data available covered only a ten-year period. Therefore we could not assess or measure further development. Given the industry trend, some such development should be expected. We chose to use the 1.113 factor directly from the industry data (see Exhibit 11.10).

Year-to-year	5 to 6	6 to 7	7 to 8	8 to 9	9 to 10
Year a					1.007
Year b				1.017	0.996
Year c			1.028	1.019	1.030
Year d		1.007	1.026	1.029	1.026
Year e	1.080	1.028	1.085	1.033	1.011
Year f	1.055	1.051	1.060	1.038	1.036
Year g	1.086	1.033	1.019	1.030	1.015
Year h	1.028	1.037	1.031	1.008	1.012
Year i	1.031	1.043	1.036	1.005	1.008
Year j	1.043	1.054	1.046	1.013	1.002
Year k	1.028	1.022	1.028	1.025	
Year l	1.034	0.991	1.021		
Year m	1.010	1.014			
Year n	1.021				
Year o					
Year p			Not yet exposed to loss		
Year q					
Year r					
Average year-to-year	e 1.042	f 1.028	g 1.038	h 1.022	i 1.014
Cumulative year-to-10th year	$n = e \times m$ 1.071	$m = f \times l$ 1.067	$l = g \times k$ 1.061	$k = h \times j$ 1.036	$j = i$ 1.014

year-to-year	14 to 15	15 to 16	16 to 17	17 to 18	18 to 19	19 to 20
Average year-to-year	e 1.010	f 1.013	g 1.009	h 1.002	i 1.004	j 1.000
Cumulative year-to-ultimate	$o = e \times n$ 1.039	$n = f \times m$ 1.028	$m = g \times l$ 1.015	$l = h \times k$ 1.006	$k = j$ 1.004	1.000

Exhibit 11.9. (continued)

One should assess the reality of each calculation along the way in a complex series of exhibits. Is this a fair and realistic series for the Mythical data? In this case the final trend is softer than the industry developmental trend (see Exhibit 11.11). It is also fairly smooth. Wild fluctuations would not seem appropriate, and if they existed, perhaps less credibility should be given to the company's own data.

Mythical Insurance Company

	Mythical data	Industry data	Merged data	10th year to ultimate	Factor to ultimate
Credibility	0.24	0.76			
	a	b	c = .24a + .76b	d	e = c × d
1st to 10th year	1.598	2.488	2.221	1.113	2.472
2nd to 10th year	1.092	1.381	1.294	1.113	1.441
3rd to 10th year	0.960	1.204	1.130	1.113	1.258
4th to 10th year	1.059	1.117	1.100	1.113	1.224
5th to 10th year	1.049	1.071	1.064	1.113	1.185
6th to 10th year	1.034	1.067	1.057	1.113	1.177
7th to 10th year	1.043	1.061	1.055	1.113	1.175
8th to 10th year	1.040	1.036	1.038	1.113	1.155
9th to 10th year	1.028	1.014	1.018	1.113	1.134
10th to ultimate	n/a	1.113	1.113	1.113	1.113

Exhibit 11.10. Calculation of Year-to-Ultimate Development Factor

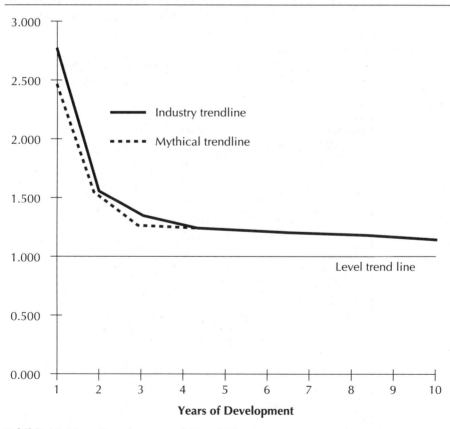

Exhibit 11.11. Developmental Trend Lines

Mythical Insurance Company

Year	Number of claims	Incurred loss + LAE	Years developed	Factor to ultimate	Ultimate loss + LAE
1	3	73,988	10	1.113	82,360
2	1	35,000	9	1.134	39,678
3	3	87,250	8	1.155	100,771
4	2	162,500	7	1.175	190,882
5	4	57,501	6	1.177	67,675
6	3	170,500	5	1.185	202,001
7	4	148,200	4	1.224	181,402
8	0	0	3	1.258	0
9	2	17,250	2	1.441	24,856
10	3	49,000	1	2.472	121,142
Totals	**25**	**801,189**			**1,010,767**

Exhibit 11.12.   Calculation of Ultimate Expected Loss

The next calculation applies the above developmental factors to the Mythical claims using the $100,000 retention. Exhibit 11.12 shows ten projections for the coming year.

A review of this chart shows that the older years have a smaller amount of remaining development and the later years have a significant amount of additional development expected. Year 8 has no losses above $100,000 at this time. It is likely, however, that ultimately year 8 will have some claims penetrate the layer reinsurance. We happen to have records of five claims that are currently reserved for amounts below the layer attachment point and above 50 percent of that amount. We could use that data to estimate the ultimate amount for year 8 (see Exhibit 11.13).

This alternate calculation indicates that there may be three claims penetrating the layer, for a total of $89,666. It could be greater or less than this amount. This amount does seem more likely than zero, however, so it seems appropriate to use. (The language we have used indicates that this decision has a subjective basis and is therefore subject to difference of opinion. In a very real sense, this process has several such points, so it is important to understand that in spite of the use of statistics, these are tendencies and trends of the past being applied to estimate future happenstance. Along the way, it is best to pause and reflect to be sure it feels realistic.) Note, this alternate calculation has been designed and used only for a single year, in an attempt to make the data realistic.

Mythical Insurance Company

Claim	Known loss + LAE	Loading factor*	Estimated ultimate	Estimated excess of $100,000
A	110,000	1.258	138,380	38,380
B	107,250	1.258	134,921	34,921
C	92,500	1.258	116,365	16,365
D	72,250	1.258	90,891	0
E	66,000	1.258	83,028	0
Total	448,000		563,585	89,666

Exhibit 11.13. Alternate Calculation for Year 8

*The loading factor for year 8 is from Exhibit 11.10—development for the third youngest year to ultimate.

Exhibit 11.14 indicates that the loss total, $801,189 is only that portion known today. There is an anticipated IBNR of $299,243 which brings the ultimate expected total to $1,100,432. Another way to look at this is that given the existing claim count of 25, today's average claim to the layer is $32,048. If the claim count stays the same, the average is expected to grow to $44,017.

What is known today is immature. One should not think of it as underreserved. The case reserves reflect current understandings, and bulk reserves (IBNR) are set to cover contingencies such as growth in the known claim amounts and additional reports of claims that occurred during these prior years.

Mythical Insurance Company

Year	Number of claims	Incurred loss + LAE	Years developed	Factor to ultimate	Ultimate expected loss
1	3	73,988	10	1.113	82,360
2	1	35,000	9	1.134	39,678
3	3	87,250	8	1.155	100,771
4	2	162,500	7	1.175	190,882
5	4	57,501	6	1.177	67,675
6	3	170,500	5	1.185	202,001
7	4	148,200	4	1.224	181,402
8	0	0	3	1.258	89,666*
9	2	17,250	2	1.441	24,856
10	3	49,000	1	2.472	121,142
Totals	25	801,189			1,100,432

Note: The ultimate expected loss for year 8 has been determined using an alternate calculation (see Exhibit 11.13).

Exhibit 11.14. Calculation of Developed Claims Excess of $100,000

Unused Capacity

Some layers, particularly those with high capacity, require a capacity charge. We have applied the term "unused capacity" since the amount of the capacity charge depends on the claim history available for pricing analysis. If there are few claims and only small claims (to the layer) the rating data is not complete. In that case, one must include a capacity charge. We shall not delve into the calculation of the capacity charge in this text.

In the Mythical Insurance case, the largest claim is $200,000, which is $125,000 into the layer. The layer capacity is $425,000. An unused capacity charge is appropriate. We shall apply a 10 percent, or 1.100, factor in the rating process.

Size Relativity

Some years had smaller volumes than expected for the coming year. In a different case some years could actually exceed the coming year's projection. In order to create parity between the prior years and the next year, it is advisable to adjust the volume so that the years will be equivalent. The factor thus determined should be applied to the loss total by year to produce losses that one might expect in the coming year (see Exhibit 11.15).

Mythical Insurance Company

Year	Subject premium	Relativity
1	4,900,330	2.449
2	5,450,960	2.201
3	6,355,461	1.888
4	7,037,056	1.705
5	7,809,634	1.537
6	8,177,232	1.467
7	9,838,112	1.220
8	9,235,145	1.299
9	10,595,256	1.133
10	10,960,000	1.095
Next year	12,000,000	1.000

Exhibit 11.15. Size Relativity

Note: Relativity is 12 million divided by the subject premium by year.

Mythical Insurance Company

Year	Change in policy years relativity	Inflationary trend relativity	Size relativity	Premium trend relativity
	Exhibit 11.5	Exhibit 11.6	Exhibit 11.15	
	a	b	c	a × b × c
1	1.097	1.598	2.449	4.291
2	1.097	1.502	2.201	3.625
3	1.097	1.409	1.888	2.917
4	1.097	1.328	1.705	2.483
5	1.020	1.256	1.537	1.969
6	1.020	1.194	1.467	1.787
7	1.020	1.132	1.220	1.408
8	1.020	1.083	1.299	1.436
9	1.000	1.051	1.133	1.190
10	1.000	1.030	1.095	1.128

Exhibit 11.16. Premium Relativities: Loss Loading Rating Method

INDICATED RATE: LOSS LOADING METHOD

The focus of the prior section was the measurement of differences between the various years collected as a basis for pricing. How does one go about putting this all together?

We have attempted to relate the measures in terms of particular aspects of the exposure. Some measures, such as inflation and coverage changes, are historical in nature. As such, the older periods must be modified to bring them to the level anticipated for the coming year. Most measures grow over time, so one might assume all these measures tend to make older claims larger in today's eyes. While that is the reality of the situation, if any of the measures happened to decrease, that factor would be applied as well. For example, if coverage was restricted such that next year's claims would not be as large, a lowering factor would be applied.

Exhibit 11.16 accumulates several trends on the premium. It includes factors for changes in policy coverage, inflationary changes, plus a size relativity. These factors have been measured to make the past experience roughly equivalent to that expected for the coming year. For example, the combined factor for year 5 is 1.969, roughly double the actual experience. This means that for rating purposes one should double the year 5 claim results to properly put it into perspective for the coming year.

Again, it is wise to step back and reflect on whether or not this portrayal is realistic. Do we believe the coverage has expanded almost 10 points from

Mythical Insurance Company

Year	Actual loss + LAE incurred	Ultimate expected loss + LAE	Premium trend relativity	Ultimate incurred at policy level
	(Exhibit 11.3)	(Exhibit 11.14)	(Exhibit 11.16)	
	a	b	c	b × c
1	73,988	82,360	4.291	353,387
2	35,000	39,678	3.625	143,844
3	87,250	100,771	2.917	293,933
4	162,500	190,882	2.483	473,936
5	57,501	67,675	1.969	133,247
6	170,500	202,001	1.787	361,072
7	148,200	181,402	1.408	255,461
8	0	57,761	1.436	82,922
9	17,250	24,856	1.190	29,576
10	49,000	121,142	1.128	136,617
Total	**801,189**	**1,068,528**		**2,263,995**

Exhibit 11.17.   Combined Relativities: Loss Loading Rating Method

year 1 to year 4? Is the loss development applicable to the exposures for this particular company? Is inflation included in any of the other measures? Are we comfortable with the end result? Can we negotiate with these numbers as a base?

In Exhibit 11.17 are ten calculations of expectancy about next year's result. They are independent because the various factors are calculated with respect to the particular year. They are very different because the actual happenstance was different in each year. Together they form a reasonable assessment for the large loss expectancy for the coming year.

The average is $230,980 ($2,309,795/10). That is not a price, it is an average expectation for loss to the layer. There remain additional factors in the rating process. One is the unused capacity charge of 1.110. Another is a provision for contingencies and profit. Reinsurers will have standard factors, perhaps with variation by kind and class, which they feel are necessary margins for the business. In this case we shall apply a 20 percent or 1.200 factor as a measure for margin.

    a. Average expected loss to the layer   = $230,980
    b. Unused capacity charge   = 1.100
    c. Adjusted for capacity (a × b)   = $254,078
    d. Profit and contingency loading   = 1.200
    e. Adjusted for contingencies (c × d)   = $304,984

    f. Subject premium for the coming year $=$ \$12,000,000
    g. Indicated rate (e/f) $=$ 2.54%

We have termed the result of this calculation the "indicated rate." The final rate is subject to negotiation. In negotiation, the cedent may win some points, and the reinsurer(s) may win others. Since this represents the starting point in negotiation, it is unlikely that the final rate will be greater than this amount.

Perspective and Negotiation

The ten-year actual incurred total is \$801,189. That means the average actual loss is \$80,119. The above method will generate \$304,984 as calculated. Note, \$304,984/\$80,119 = 3.873. In contrast the burning cost method, with a 200 percent load, would generate \$80,119 $\times$ 2.000 = \$160,238. There is a 90 percent difference (being \$304,984/160,230) between the methods. More importantly, however, the loaded loss method illustrates in real terms just how life affects these claims. It provides reinsurers with tools that can be employed in the negotiation process.

    Let us suppose the cedent disputes the measure of change in the terms of the contract. The discussion can focus on just why that discomfort exists. The cedent may hold information that indicates the impact was 8 percent overall rather than the 9.7 percent illustrated above. The difference is 1.7 percent, and one figure or the other, or perhaps the midpoint, may prevail in the negotiations. This is an appropriate discussion. It focuses on facts and the interpretation of those facts rather than the magic factor, which is the basis of the burning cost method. For example, the cedent may believe that the change-in-terms measure is overstated because larger policy limits are associated with greater deductibles, on average; thus, for the excess of loss reinsurance a smaller factor should be used. The next question is whether or not the calculation of this factor has considered deductibles. A discussion as to the validity of the consideration about deductibles might follow.

    The object is to reach a fair price. One might suggest using a burning cost method with a 300 percent load for unsophisticated cedents and a loss load with a 30 percent profit factor for more sophisticated potential customers. While that may seem like a logical ploy, in reality, there is competition to consider. If a reinsurer treats a small carrier as unsophisticated, competitors will exploit this. If the method is far too sophisticated, it will not be fully appreciated, and competitors will exploit that perceived shortcoming.

    Negotiating in a competitive mode usually reaches an appropriate middle ground. Security is also critical in reinsurance, since there are very long terms involved. Quality is a key determinant. The cheapest is not the best. So within the negotiating process, quality considerations have an immense impact. Is reinsurer A deliberately underpricing this year's coverage in order to secure the account with the hope of a long-term relationship? Is the intention to price this year low and next year high? Which alternative is really best? If the indicated price is not realistic, the negotiations will not secure the account. There are always competitors who will expose a padded rate, thereby undermining any existing trust the renewing reinsurer may have developed over the years.

Alternatively, reinsurers who have held an account for several years and who hold profits accumulated from, say, four of the last six years, have an advantage in renewal. The cedent will not want to shift to a new reinsurer and forego that profit bank. With a bank, the reinsurer will be less likely to radically adjust the rate.

Reinsurers in a deficit position, say, with losses outnumbering profits in four of the last six years, will naturally look for payback. The price will include some measure for the past losses. Most likely, competitors without the past losses will quote lower rates. Does the carrier wish to cut existing reinsurers in favor of a new low rate? Payback is important. One cannot leave a trail of reinsurers in deficit. There is a finite number of quality reinsurers, so burning one's bridges is an unwise strategy.

There are times when the negotiations are not interpreted as fair by both sides. Differences in what is realistic can be divisive in negotiations. There are some principles to consider:

- Offering continuity is an advantage.
- Holding excellent financials is important.
- Market reputation is a factor critical enough to work hard to maintain.
- Personal contact between the account executive and cedent is most often the telling factor in negotiations; this is trust.
- A realistic indicated rate starts the process in the right direction.

With the loss loading method, the discussion focuses on fact and technique rather than on a subjective judgment within the process. So the improvement in choosing the loss loading method over the burning cost method is realized both in terms of price relativity and the ability to support the indicated price. The price negotiations tend to be a learning experience rather than an adversarial debate.

It is necessary to demonstrate that the various factors applied in series do not accumulate based on some common trend. Negotiations have been mentioned at several points in this text. The purpose is to take the opportunity of a particular point and illustrate how it might work into the negotiations.

LIMITS EXPOSING METHOD

Earlier, we introduced a limits profile based on policy counts. It is certainly possible to build the exhibit based on policy premiums. Consider the following profile based on premium volume (see Exhibit 11.18).

The profile by count had 60.1 percent of the policies under $100,000 and, alternatively, 39.9 percent with some portion of the exposure within the layer. This exhibit indicates 53.9 percent is below the attachment point and 42.1 percent exposing the layer. That appears to be a significant difference. There will always be a difference between these two measures of the limits exposure. When the larger limit policies hold a substantially greater premium differential, the profiles will show a greater disparity. Also, the distrib-

Mythical Insurance Company

Range boundaries		Policy	Price	Policy	Premium	Cumulative
Lower	Higher	count	relativity	premium	profile	percentage
0	24,999	0	0.000	0	0.0%	
25,000	49,999	6,136	1.000	1,846,936	12.8%	1
50,000	74,999	11,250	1.240	4,198,950	29.0%	4
75,000	99,999	4,493	1.292	1,747,292	12.1%	5
100,000	124,999	3,234	1.321	1,285,906	8.9%	6
125,000	149,999	0	0.000	0	0.0%	6
150,000	174,999	2,155	1.324	858,819	5.9%	6
175,000	199,999	0	0.000	0	0.0%	6
200,000	224,999	1,899	1.524	871,117	6.0%	7
225,000	249,999	0	0.000	0	0.0%	7
250,000	274,999	1,644	1.611	797,194	5.5%	8
275,000	299,999	0	0.000	0	0.0%	8
300,000	324,999	1,571	1.630	770,780	5.3%	8
325,000	349,999	2	1.651	994	0.0%	8
350,000	374,999	0	0.000	0	0.0%	8
375,000	399,999	0	0.000	0	0.0%	8
400,000	424,999	1,826	1.653	908,532	6.3%	9
425,000	449,999	0	0.000	0	0.0%	9
450,000	474,999	26	1.721	13,469	0.1%	9
475,000	499,999	0	0.000	0	0.0%	9
500,000	524,999	2,192	1.750	1,154,636	8.0%	10
525,000	and over	0	0.000	0	0.0%	10
Total Count		**36,428**		**14,454,625**		

Exhibit 11.18. Increased Limits Profile: Exposure Premium Method

Mythical Insurance Company

| Range boundaries | | Price | Relativity | Relativity |
Lower	Higher	relativity	under $100K	over $125K
0	24,999	0.000	0.000	0.000
25,000	49,999	1.000	1.000	0.000
50,000	74,999	1.240	1.240	0.000
75,000	99,999	1.292	1.292	0.000
100,000	124,999	1.321	1.292	1.022
125,000	149,999			
150,000	174,999	1.324	1.292	1.025
175,000	199,999			
200,000	224,999	1.524	1.292	1.180
225,000	249,999			
250,000	274,999	1.611	1.292	1.247
275,000	299,999			
300,000	324,999	1.630	1.292	1.262
325,000	349,999	1.651	1.292	1.278
350,000	374,999			
375,000	399,999			
400,000	424,999	1.653	1.292	1.279
425,000	449,999			
450,000	474,999	1.721	1.292	1.332
475,000	499,999			
500,000	524,999	1.750	1.292	1.354
525,000	and over			

Exhibit 11.19.   Increased Limits Relativities: Exposure
Premium Method

ution of policies by limit also has an impact. Neither is better. Both have advantages that should be considered in the choice of basis.

There is a secondary observation. The data in Exhibit 11.18 seem to imply that one could split the premium by that portion exposing only the lower limits and that portion exposing the reinsurance layer. In order to accomplish this calculation all low limit policies would not expose the reinsurance layer. Also, that portion of each high limit policy that would be allocated to the lower limit should also be segregated. In this case 1.292 is the price differential for the lower portion. Note there are no policies with limits in the $100,000–$124,999 range. That does not mean there is no benefit to increasing the retention. Remember that this shifts $25,000 of each large loss from ceded to net. In this case, it happens to be a 25 percent increase in the attachment point.

We have illustrated how the factors can be split into two parts. Clearly, the product generates the actual price relativity. In a similar manner, we can calculate the premium applicable to two parts.

In this chapter we have demonstrated the burning cost method, the loss loading method and the limits exposing method for pricing reinsurance. The limits exposing method was illustrated without final determination of a rate for this case. All three have applicability and can be seen in widespread use. There are advantages and disadvantages to each. Certain situations lack credibility for the full calculations of the two longer methods and are appropriately priced using the burning cost method. The loss loading and limits exposing methods include measurement aspects that help one discover how the exposure is growing and changing. There is complexity in the choice of methods and obvious complexity within the methodology as well. We have attempted to illustrate just how a calculated rate emerges from the negotiating process. There are endless variations within this process. The purpose here was to expose the reader to these options and to maintain a written record that may serve readers' future situations.

12

REINSURANCE ACCOUNTING

THE OBJECT OF ACCOUNTING
BASIC COMPONENTS
THE INFORMATION HEADER
- **Communication and Corrections**
- **Sample Information Headers**
- **Data Processing**
- **Facultative Information Headers**
- **Treaty Information Header**
- **Premium Coding Abstract**
- **Claim Coding Abstract**
- **Funds Held**
- **Net Cash**
- **Other Checkpoints**
- **Processing Evolution**
- **Facultative Reporting**
- **Treaty Reporting**

This chapter covers all the data and all the cash handled by reinsurers. In a large operation, these aspects may be divided into several functional areas, with professional attention directed to the various specialty needs. Keeping our fundamental perspective, we shall approach this topic as if it were a small operation where a small staff is held responsible for the full scope.

THE OBJECT OF ACCOUNTING

The object of accounting is to book the business, control the funds, and maintain a proper record for both management and outside observers. Outside observers may be regulators, stockholders, potential clients, rating orga-nizations, mortgagees, and policyholders. Control means matching pennies of billings and receipts and much more. The management and the board of directors want to be in a position to observe profitability and growth in each department. They therefore must compile data in a manner that permits iden-tification of problems before they become crises.

If management is looking at its automobile business, it must be able to as-certain how personal lines compare to commercial lines and if there is a par-ticular problem with long-haul trucking, or taxi business, or fleet business, or its rental component, etc. The information must be sufficient for the man-agers to identify the source of problems. Does a concern arise in the kind, class, price, or quality of submissions? If management is able to identify the source of the concern, it should feel confident of finding a resolution. Yes, they may undertake more than one change to effect improvement. For exam-ple, they may address the quality of submissions with the agency force as well as raising rates on certain kinds of business. The ability to fine-tune reparations rests on the available data in the company's information system.

The accounting methodology is regulated; in addition, internal and exter-nal auditors review processing and all figures in detail. These are private re-views, not open to the public except as included in annual reports and the an-nual statutory statement or in other public releases of the company's own data.

Let us digress briefly from accounting to discuss regulation. Much, but surely not all, of the regulation of primary business is motivated by the pub-lic interest in helping consumers who do not know as much about the insur-ance products as the corporate insurers who design and offer those policies. Reinsurance is between insurance corporations and is thus deemed to be be-tween parties of equal stature. The logic follows that the terms and prices should be relatively free from regulatory supervision but that the recording of the agreements should meet standard accounting principles and practices. Ethics and conformity are the dual concerns. The books should be main-tained honestly and the recording should meet accepted industry standards. Thus the regulatory concern is on solvency rather than types or terms of busi-ness written.

Accounting is a large and important aspect of the business. If this function is shorthanded or inaccurate, all of the other functions or departments of the reinsurer will suffer in some manner. For example:

1. If the authorization is slow, a share may not be available.
2. If processing is inaccurate, the clients and intermediaries will not have faith.
3. If loss payments are slow, cedents will curtail cessions or not select the reinsurer for core cessions.

4. If contract wording approvals are untimely, the discomfort will affect renewal as well as additional cessions from the cedent and intermediary.

Payment patterns are tracked by cedents and intermediaries alike. Constant dunning for payments or signed agreements increases frictional costs. Frictional costs are those added expenses that arise because the company was not able to book or handle the item in one step or setting. Revisiting and reworking the same item adds time in handling and also expands other expense categories, which are collectively termed "frictional costs." If the work flow is smooth, frictional costs are low. However, all parties appreciate a carefully considered question or criticism intended to improve or clarify the agreement. Thus, delay caused by inquiry is not viewed in the same way as inaction.

One feature out of line with the norms within the industry can cause problems in securing or renewing business. If a company is known for its habitual slow payment of claims, for example, business offerings will drop or the reinsurer will experience a deterioration in the quality of submissions. The business flows to those companies that keep pace with industry norms and standards.

BASIC COMPONENTS

We shall begin by describing how reinsurers set forth the parties, terms, and conditions of each treaty or certificate.

The *header* of a letter contains the name and address of the correspondent along with phone number, facsimile, and logo. We use the term header to apply to the characteristics of the business deal: policy information, details about the facultative certificate, and terms and conditions of the treaty. The reference number uniquely assigned to that base data links the policy to its results for the insurer, the certificate to its results for the facultative reinsurer, and the treaty to its results for the treaty reinsurer. The information includes the following:

1. The kind, class, quality, and nature of the exposure and business ceded.
2. Premiums of all kinds.
3. Claims, including counts, reserves, payments, and expenses for both individual cases and bulk reserves.
4. Cash flow, which includes receivables and payables, along with collections and that amount of additional income which derives from funds in hand before they need to be paid out.

THE INFORMATION HEADER

The policy declarations page is an example of what a header might be for a primary policy. It lists the policyholder's name, address, and characteristics in addition to the selected options for the coverage afforded.

Typically a treaty reinsurer will have an in-force treaty count ranging from several hundred to perhaps a few thousand. The contract or certificate counts for a facultative reinsurer are substantially greater, say 20,000 to more than 200,000 in-force certificates. To maintain the perspective, an insurer with just 100,000 policies would be a small operation; generally insurers handle several hundred thousand policies, with the large carriers having counts into seven digits. These figures are not averages; they are given to underscore the different perspectives with respect to the database of the business held by primary carriers, facultative reinsurers, and treaty reinsurers.

Further, insurance policies tend to arise in homogeneous types. A carrier may have one or two policy options for each kind of business principally due to the regulatory approval of forms and rates. There may be a couple of dozen endorsement options for each type, but the population tends to select the same options. So we have a situation where there are many policy counts in each "pigeonhole" of the primary company data processing system. Reinsurance contracts have more options on each deal, thus their system conceptually has many "pigeonholes" with a few treaties or certificates in each.

Line of business, type of policy, year, form, endorsement list, source, limit, deductible, price, commission, etc., are some of the data recorded for each contract. We refer to the whole of this data as the header. All the premium and loss transactions are linked to the policy header via the policy number.

A facultative certificate header is substantively the same as that of a primary policy, except that it also includes the carrier's name (rather than the agent source) and perhaps the intermediary's reference as well. In addition, there are a few codes necessary to describe the kind of certificate and the rating scheme.

If a copy of the facultative certificate header were handed to a clerk at the cedent's firm, that clerk could read and understand it and, with their policy in hand, might also be to able check the accuracy of the coding. The point is that common references, terminology, and concepts to measure and monitor exist between primary insurance and facultative reinsurance. Since the primary carrier solicits and receives quotations for reinsurance before binding its policy, the primary carrier understands the layering, the terms, and the pricing. The information is policy-specific, and such information should be readily understood by processing staff at both the cedent's and reinsurer's offices.

A treaty header is quite lengthy. Further, there is a substantial amount of variance from reinsurer to reinsurer as to how the business is partitioned within the system. For example, consider a quota share participation in some umbrella business. The umbrella is essentially a casualty cover that is excess to the normal primary policies. Should that reinsurance be considered proportional or excess? That's a rhetorical question, for in actuality one can find it coded either way.

Chapter 5 outlined the major structures used in reinsurance and made the point that simple structures are best when the business itself is complex. That is given as one reason most facultative business is written on a quota share or excess basis. The codification is another reason. It is not advisable for the facultative reinsurer to make the accounting overly complex through its offering of a variety of types and classes of certificates.

In contrast, the nature of treaty reinsurance is to address specific needs of each individual carrier and tailor the reinsurance coverage to those needs. There may be special features added to help resolve particular problems or needs. These features can make a treaty quite complex. Thus the codification structure must be sufficiently broad to capture the vital components of each treaty situation.

Larger treaty reinsurers tend to have greater shares on each contract as well as exposure to far larger programs rather than simply more treaties. Obviously that statement must be interpreted with some caution. Very likely, a large reinsurer will have greater numbers as well as greater shares in larger deals. However, if one reinsurer has 850 treaties and another has 1100 treaties, we do not yet have a clear indication as to which reinsurer is larger.

It follows that the accounting of the treaty reinsurance business must characterize the variances from one treaty to another. In contrast, the facultative certificate accounting is directed toward characteristics of the underlying policy rather than the minute details of the deal.

The control and containment analysis for treaty reinsurers is of the vital and definitive characteristics of each treaty. It will record classifications held in common with other deals and specifications that make each treaty different. The object is to measure success and to seek out those characteristics that are associated with poor results so as to differentiate them from the characteristics of profitable business.

The header is the data that allows management to profile and review results. For example, the policy limits detail in the policy header is used by insurers to create statistical profiles of the limits written to assess whether there is some sort of imbalance within the portfolio on the books. Managers can also review loss ratio by limit to determine whether the additional rate charged for that extra limit was adequate. Obviously, one or two very large or unique claims might skew the data, so insurers review trends as well as long-term patterns.

Communication and Corrections

The coding of the header information is the responsibility of the underwriter. The underwriter has agreed to the terms and therefore is the resident authority of the intent and understanding over all the terms. This is an important feature in the corporate control of its business. If anyone other than the underwriter perceives an error, even so small as a spelling error, that person should not initiate or make the change; rather he or she must bring the item to the attention of the underwriter. In turn, the underwriter makes the judgment and makes the change, if necessary. In this manner the underwriter is advised on anomalies that occur in normal processing that may not suit the understanding of the agreement.

Note in the previous paragraph the emphasis has purposefully been on the understanding of the agreement rather than the actual contract. Even if someone finds a transaction not reported in accordance with the contract, he or she must bring the matter to the attention of the underwriter for assessment. If the contract is correct, the underwriter then must make sure the header outline reflects the proper methodology. If the underwriter feels the contract wording is not correct, he can take steps to discuss the situation with the intermediary or account executive and make sure the contract reflects the terms as agreed.

These procedures are not merely steps to spread out work that may seem tedious. It is an important control factor. It is a necessary and indeed the most effective structure for communication within the reinsurance company.

For example, one item in many treaty headers is an estimate of the anticipated loss ratio. If the treaty is a high excess with no real expectancy for loss, the figure may be 1 or 2 percent. Conversely, if the cover has been priced with an average loss ratio over the past few years at 62 percent, that figure should be recorded as expected. This permits the accounting or claim staff to realize when the developing loss ratio is out of expectation, either too high or too low. It is vital that they communicate such information to the underwriter. It can be accomplished quickly, days before an edit in the system might highlight such a difference.

If it happens to be a low loss ratio, the underwriter may wish to send along compliments to the cedent for a good start or good quarter. If the loss is well above expectations, an early effort may be initiated to learn about the cause and to see if some reparations might be suggested to forestall deteriorating results.

The header information is the underwriter's outline to the rest of the reinsurer's staff about the terms for a particular deal. It is the basis for many decisions. In fact, there are two sources that need to be checked. The treaty wording or facultative certificate are thought by many to be the ultimate authority for checking terms and conditions. Yes, it is the signed agreement, and as such, carries a great weight. If an issue develops into a dispute, the intent of the parties carries weight also. The words in the contract are subject to interpretation, and that goes back to the underwriter. Further, the contract is a lengthy form of communication, and it is vital to keep information flowing properly. Thus, others checking the basis for a particular transaction should review both the contract header and the contract wording. Doubts in interpretation, assessments, judgments, and apparent errors or omissions should be brought to the attention of the underwriter. In this manner, concerns are brought to the table, visible to all.

The setting of the underwriter as holding the responsibility for judgments should not be regarded as a basis for staff hierarchy. The jobs faced by the accountant, the claims handler, and the underwriter are all tough jobs, requiring specialized knowledge, a high level of professionalism, and business acumen. The object is to run the business, not to cast blame, fight, or play mind games. Successful companies can exert pressures to curtail negative working relationships and indeed *should* do so. Teamwork leads to achievement of corporate goals and to success.

Sample Information Headers

The following are sample coding headers for treaty reinsurance and for property and casualty facultative reinsurance (see Exhibit 12.1, 12.2, and 12.3). In displaying these header formats we hope to illustrate the type of information desired in each type of reinsurance. It is not our intent to discuss each coding box or to define each field. And we shall not define the headings, some of which may be abbreviated in a manner such that interpretation is difficult. Rather, the focus here is on the big picture. These formats differ greatly from company to company. We shall relate the major types of information recorded in a typical reinsurance contract header.

The header is constructed to have fields or information categories that suit most situations. There should be space for remarks that inform any reader if aspects are not typical. Further, since some fields suit a particular type of contract, one should not expect each and every field to be completed.

Note, everything is condensed in the coding. The idea is to classify the account and supply measurement points, for example, the contract is rated, the base is written premium, the rate is 3.5 percent, reporting is quarterly, etc. Matters requiring a longer explanation should be checked in the reinsurance contract or in the original submission of the account and attendant negotiations.

Data Processing

The form is illustrated here as a manual coding sheet. It is likely that a reinsurer's printed form will be designed in similar fashion. It is shown here as

PROPERTY FACULTATIVE—HEADER CODING

Date Coded	Add/Change/Update

CEDING COMPANY   1 _____

INSURED COMPANY   2 _____

LOCATION (Key)   3 _____

COVERAGE   4 _____
   CLASS   5 _____ PRIMARY   8 _____
   TYPE   6 _____ PRO RATA   9 _____
   KIND   7 _____ PART XS   10 _____
                EXCESS OF LOSS 11 _____

OPERATIONS   12a _____
           12b _____
           13 _____
           14 _____

LIMITS
   INSURED'S LIMIT   15 _____
   CEDENT'S LIMIT   16 _____
   ATTACHMENT   17 _____
   LAYER LIMIT   18 _____

PRICING
   INSURED'S COST   19 _____
   CEDENT'S COST   20 _____
   LAYER COST   21 _____
   LAYER RATE   22 _____
   SUBJECT PREMIUM   23 _____
   CEDING COMM   24 _____
   BROKERAGE   25 _____

LOSS HISTORY   26a _____
           26b _____
           26c _____
           26d _____
           26e _____

MULTIPLE LOCATIONS
   TOTAL # BUILDINGS 27a _____
   TOTAL # SITES   27b _____
   KEY LOCATION $ 27c _____
   TOTAL $ INSURED   27d _____

REMARKS

63a
63b
63c

CERT NUMBER   28 _____

REINS SHARE   29 _____

REINS LIMIT   30 _____

REINS PREMIUM   31 _____

INTERMEDIARY   32 _____
OFFICE   33 _____
PRODUCER   34 _____
TELEPHONE #   35 _____

UNDERWRITER   36 _____
DECISION DATE   37 _____
NEW   38 _____
RENEWAL   39 _____
DECLINED   40 _____
AUTHORIZED   41 _____
QUOTED   42 _____
BOUND   43 _____
EFFECTIVE DATE   44 _____
TERM   45 _____
NOC   46 _____

POLICY COVERAGES

	YES/NO	SUBLIMIT
Earthquake?	47a	47b
Flood?	48a	48b
Annual Aggregate?	49a	49b
Contents?	50a	50b
Bis Interruption?	51a	51b
Liability Coverages?	52a	52b
	53a	53b
	54a	54b

EXPOSURE CHARACTERISTICS

	YES/NO	REMARK
Sprinklered?	55a	55b
Fire Resistive?	56a	56b
Fire Protection?	57a	57b
PML?	58a	58b
Amount Subject?	59a	59b
	60a	60b
	61a	61b
	62a	62b

Exhibit 12.1.   Property Facultative Header Coding Abstract

Date Coded	Add/Change/Update

CASUALTY FACULTATIVE—HEADER CODING

CEDING COMPANY	1		CERT NUMBER	28
INSURED COMPANY	2		REINS SHARE	29
LOCATION	3		REINS LIMIT	30
COVERAGE	4		REINS PREMIUM	31

CLASS	5	PRIMARY 8	
TYPE	6	PROPORTIONAL 9	INTERMEDIARY 32
KIND	7	PARTICIPATING XS 10	OFFICE 33
		EXCESS OF LOSS 11	PRODUCER 34
			TELEPHONE # 35

OPERATIONS 12a
12b

GROSS SALES 13
PAYROLL 14

UNDERWRITER 36
DECISION DATE 37
NEW 38
RENEWAL 39

LIMITS
INSURED'S LIMIT 15
CEDENT'S LIMIT 16
ATTACHMENT 17
LAYER LIMIT 18

DECLINED 40
AUTHORIZED 41
QUOTED 42
BOUND 43
EFFECTIVE DATE 44
TERM 45

PRICING
INSURED'S COST 19
CEDENT'S COST 20
LAYER COST 21
LAYER RATE 22
SUBJECT PREMIUM 23
CEDING COMM 24
BROKERAGE 25

NOC 46

POLICY COVERAGES

	YES/NO	SUBLIMIT
Aircraft	47a	47b
Watercraft	48a	48b
Host LLL	49a	49b
Inc. MP	50a	50b
Broad From PD	51a	51b
Personal Injury	52a	52b
Blanket Contractor	53a	53b
CC&C	54a	54b
ERISA	55a	55b
Punitive Damages	56a	56b
E&O	57a	57b
D&O	58a	58b
Products	59a	59b
	60a	60b
	61a	61b

LOSS HISTORY 26a
26b
26c
26d
26e
26f

REMARKS 27a
27b
27c
27d

UNDERLYING COVERAGES

	GL/BI	GL/PD	AUTO/BI	AUTO/PD	OTHER COVERAGES	
LIMIT	62	65	68	71	74	77
INSURER	63	66	69	72	75	78
PREMIUM	64	67	70	73	76	79

Exhibit 12.2. Casualty Facultative Header Coding Abstract

an input document. The computer will generate a printed form that is supplied to other staff. In many cases the data is accessible on-line through the office computer system. Companies are also attempting to changeover to paperless processing. The basic information of any reinsurance system will parallel that illustrated in this chapter.

Facultative Information Headers

There is substantial similarity between property and casualty versions in so far as the kind, class, type, and terms for the reinsurance. They differ greatly in the descriptions of the exposures faced.

Location might be something like "Sioux City, Iowa," for property business but something like "worldwide" for casualty. Multiple locations should be noted in both classes. That may be obvious for property. In the case of liability exposures, the laws are different in different states, and multiple locations increase exposures to claim frequency, etc.

Operations is a brief description of the industry, or the product/service that may be offered. It includes revenues and payroll as standard measures of the size of the operation, other factors should be included in the remarks areas.

Limits and *pricing* relate to the terms of the certificate.

The *loss history* is normally quite brief in a facultative header. It is a case of many or few. If the account has loss frequency or is situated in an active layer, a small space will not be sufficient. In many cases the accounts have just one or two notable claims in their past history, so the form is designed for that situation, but may fall short in others. The top right-hand column in the facultative samples relates to terms of the certificate, items 28 through 31.

The lower right-hand corner relates characteristics of the policy or underlying policies. The listing of these characteristics enables the reinsurer to analyze its business. It is possible, for example, for a property reinsurer to partition its results into sprinklered and nonsprinklered properties. Likewise, a casualty reinsurer might wish to review a profile showing how many of its certificates have exposure to punitive damages.

There are two uses for the above profile displays. One is in the assessment of the aggregate exposure assumed in the entire portfolio of certificates, to see if there is balance and spread, or if there might be an uncomfortable concentration within the business. The second is in assessing pricing.

Cook County, Illinois, which includes Chicago and a few suburbs, is one of the more highly populated areas of the country. It happens to carry one of the highest average award levels for cases litigated in its courts. That is not necessarily bad, it is just fact. City averages are higher than rural averages, and

TREATY REINSURANCE—HEADER CODING

DATE CODED	[ ]	TREATY #	[ ]	U/W YEAR	[ ]

ADD	[ ]	REINSURED	
CHANGE		INTERMEDIARY	BROKER REF#
UPDATE			

		TREATY TITLE	
CLASS	[ ]	T.Y. EFFECTIVE	T.Y. EXPIRATION
TYPE	[ ]	AUDIT DATE	TYPE AUDIT
P/R OR XS	[ ]	TERM	
LAYER	[ ]	CANCELLATION	N.O.C. DATE
KIND	[ ]		
MGA	[ ]	PRICING FORMULA	
RETRO	[ ]	PRICING BASE	
		PRICING TYPE	

CAL EQ	Yes/No		A
WIND SPLIT			B
ZONE #1	[ ]	PRICING	C
ZONE #2	[ ]	REMARKS	D
ZONE #3	[ ]		E
ZONE #4	[ ]		F
ZONE #5	[ ]		
ZONE #6	[ ]	PORTFOLIO IN	PORTFOLIO OUT
		FEES	BROKERAGE
LAE INCLUDED	Yes/No	ACCOUNTS DUE	
IBNR REPORTS	Yes/No	CASH TERMS	CASH LOSS
REINSTATE	Yes/No	SPECIAL HANDLING	
OCC LIMIT			
AGG LIMIT	[ ]	REMARKS	
		A	
CURRENT RATINGS		B	
A.M. BEST'S	[ ]	C	
STD & POOR'S	[ ]	D	
DEMOTECH	[ ]	E	

TERMS	100% TREATY TERMS			GROSS ASSUMED	SPLIT #1	SPLIT #2
INCEPTION DATE		INCEPTION DATE				
COVER %		SHARE%				
LIMIT		LIMIT				
RETENTION						
SUBJECT PREMIUM						
ESTIMATED PREMIUM		ESTIMATED PREMIUM				
ESTIMATED LOSS RATIO						

BRIEF TREATY HISTORY	WRITTEN PREMIUM	SHARE	COMM+BKG	INC LOSS+LAE	COMBINED	RATIO
YEAR #1						
YEAR #2						
YEAR #3						
YEAR #4						
YEAR #5						
TOTAL						

Exhibit 12.3.   Treaty Header Coding Abstract

big cities carry even higher averages than smaller cities. A geographic concentration of liability business in this city might contribute to a higher average claim. It might also imply that accounts carry higher premiums. So assessment of concentration is not an easy matter. But a company needs to be able to test how much happens to be written in the area and how its profitability stands. That is an example of using the statistical base to make decisions about pricing and also strategical decisions about the kind, class, or area.

Treaty Information Header

The language and focus is different in the treaty form (Exhibit 12.3) when compared to the facultative forms. Most reinsurers strive to include a brief summary of past experience on the form. Thus most of this form applies to the current treaty year, while the bottom section lists the past history. That is different from the facultative forms, since many treaties are expected to have losses every year, with some expectation of frequency. Here the left-hand column lists some details that may or may not apply to each specific type of treaty. The broad right-hand column displays the key terms. The pricing formula area may be of interest. This block of information has been created to suit the pricing schemes used most often. (Exhibit 12.4).

The following are a few examples of how these few codes can be used to describe a particular pricing scheme.

```
┌─────────────────────────────────────────────────────────────────┐
│  Pricing Formula        Format: A (1 digit alpha)                │
│      A  = Set dollar amount (No adjustment)                      │
│      B  = Volume adjustable                                      │
│      C  = Loss adjustable                                        │
├─────────────────────────────────────────────────────────────────┤
│  Pricing Base           Format: A (1 digit alpha)                │
│      W = GNWPI or written premium                                │
│      E  = GNEPI or earned premium                                │
│      N = Net/nett or gross premium less acquisition cost         │
│      Z  = See contract                                           │
├─────────────────────────────────────────────────────────────────┤
│  Pricing Type           Format: NN (2 digits numeric)            │
│         11 = Flat commission                                     │
│         12 = Commission with contingent                         │
│         13 = Sliding scale                                       │
│         21 = Flat rate                                           │
│         22 = Rate with contingent                               │
│         23 = Retrospective rate                                 │
│         24 = Rate with M&D                                       │
│         31 = Set dollar amount                                   │
│         32 = Other scheme                                        │
└─────────────────────────────────────────────────────────────────┘
```

Exhibit 12.4.   Basic Pricing Identification Codes

Example 1: A proportional treaty may use a provisional commission on a quarterly basis with an annual adjustment. A casualty contract, as illustrated in Exhibit 12.5, has an adjustment that is to be delayed for 24 months, with an agreed IBNR applied. If a deficit existed, it would be carried forward into the calculation of the subsequent year's adjustment, which would be calculated another 12 months later. In this case the commission is 27.5 percent on reported accounts through 24 months. Thereafter, a profit may be applicable, 15 percent of the calculated profit that exists after a formula expense factor of 10 percent. In other words, if the treaty year had an 18 percent profit, the reinsurer would be paid 15 percent of (18 percent − 10 percent or 8 percent), that is, 1.2 percent.

Pricing Formula	C	Loss adjustable	
Pricing Base	W	GNWPI	
Pricing Type	12	Commission with contingent	
1	Provisional commission		27.5%
2	Profit commission		15.0%
3	Formula expense factor		10.0%
4	Contingent period = Annual with a 24-month delay		
5	Carryforward of deficit into next year		
6			

Exhibit 12.5.   Sample Coding: Flat Commission with Contingent

Example 2: A sliding scale commission is one of the typical schemes used for proportional property treaties. The contract may specify a limited number of commission adjustments, spaced six months apart. Here, the calculation is to be calculated three months after the end of each year and repeated semiannually for three years. The initial reports are done with a 26 percent commission. Once the losses and premiums have matured to 15 months, the actual loss ratio is cal-

Pricing Formula	C	Loss adjustable	
Pricing Base	E	GNEPI	
Pricing Type	13	Sliding scale	
1	Provisional commission		26.0%
2	Minimum commission		20.0%
3	Maximum commission		38.0%
4	Commission period = Annual with 3-month delay		
5	No deficit or credit carryforward into next year		
6	Adjustments at 15, 21, 27, 33 and 39 months		

Exhibit 12.6.   Sample Coding: Sliding Scale Commission

culated, and the commission is adjusted to a minimum of 20 percent if losses are heavy or to 38 percent if claims are low. Note, this describes the basic calculation but does not supply all the data necessary to complete the calculation. Remember, it is an outline of the boundaries, not an expression of the precise formula. It supplies data that may have general interest, but not all data.

Example 3: A rated treaty may have the premium calculated on quarterly reported subject premium or, as in this example, a deposit paid quarterly and subject to a minimum premium when the full premium is reported after the treaty year is 15 months old.

Pricing Formula	B	Volume adjustable	
Pricing Base	W	GNWPI	
Pricing Type	24	Rate with minimum and deposit	
1	Rate		6.0%
2			
3			
4	Deposit = $24,000		
5	Minimum = $20,000		
6	Deposit payable 1/4th per quarter.		

Exhibit 12.7. Sample Coding: Rate with Minimum Plus Deposit

Referring back to Exhibit 12.3 please note the two bottom sections. One lists some vital statistics for 100 percent of the treaty and for the share assumed. The sections "Split #1" and "Split #2" are reserved for corporate divisions, but a similar display could be applied for specific retrocessions.

The last section displays a brief summary of experience if the contract has been on the books for a while.

Premium Coding Abstract

The initial lines, two lines in this sample abstract (Exhibit 12.8), link the abstract to the reinsurance contract. Among other things, this detail allows the reinsurer to edit when there is more than one report for a quarter and indicates that there are indeed four quarterly reports each year. These sort of edits are embedded within the delinquency checks, and will be discussed later in the chapter.

There may be several active years reported at the same time. Each sheet is designed to measure the amounts for a single year of account. Thus with three active years, three sheets would be coded each quarter.

PREMIUM CODING ABSTRACT

COMPANY _____

IDENTIFICATION _____

COMPLETED   DATE _____ BY _____

TYPE   PROPORTIONAL _____ EXCESS OF LOSS _____

ENTRY MO. | YR.	TREATY NUMBER	ABSTRACT NUMBER		TRANS TYPE	COMM TYPE	PREM LOB

ACCOUNT PERIOD FROM MO.| YR.	TO MO.| YR.	TREATY TERM YR.	REPORT DESCRIPTION	INVOICE REFERENCE	CURR TYPE	EXCHANGE RATE
		1 9				

WRITTEN PREMIUM (+)	PRIOR UNEARNED (+)	CURRENT UNEARNED (−)	EARNED PREMIUM (+)
a	b	c	d

COMMISSION (−)	
	e

BROKERAGE (−)	
	f

TAXES (−)	
	g

NET PREMIUM (+)	
	h

NET PAID LOSS (−)	
	i

NET CASH (−)	
	j

NOTES & CALCULATIONS

FORMULAS

Earned Premium $d = a + b - c$
Net Premium $h = a - e - f - g$
Net Cash $j = h - i$

Note: Funds held excluded from this worksheet.

Exhibit 12.8.   Premium Coding Abstract

All figures are normally coded as positives. The (+) and (−) indicators essentially repeat the formulae noted at the bottom of the coding sheet. On occasion, there will be a return premium, return commission, return brokerage, reserve reduction, etc. In a high-volume period, these items will be included with the normal processing, and as such, not evident in the figures. Obviously the normal positive numbers would outweigh the smaller negative figures. Later however, when the normal volume drops, corrections and returns can be evident in the reports. On the abstract, the negative figures are typically *circled.*

There are three formulae in this abstract. These work in two ways. First, they are a necessary calculation for interpretation of the report that has been registered with the abstract. Second, they incorporate the new report with the ongoing results.

Earned premium was introduced in Chapter 2. At each subsequent measurement point in time, the prior unearned is recorded as now earned, with a new amount set as an unearned reserve. To calculate the total written premium, the following formula is applied:

Total written premium in a period *equals* the amount of new business written in a period, *plus* the prior unearned premium, *less* the current unearned premium.

Net premium equals the total for the quarter, or report period, less amounts paid to the cedent and/or intermediary. Taxes are just another item that is deducted in calculating the net.

Earned = Written − commissions − brokerage − taxes, if any.

Net cash equals net premium *less* the paid loss. The abstract properly registers the paid loss as a net figure. This essentially means that any returns have been subtracted. Reserve reductions may be fairly common, but payment returns are extremely rare. The abstract must have the capability of reflecting all odd amounts.

Odd amounts, which may be defined as entries which are opposite or negative from the normal coding, should be subject to an edit within the accounting system. This requires that a second accountant review the report to check that it has been properly reported and recorded. Either the initial or second clerk may check with the client/intermediary to be sure the report is correct.

Copies of the coding form should be placed in file with the report and handed to the data entry staff to incorporate into the computer files.

Claim Coding Abstract

There are two kinds of claim abstracts, the claim detail header and the loss coding abstract. Essentially, the header performs the same function as the treaty or certificate header, to record essential detail. In the case of a claim

LOSS CODING ABSTRACT

COMPANY _____

IDENTIFICATION _____

COMPLETED   DATE _____ BY _____

TYPE   PROPORTIONAL _____ EXCESS OF LOSS _____

ENTRY MO. YR.	TREATY NUMBER	ABSTRACT NUMBER		TRANS TYPE	COMM TYPE	PREM LOB

ACCOUNT PERIOD FROM MO. YR. TO MO. YR.	TREATY TERM YR.	REPORT DESCRIPTION	INVOICE REFERENCE	CURR TYPE	EXCHANGE RATE
1 9					

CLAIM #1	DATE OF LOSS	CAT NO.	CLAIM NUMBER	CLIENT OR BROKER CLAIM NUMBER	LOSS L.O.B.	DATE OF 1ST RPT	TRANS CODE

	PAID LOSS	CURRENT OUTSTANDING RESERVE	PRIOR OUTSTANDING RESERVE	INCURRED LOSS
LOSS				
LAE				

CLAIM #2	DATE OF LOSS	CAT NO.	CLAIM NUMBER	CLIENT OR BROKER CLAIM NUMBER	LOSS L.O.B.	DATE OF 1ST RPT	TRANS CODE

	PAID LOSS	CURRENT OUTSTANDING RESERVE	PRIOR OUTSTANDING RESERVE	INCURRED LOSS
LOSS				
LAE				

CLAIM #3	DATE OF LOSS	CAT NO.	CLAIM NUMBER	CLIENT OR BROKER CLAIM NUMBER	LOSS L.O.B.	DATE OF 1ST RPT	TRANS CODE

	PAID LOSS	CURRENT OUTSTANDING RESERVE	PRIOR OUTSTANDING RESERVE	INCURRED LOSS
LOSS				
LAE				

L+LAE	ABSTRACT TOTAL PAID LOSS	ABSTRACT TOTALS	ABSTRACT TOTAL INCURRED LOSS

Exhibit 12.9. Loss Coding Abstract

this essential detail describes the event and circumstances. In the case of the treaty or certificate header the detail sets the terms and boundaries of the contract. The claim header will be described in Chapter 13.

The loss coding abstract (Exhibit 12.9) has space for three claims. Many companies have forms with a single claim per page. However, with proportional contracts the figures are normally reported in bulk for the quarter or reporting period. There may be a few large or unusual claims that are specially tracked within these proportional reports. This form allows for that sort of situation, while in most cases just one loss line would be coded for a given report.

It is common practice for reserves, both unearned and outstanding, to be reported as whole dollar figures. These abstracts have the capability of recording pennies but do so in a shaded field to alert the clerk to double check against the report.

The abstract total figures may not be part of the data entry, but there are alternative reasons for their inclusion on the abstract. The *abstract total net paid loss* is transferred to the premium abstract since this figure is part of the calculation of the net cash.

Funds Held

The abstracts displayed in this chapter suit domestic business. Many international contracts include provisions for cash flow. The international transfer of funds is slower than that which we are accustomed to in the United States. This is true for reinsurance ceded to foreign reinsurers as well as reinsurance assumed from foreign cedents. The distance and the borders create hindrances. Thus it is fairly common to hold some of the funds normally transferred internationally. The funds held are agreed portions of the reserves. The agreement stipulates a simple, straightforward formula.

Adjustments in reserves do affect the amounts of funds held, either positively or negatively. This makes the cash flow formula for international business somewhat more complex than the one for domestic insurers and reinsurers.

The specifics of the funds held calculation are not within the scope of this text. However, the funds held formula can turn a positive cash report into one where funds flow in the other direction.

Net Cash

This discussion does not include reference to funds held. We focus here on how cash flow relates to the accounting of domestic reinsurance business.

Cash flow considerations are pervasive in reinsurance business. The payee is motivated to keep cash flow slow and the recipient strives to make it quicker. The bigger the dollar amount the more pressure both sides exert on the flow. If the cash did not flow, there would be no motivation to continue the business.

Cash flow is particularly vital in reinsurance since premiums flow from the insurers to reinsurers fairly quickly. On the other hand, loss payments to policyholders tend to be much slower in casualty business, so payment requests to reinsurers occur later. It is the timing between the request by the cedent and the actual payment by the reinsurer that is monitored. Both cedents and reinsurers monitor how swiftly the premium flows from policyholders to insurers and in part to reinsurers. Also, both parties watch how fast requests for claim payments are satisfied.

The total premium typically flows through the chain to reinsurers in 18 to 24 months. There may be small amounts and corrections for several quarters beyond that period. Claims flow more slowly. Property claims are generally closed and paid within 24 months, with some activity for another 15 months. Liability claims have a slower pattern, commonly referred to as a long tail. Automobile business has a tail of five to ten years. The general liability tail stretches from 15 to 20 years. Accountant legal liability and medical malpractice are examples of coverages that have even longer developmental tails.

Yes, reinsurers appear to have an advantage here, since premiums flow faster than loss dollars. Yes, reinsurers generate considerable amounts of interest on the funds in their possession. Those are simplistic views, however. Consider these facts:

1. The competitive nature of reinsurance ensures that interest is considered in pricing coverages. Otherwise, competitors would aggressively cut up-front cost to take over contracts, with the hope of building interest to make the deal work.

2. Cedents may hold a large amount of premium to be ceded for periods from one to three months. There is an offsetting interest consideration in that period. This is interest on large amounts for short terms.

3. Reinsurers hold only the net for interest. A great number and amount of the claims are paid out fairly swiftly. Reinsurers only invest the net amount held. Over time that net gets smaller as losses are paid. While reinsurers hold a diminishing net, they are able to invest for a longer period.

4. The developmental tail is a natural phenomenon in the business. Having funds for some period is a common feature for both cedent and reinsurer, as is coincidental interest income gained on those funds.

5. Transferring funds is another aspect of this matter. If a cedent or assuming reinsurer is recognized as being "slow," it will find future negotiations over price much stiffer. Thus the speed at which parties respond to requests for payment on claims (or premiums) is one of the main factors measured in cash flow considerations.

Cash flow has other considerations. There is a check or draft that follows each and every report. If premiums exceed paid losses, the cedent will forward funds. If losses exceed premiums the amount is due from reinsurers. Also, reinsurers are obligated to pay cash calls and excess of loss claim payment requests. The speed of all those payments are monitored. This is the "collections" aspect of the business. Delinquents are pressed for faster action.

Accountants match payments to reports. This is a fundamental check for the accounting process. Does the cash match the requests for payment? And does the cash plus reserve match the amount reported to date? That is a very basic consideration of any business, but the cash flow focus of reinsurance gives it prominence.

This is why the premium and loss abstracts are combined to determine how the funds are to flow. *Net premium less net paid loss equals the net cash.* If positive, it is receivable; if negative, it is payable.

Reconciling the cash with the booked reports is the main checkpoint for measuring accuracy within the accounting system. For the most part, it keeps the cedent's books square with those of its reinsurer or reinsurers with respect to the ceded business.

Other Checkpoints

Account handlers take time to look over reports to see if each transaction is suitable for the agreement and meets all of its terms and conditions. They use both the information header and the contract wording to make judgments.

1. Does the arithmetic within the report and within the abstract check?
2. Are there any excluded lines of business?
3. Does the report fit the same pattern as previous reports? (same report format, similar types of content, similar volume, etc.)
4. Are there unusual or uncomfortable claims?
5. Are there any large claims?
6. Are there any tracked claims?

In order to check these aspects, the account handlers must be versed in the industry standard processing methods and understand the reinsurance business. It is necessary to train new people beyond the steps of recording numbers. In some companies the underwriter looks over the first few reports of a new treaty, to get familiar with the cedent's manner of recording the business transferred. But the responsibility for accuracy and detail is in the hands of the accounting staff.

Processing Evolution

The evolution of processing is plainly evident in reinsurance. In the 1970s, one might find an occasional handwritten report from smaller cedents. The intermediary summary and cover letters have been computer generated for a much longer time, as have reports from direct writers.

Likewise, both types of reinsurers would action stamp the cover letter submitted with each report. There would be a date received stamp. Another stamp would indicate "report booked," with an initial and date. On occasion one might find stamps indicating reviews by supervisors or internal auditors and by underwriters who might have been passed a report for review.

The next evolutionary step was to incorporate coding forms for entry of data into the reinsurer's system. There were premium forms, claim forms, cash transaction forms, etc. This has changed. Some of this material is now transferred electronically. Some are coded directly from report to the computer. The use of stamps or coding forms has been reduced.

The sample forms illustrated earlier in this chapter are from the intermediate stage, when coding forms predominated. It is important to remember that the base data is the same. There has been some improvement in the header and in the ability of management to track and analyze data. There are some new commission and rating schemes. However, the base data, premiums written and earned, losses incurred, etc. remains the same.

The review is a critical aspect in the transfer of business from cedent to reinsurer. Any divergence from either standard practices or the terms of the specific agreement need to be noted and discussed as soon as practical.

Facultative Reporting

Facultative reporting is accomplished by endorsements to the certificate. The basic agreement foresees passing through the agreed portion of any premium, less agreed commissions, taxes, and fees. The timing is *as soon as practical.*

A midterm cancellation or change to the underlying policy would necessitate an endorsement. Many property certificates that cover multiple locations have frequent endorsements as locations are added or deleted. These would require additional premium or a return premium. As many endorsements require a premium change, it is the vehicle used for both accounting and underwriting. As a result, most facultative reinsurers use a common file for both underwriting and accounting. Each endorsement has a rather simple accounting procedure, premiums less commissions and brokerage, prorated for the percentage of the year remaining.

Treaty Reporting

Treaty reporting is normally accomplished either monthly/quarterly or on a minimum and deposit basis. Claims can be reported individually or in mass.

Individual claim reports tend to have more detail. In turn they require far more processing effort, since much of the detail will be recorded for analysis.

Bulk reporting is called reporting by *bordereau.* If a reinsurer accepts a cession from one of the giant insurers, the policy list may be volumes long. Since many policies have multiple claims, there would be a massive transfer of data. Keeping up would be most difficult. Given that the giant insurers are necessarily expert in the coverages offered and fully knowledgeable about the business and exposures, there is a question of what purpose the recording of data might accomplish. If a problem arises, would it not be better to have the giant insurer access its own data bank to research possible solutions?

To a certain extent this assessment is the same for certain kinds of reinsurance, regardless of the size of the company. This is an important realization. The reinsurer is limited in the perspective it can contribute to improving certain types of business. Granted, the assessment/advice aspect is a significant part of the reinsurance business, and reinsurers compete on their ability to effect improvements as necessary to assure and advance success.

For example, with homeowner's or private passenger automobile business, the rating and policy forms are highly regulated. Insurers are restricted in the number and kind of declinations or nonrenewals they can issue. If the results are not profitable, it is unlikely that any advice from the reinsurer could be executed and approved by regulators. Then too, the treaty or facultative reinsurer may hold a share of as little as 1 percent or so, while the cedent holds a much larger retention. Thus, the bottom line motivation is stronger for the primary insurer.

Short Form Reporting

The monthly or quarterly report (see Exhibit 12.10) is a simple summary of premiums and losses recorded by the cedent during the term. Note, the report does not supply detail about the policies ceded or about specific claims. Information about the kind, class, and limit ceded are typically supplied at renewal.

SAMPLE REPORT FORMAT

Company _____

Treaty Title _____

Cedent Reference _____

Reinsurer Reference _____

Period   From _____   To   _____

Invoice Number _____

	CURRENT PERIOD	TREATY YEAR TO DATE
Written Premium	_____	_____
Prior Unearned Premium	_____	_____
Current Unearned Premium	_____	_____
Earned Premium	_____	_____
Commission	_____	_____
Brokerage	_____	_____
Taxes	_____	_____
Net Premium	_____	_____
Net Paid Loss & LAE	_____	_____
Net Cash Due	_____	_____
Outstanding Loss Reserve	_____	_____
Outstanding LAE Reserve	_____	_____
Prior Loss Reserve	_____	_____
Prior LAE Reserve	_____	_____
Total Loss and LAE Incurred	_____	_____

Exhibit 12.10.   Sample Report Format

These are profiles about the business, not specific information about each and every account.

Typically there will be a provision for separate payment requests involving very large claims. These are referred to as cash calls. The requests are submitted with detail about the large claim and settlement terms that necessitate the large payment. The next monthly or quarterly report would show the cash call as a credit to that report.

This short form reporting relies heavily on the cedent for fair dealing. Reinsurance is called a contract of utmost good faith, and this is just one of the characteristics of the relationship.

Bordereau Reporting

The alternative is to supply listings of each and every policy (see Exhibit 12.11). There are contracts that by their very structure or composition necessitate this transfer of information; property surplus or semiautomatic facultative cessions treaties are examples.

Occasionally, one will see a handwritten list of policies bound. Although frequent in the distant past, they are seldom seen today, replaced by computer printed listings. The original concept grew out of operations such as Lloyd's of London, where the underwriter in the box had ready access to intermediaries and in the course of recording transactions compiled the list of all approvals, supplying the policy number and listing a few details about the specific source, policyholder, and risk/exposure.

Today the bordereau will display far more information and will be more difficult to interpret. Typically they are compiled on premium recorded in the term, by policy. Thus there are often hundreds of miniscule transactions, recording additional or return premiums. They tend to be so detailed and long that usage is hindered.

For example, if a loss arises from a specific policy, the underwriter may have to search line by line through several bordereaux to check to see if the cession was made and to determine if the amount shown in the claim tracks with the portion of premium ceded. The problem arises as cedents design the bordereau to their specifications, rather than those of the reinsurers.

Auditing

With short form or bordereau reporting the information supplied often lacks an audit trail (see Chapter 15). Given the size, type, kind, and class of the account ceded, the reinsurer should audit results, in addition to securing reports. This can be accomplished by sampling, the object being to make sure that procedures are applied as intended and that the cessions match requirements of the treaty.

Often, for example, the cessions are automatic and thus require the cedent to cede a fixed or variable cession on each applicable policy, except for

Company _____ - _____ Bordereau Dates _____ From _____ To _____

Treaty: _____

Item	Policy Number	Policy Dates		Trans. Type	Prem LOB	Invoice Reference	Currency Type	Written Premium	Commission Paid	Taxes Paid	Net Premium
		From	To								

Identification

Page Totals ☐ ☐ ☐ ☐ ☐

Report Totals ☐ ☐ ☐ ☐ ☐

Policy Count ☐

☐ Unearned at end of period

☐ Unearned at beginning of period

☐ Earned premium for period

Exhibit 12.11 Sample Premium Bordereau

Company _____   Bordereau Dates   From _____ To _____

Treaty: _____   Identification _____

| Item | Policy Number | Policy Dates | | Trans. Type | Claim LOB | Claim Type | Invoice Reference | Paid in Period | Paid To Date | Reserve Change | Current Reserve | Current Incurred | Claim Status |
		From	To										

Page Totals

Report Totals

Claim Count

Outstanding Reserve at end of period

Outstanding Reserve at beginning of period

Incurred to date

Exhibit 12.12. Sample Loss Bordereau

excluded classes. A report tells what was ceded but is silent about what was not ceded. An auditor can work back from the premiums reported in the annual statement to those ceded to the treaty. The difference should be accountable by a series of policies from a program not ceded to the treaty or by policies that fall into excluded classes.

It is obvious that short form reporting should be audited in most cases. Again, it need not be done every year, as the auditor can test more than one year during a single visit. In actuality, most audits do test developments in prior years as well as apply measurements to the current year.

13

REINSURANCE CLAIMS

This is the point where reinsurance gets interesting! All the material in the previous chapters is routine when compared to the activity in the area of claims. In carrying out their daily tasks, reinsurers participate in the industry's renowned claims, all the serious and atypical events, plus losses that inspire recall years later. Claims such as the *Titanic* and *Andrea Doria* shipwrecks, the MGM Grand Hotel fire, the Guess? jeans dispute, WSPPS bonds, recovery of two failed satellites, the Sky Walk collapse, the 1994 Los

Angeles earthquake, and Hurricanes Betsy, Hugo, and Andrew all inspire great tales in the insurance business. Every region has its own such claim. The claim logs of most companies are full of interesting, controversial, and challenging cases that make up the historical fabric of the reinsurance industry. The industry is all about containing and controlling the financial effects of such events.

Part of the interest is in the circumstances involved in the event. Reinsurers can relate how events affected certain clients and how the devastation came to happen. Another part is the record keeping. For example, the sinking of the *Andrea Doria* occurred in 1956 but the details of the incident were reported well into the 1980s. Thus, the events seem very recent in the reinsurer's mind.

Yet another interesting aspect is the manner in which events become fully realized. For example, reserves for Hurricane Frederick, a 1979 storm, continued to develop into the mid-1980s, which is unusual for what is essentially a property loss. This process keeps these events in the memory of most of the reinsurance staff, years after the event occurred.

Some claims are especially complex. The debate over asbestosis has continued into its third decade. What was the cause? Who was to blame? When did the injury happen? How will the claims be paid? Such claims are not easy to resolve. In a claim involving Guess? jeans, the defense expenses surpassed the indemnity damages. This was a director's, officer's, and owner's dispute over a product line manufactured in multiple countries and sold worldwide. The multitude of corporate entities necessitated a worldwide investigation and complex financial measurement. Settling the claim was not easy to understand and involved hard work.

Remember that reinsurance is a risk/exposure transfer mechanism. It responds to claim events. Because of the nature of the cessions, reinsurance tends to be involved in events that are critical to the company, significant to the industry, and meaningful to the staff. After a major catastrophe, estimates and rumors fly through the industry as everyone attempts to measure their financial piece of the event and compare it to the whole. For example, the eleventh-largest insurer in a state may compare its estimate with that of the eighth- to fourteenth-largest insurers, to see if the loss cost distribution matched market share. Everyone on the staff eventually deals with the claims, even if they are not part of the claim handling process.

REINSURANCE HANDLING VERSUS PRIMARY HANDLING

Reinsurance is a contract of indemnity rather than a liability contract. Many primary insurance policies are liability contracts (although there are some primary indemnity policies). In the liability cases, the primary carrier is obligated for 100 percent of the claim, even though it may have ceded a sizeable share.

Then too, the primary carrier is obligated to defend against assertions claimed, even if the connection to its insured is oblique. In contrast, reinsurance responds to the payment of claims and, to some extent, to the reserving as well.

Once the insurer posts a reserve, it has incurred some economic damage. Reinsurers in turn may post reserves for that portion for which they may be ultimately held accountable. Interestingly, the reinsurers may reserve amounts greater than or less than that recorded as primary reserve. True obligations arise when claim payments are made by the cedent, within the layer of the reinsurer's involvement.

We must understand that the insurer/reinsurer relationship is far different from the relationship that necessarily exists between a primary carrier and an excess or umbrella carrier. An excess carrier holds a separate policy, with its own terms and conditions. It need not follow the underlying carrier's settlement logic. A policy wording difference may seem slight, but can pose significant differences in the handling and settlement. At times, there may be conflicts in the interests of the primary and excess carriers.

This difference between primary and reinsurance perspectives affects the entire claim handling process. The insurer holds primary authority and accountability for 100 percent of the claim. Reinsurers are obligated by the actions of the cedent. Normally, reinsurers may be asked for advice or may offer some when presented with the facts of a specific claim. Observing the cedent's claim handling expertise is part of the underwriting process, so reinsurers often have done their homework in advance, choosing to do business with capable insurers and avoiding those that present weak credentials.

In most situations, the reinsurer is obligated to follow the decisions and covered expenditures of the primary carrier or cedent. In those situations where the reinsurer chooses not to follow, there is a significant departure. This means denial by the reinsurer to pay a claim. It is a step that most often leads to arbitration between the parties of the contract. Time is important, because it may prove that the primary carrier's judgment is the correct approach. If so, the reinsurer will fall back into place, having lost a significant amount of trust. If the cedent fails to prevail, arbitration is likely.

It is important to understand that dispute over a specific claim, however settled, will not alter the basic relationship. The reinsurer will continue to follow most decisions. It may audit more frequently and surely will watch closely. The relationship and mutual trust may be altered by the disagreement, but the basic relationship will hold through renewal, at the very least.

CLAIM REPORTING

Let us briefly review the typical claim reporting requirements by type of treaty. *Case reporting* refers to claims that are individually reported to reinsurers.

Bulk reporting means either *bordereau reporting* or *summary reporting*. A bordereau report is a computerized report that essentially lists the information for each and every claim as a single line entry—it is very brief. A summary report lacks specific claim detail and provides only the monthly or quarterly totals.

Type of Treaty	Typical Reporting Format
Quota share	Bulk reporting
Surplus T	Bulk reporting
Excess of loss	Case reporting
Catastrophe excess	Summary reporting
Aggregate excess	Summary reporting

It is important to understand that the routine reporting in all of these formats is quite brief. Obviously the summary report may not supply any data on specific cases. The bordereau will likely list just 6 to 12 items of information for each claim. Individual reports will contain much more data. Individual claim reports have two levels of reporting: the reporting of the event with policy detail and the reporting of the story behind the claim.

Claim Review Worksheets

Once a case is reported to a reinsurer, the reinsurer needs a system to record and monitor reported claims.

Exhibits 13.1 and 13.2 are forms for both treaty and facultative claim reviews by reinsurers. Both have been condensed onto single pages, and in doing so, lack space to fully record responses in the allotted fields. These have application as internal data processing abstracts, or input sheets, and as field audit work sheets. They comprise the claim information header maintained by reinsurers for controlling and tracking each claim. These work sheets are part of the first level of reporting; they omit the story behind the claim.

The major difference between the treaty and facultative forms is that the facultative work sheet focuses on the layering, while the treaty form focuses on the developmental aspects of the claim. Also, it is likely that both versions may have separate formats for property and casualty claims.

Some of the fields in these work sheets are explained below.

Cedent Information (2–19)
This is a compilation of information about the insured as supplied by the cedent. It contains policy numbers (14), policy limits (4), claimant count (11), etc.

Treaty Claim Review Work Sheet

Control #

1. Project:

Cedent Information

2. Insurer:	8. Type:	14. Pol #:
3. Insured:	9. Description:	15. Claim #:
4. Policy Limits:	10. Injury/Damage:	16. Date of Occurrence:
5. Location:	11. No. Claimants:	17. Date Reported:
6. Description	12. % Paid:	18. In Suit: Yes ___ No ___
7. Class: Property _____ Casualty _____ Other _____	13. Kind of Business	19. Status: O __ C __ ? __

Reinsurer Information

20. Treaty:					21. Term:		35. U/W Year:
22. Broker:					23. MGA/MGU:		36. Treaty #:
24. Limit:					25. % Share:		37. Date of Occurrence:
26. Retention:							38. Date Reported:
27a. Q.S.	b. S.T.	c. XS/XOL	d. CAT XS	e. AGG XS	f. OTHER	28. In-force/Terminated:	39. Single Treaty:
29. Expenses:							40. Multiple Treaty:
30. Remarks:							41. Critical Claim?
							42. Tracked Claim?
31. Coverage Questions:							43. A.C.R.
32a. Precautionary	b. Open/Reserved		c. Reopen	d. Paid/Closed		f. Closed/No Pay	44. Special Handling:
33. Settlement Value:				34. Verdict Value:			45. Resisted/Denied

CLAIM HISTORY

EVALUATION DATE:	46a. ___/___/___	47a.	48a.	49a.	50a.
CLAIM AMOUNT:	46b.	47b.	48b.	49b.	50b.
EXPENSE AMOUNT:	46c.	47c.	48c.	49c.	50c.
INCURRED AMOUNT:	46d.	47d.	48d.	49d.	50d.
PERCENTAGE PAID:	46e.	47e.	48e.	49e.	50e.
TREATY SHARE AMOUNT:	46f.	47f.	48f.	49f.	50f.

Exhibit 13.1. Treaty Claim Review Work Sheet

Date of Loss (16, 17, 37, and 38)

As related in Chapter 3, reinsurers track date of loss (16), date reported to the cedent (17), and the date the claim was first advised to reinsurers (38). Note also, this form has a date of loss from the perspective of the treaty (37) as well as the date of loss reported by the cedent (16); they are rarely different.

Facultative Claim Review Work Sheet

Control #

1. Project:

Cedent Information

2. Insurer:	8. Type:	14. Pol #:
3. Insured:	9. Description:	15. Claim #:
4. Policy Limits:	10. Injury/Damage:	16. Date of Occurrence:
5. Location:	11. No. Claimants:	17. Date Reported:
6. Description	12. % Paid:	18. In Suit: Yes ___ No ___
7. Class: Property ___ Casualty ___ Other ___	13. Kind of Business	19. Status: O ___ C ___ ? ___

Reinsurer Information

20. Company:		21. Term:	35. U/W Year:
22. Broker:		23. MGA/MGU:	36. Cert #:
24. Limit:		25. % Share:	37. Date of Occurrence:
26. Retention:			38. Date Reported:
27a. Proportional:	27b. Excess:	28. Not Used	39. Single Certificate:
29. Expenses:			40. Multiple Certificate:
30. Remarks:			41. Critical Claim?
			42. Tracked Claim?
			43. A.C.R.
31. Coverage Questions:			44. Special Handling:
32a. Precautionary	b. Open/Reserved	c. Reopen	d. Paid/Closed	f. Closed/No Pay	45. Resisted/Denied
33. Settlement Value:		34. Verdict Value:	

46. Evaluative Date:	CLAIM AMT	EXPENSE AMT	INCURRED	% PAID	CASE IBNR
SIR Deductible:	47a.	48a.	49a.	50a.	51a.
Primary:	47b.	48b.	49b.	50b.	51b.
Underlying:	47c.	48c.	49c.	50c.	51c.
Reinsurance:	47d.	48d.	49d.	50d.	51d.

Exhibit 13.2.   Facultative Claim Review Work Sheet

MGA/MGU (23)

This field refers to the involvement of a managing general agent or managing general underwriter, at any point in the policy or claim. This does not refer to an independent adjuster. This appears as a separate field since some MGAs have in the past been the source of confusion, lapses in handling, and other problems. Obviously, the concern does not apply to all MGAs. This field is intended to acknowledge the involvement of an MGA or MGU so that this feature can be monitored.

Type of Reinsurance (27)

This is a quick check for the structure. For facultative it is simply proportional or excess. In contrast, there are a variety of codes used for treaty reinsurance.

In-force/Terminated (28)

This is a field applicable to treaty but not facultative. It relates the status of the particular treaty. If in force, the claim handler should pay particular attention to the treaty effective date, notice of cancellation (NOC) date, and expiration date. If the claim happens to be large or unusual, the claim handler should inform the underwriter (and account executive for direct writers). If the treaty is in force and the NOC date or renewal is approaching, the handler should send the information to the underwriter quickly.

Expenses (29)

This is a critical field as related above. Expenses can be handled as an additional amount, included within the total loss or ultimate net loss. Alternatively, expenses can be shared *pro rata* in addition to the incurred amount of the claim. The appropriate method for the particular treaty or certificate is highlighted by this field.

Coverage Questions (30)

This is a field that is seldom used; however, experience has led reinsurers to include within the database. Listing the concerns, even if resolved, helps create a pattern that has applicability for the analysis of future claims in a specific account. Further, the process of facing the inquiry every day for each and every claim keeps the effort a high priority. Is there anything about this claim that should be questioned?

Claim History/Current Evaluation (46–51)

This is purposefully displayed in a different manner for facultative and treaty claims.

Facultative focuses on the layering. The particular certificate may represent a 5 percent share in a fourth layer, so it is vital to know how much capacity underlies the certificate and how it fits into the particular layer. In this particular display, all the underlying layers are compressed into one statistic, "underlying." It is far better to display all the layering, as space permits.

The treaty focuses on what the current evaluation is and how it compares to prior evaluations. Obviously, this has more applicability for casualty claims. However, the format can be used for property as well, with the expectation that a great many cases will carry the same figures across the page.

Claim Status (32)

This is accomplished in many different formats. That which is displayed in these work sheets is intentionally simplistic. For example, some reinsurers prefer to identify separately settled claims that remain open. This is another measure that effectively measures the maturity of a claim, percentage paid. The closer this is to 100 percent, the closer the claim is to its ultimate development. Of course, it can be distorted on occasion; however, when accumulated over a large portfolio, it becomes a very credible measurement.

In the facultative work sheet, % Paid appears as items 50a–d. Note the percentage paid should be at or near 100 percent for each layer before the next one begins to require payments. In the claim maturation process, one can envision how close the certificate is to requiring payments. In addition, this statistic is a lead indicator of the ultimate settlement value as the %. Paid elevates through the loss as the claim ages.

For treaty evaluation, the % Paid is displayed as a row of data, 46e to 49e. Rows 46a, 46b, and 46c display the 100 percent from-ground-up (FGU) claim amounts. Thus the % Paid represents that portion of the total claim that is paid at the particular evaluation point. In this respect, the % Paid is an excellent measure of the maturation of the particular claim as viewed across the page.

Single/Multiple (39 and 40)

This is one way to indicate whether the particular claim has been reported to one certificate/treaty or to multiple certificates/treaties. If it is reported to multiple treaties or certificates, the advice from one cedent may have implications for other claim files. This is not a breach of confidentiality, for the information is just applied in-house. Clearly if the reinsurer participates on several treaties or certificates on a particular account, a reported increase from one cedent may have applicability to other claims on the same event. This field simply indicates that other claims exist; the handler will have other procedures for searching for those linked claims. If the claim is reported to a single treaty or certificate, the claim handler knows to focus on this one report.

Special and Tracked Claims (41, 42, 43, 44, and 45)

As there are several tracking categories, this format applies to several fields; most are yes/no formats.

Critical Claim (41)

This is intended to identify large claim situations. Often the criteria include the occurrence of serious bodily injuries, which, because they may arise under liability that has a questionable linkage to the policyholder, may not carry a high reserve. Because of this possibility, the term *critical claim* seems appropriate.

Tracked Claim (42)

The domestic industry tracks property catastrophes that arise from 1000 policies and more than $5 million in insured damages. These are assigned two-digit tracking numbers. The claim counts and loss amounts are recorded across the country. The tracking number is written in this field, as and if applicable.

Casualty claims are more complex and are not currently accumulated by the industry. However, most reinsurers do track their own large, multiple contract claims and such claims as pollution, asbestosis, toxic shock syndrome, etc. They may include claims such as WSPPS bond claims, even if they have few, if any, incidents from such events, if only to display to retrocessionaires that they were not affected by these events. Typically casualty tracking is accomplished using a three-digit tracking number assigned by the reinsurer's own staff.

A.C.R. (43)

This refers to *additional case reserves*. This code highlights the fact the reinsurer's reserves have been posted differently from those of the cedent. The term and the practice are such that lower reserves are rarely posted by reinsurers.

Special Handling (44)

This is a field that highlights those claims that are unusual or that arise in complex treaties. A special handling indicator may mean that the supervisor reviews each report. The code indicates that special steps must be followed, which are outlined in the specific claim file.

Resisted/Denied (45)

Like special handling, this code highlights those claims that are being resisted for one reason or another. Some reinsurers complete this field also to specifically identify claims that had expense payment requests submitted which were rejected following the logic outlined earlier.

We have emphasized the two parts of reporting, because the reinsurer has two functions: recording the event and monitoring the settlement.

Individual Claim Reports

The second part of the report is the "story behind the claim." Individual claim reports may include very detailed information. There are many files in the reinsurer's hands that contain hundreds of pages. Our focus here will be on compiling the necessary data to comprehend a typical claim.

The reinsurance contract generally requires supplementary reports of serious and substantial claims. These may be defined as serious bodily injuries, death cases, industrywide tracked catastrophes, claims that approach half of the retention, etc. The object is to gather more information on those cases that materially affect the overall results of the treaty.

Normally there are no specific requirements for reporting these special cases because the cedent and reinsurers generally cooperate in supplying data and responding to inquiries. Since the events vary to a great degree, it is not practical to have a standard format for these reports. Then too, by providing a complete file, the cedent may secure the advantage of an informed critique by the reinsurers to help its case.

CLAIM RESERVING

The claim reserving process and some of the terminology was introduced in Chapter 3. It is important to appreciate that the cedent and the reinsurers are required to set aside reserve funds which approximate the amount(s) they will be required to pay in the future on these claims. The primary insurer must set reserves for the entire exposure perceived in each specific claim.

If the claim happens to be an auto accident with personal injury, the insurer must estimate the cost of repair, the amount to be paid for the medical needs of the injured parties, plus an amount for pain and suffering. All of this is speculative, as the costs are not certain. Even the repair cost is approximate, because every part may not be visible, and the labor may exceed the normal time. In setting reserves, some cases are far more elusive than others. Also, in the case of liability claims, the insurer may factor in shared or contributory liability of other parties involved in the claim.

The reinsurer posts reserves for its contractual liability for the indemnity that exists within the reserves posted by the ceding carrier. If there is any question as to whether the reinsurer's liability directly attaches to the original claim, the reader should refer to the section on claims in Chapter 2. Theoretically, when the event happens, the reinsurer has no damage. The reinsurer's damage arises when the insurer posts the reserve. This subtle but important condition exists because the reinsurance contract is an indemnity contract, attaching to the insurer's economic loss rather than to the events or exposures themselves. This subtle language prevents the policyholder from including the reinsurers in suits. Although this is a basic tenet in reinsurance, reinsurers will often discuss the event and the exposures without mentioning this condition.

In summary, the insurance company sets reserves for the perceived indemnity costs plus reserves for defense and loss adjustment expenses. The reinsurer sets reserves for the economic damage posted by the ceding carrier.

A *reported claim* will be a verifiable claim made against a specific policy of the cedent by a policyholder or third party. It must arise from a policy included within the terms of the reinsurance treaty. The claim attains "recognized" status once it is judged to meet all the terms of the treaty and is not excluded thereunder. Thus, *recognized claims* are a subgroup of all reported claims, as a few reported events may be dismissed because they do not meet all of the terms and conditions of the treaty or certificate.

The reported/recognized claims will be monitored through subsequent reports of evaluations, negotiations, and developments. At some point, the amount reserved by the reinsured may exceed the attachment level of the reinsurer. That portion of the claim amount in excess of the attachment level may be then considered as an *incurred claim* by the reinsurer.

Those cases that are reported as reserved within retention, but not yet incurred to the specific treaty, are *precautionary claims*. If, for example, the attachment point is $100,000, the cedent may be required to send advices of events that they reserve at 50 percent of that amount, that is, $50,000. Where the policy limits of the individual case are not sufficient to exceed the attachment point or retention (e.g., $100,000) the cedent should submit a one-time advice indicating the reason for the report and that the case will not develop sufficiently to reach the layer. This would-be a $55,000 claim on a policy with a $75,000 policy limit. That is good communication and it should not affect the treaty pricing.

If the policy limit is sufficient for adverse development to affect the treaty, the report will be recorded by the reinsurers for subsequent monitoring. Continuing the example, if the reserve was $60,000 on a policy that had a $125,000 limit, a precautionary advice should be forwarded. Some reinsurers do not treat precautionary claims as open claims. Thus a precautionary advice may not be viewed in the same way as an open or reserved claim. Technically, this can be one of those situations where the open or incurred claim count does not equal the reported claim total. This is not handled in the same way by all reinsurers.

The aforementioned process is to collect advices on claims that affect the treaty or appear to be sufficient to do so and to check to see if the policy type, kind, and class are indeed subject to the treaty. That is the recognition process.

With a reported claim that happens to be reserved by the cedent for an amount that exceeds the treaty attachment point or retention, the reinsurer sets up its portion of the suggested reserve, and simultaneously, the reinsured may credit an equivalent amount as receivable. Thus, the cedent posts the total reserve and a credit for the amount transferred to the reinsurer. The claims are then incurred on the books of both companies.

There are duties for each party. The reinsurer may want to inquire about the claim or the handling by the reinsured. Normally, the reinsurer works behind the scenes, giving advice on occasion, but generally relying on the ceding carrier to handle and settle the claim properly. This monitoring process is important, as reinsurers may have seen a greater number of similar claims and can help the carrier effect the best resolution. The ceding carrier is obligated to negotiate the entire claim in fairness to its reinsurers. It is important to understand that the total reserve exists at all times on the books of the ceding carrier.

The reinsurer may choose to set a different reserve, either higher or lower, than that set by the cedent. It is proper that the reinsurer advise the cedent of such an event regardless of whether such advice is required by the contract. The reinsurer records the amount incurred in its statutory statement under Schedule F, Assumed Reinsurance. The amount should match the records of the cedent within its own statutory statement under Schedule F, Ceded Reinsurance. There are general interrogatories within the statutory statement that require any amount disputed to be specifically listed if in excess of 3 percent of the cedent's premium. Let us briefly digress to discuss the terms "different reserve" and "disputed reserve."

Different Reserve Situations

Differing views on the evaluation of a claim may reflect reserving philosophy, judgment, or timing. It can be a matter of communication rather than disagreement. One would generally view these situations as perspectives about the potential given the information at hand at the time of the decision. Once further information becomes known, such differences tend to disappear. This is natural, and need not be viewed as problematic. It is important to keep up the communication. If it is a material amount, there will be some learning from the process. Also, these need to be accounted for in the renewal process. Both parties understand how prices are calculated.

As a matter of practicality as well as procedure, many reinsurers do not set reserves below the amount reported by the cedent. Rather, they follow the course of posting that amount and discussing the amount with the cedent. Experience has shown that, as often as not, this process brings more information to the reinsurers' hands to the extent that they concur on the amount set by the cedent.

If the reinsurer chooses to post a larger amount, it does so as an additional case reserve (ACR). That amount is on the reinsurer's books but not the cedent's. Remember, this larger amount will be used by the reinsurer in any pricing work. It should always be identified as an ACR, however, so that the parties understand. In such cases the reinsurer's assumed Schedule F does not match the cedent's.

Claims Disputed by the Cedent

It should be understood that claims that are denied or resisted by the cedent under its insured policy are typically supported by the reinsurers. These represent an entirely different category than those that are disputed by the reinsurers.

Generally, reinsurers support cedent actions due to the obvious common benefit. It is quite important that cedents maintain appropriate levels for claim settlements. If the level is too high, the cedent may become a target litigant, driving up many of its settlements. If the pressure is far too severe, always pressing settlements downward, negatives can also arise. In actions where the cedent is pressing settlement on behalf of the policyholder to a third party, it is possible that the policyholder will assert that his insurer is operating in bad faith and not in the policyholder's best interests. Whether or not bad faith awards fall into the reinsurance treaty should be closely reviewed in each specific case. Generally, such awards are covered by reinsurance. These sort of cedent actions are part of the business. Reinsurers monitor them as well as the routine cases.

Claims Disputed by Reinsurers

Claims can fall into gray areas or gaps in the reinsurance contract. There can be cases where a clerical error has assigned a particular claim to the wrong treaty. Most disputes arise because the claims fail during the "recognition" process and because of the nature of the coverage afforded.

Sometimes the policy to which the claim is applicable probably was not or should not have been ceded to the treaty. Further, such a problem is more likely than errors in processing or claim handling to be the cause of disputes.

Typically, disputes tend to move very slowly, and the parties tend to hold close control over the passage of communication. It is hard to work through any problem with these two conditions. Generally, the disputed item is separated in the accounts, and the other reports and payments usually continue with due process.

Reinsurance contracts contain an arbitration clause that guides the resolution of formal disputes. The process was once considered to be swifter and less costly than going through the courts, and it did keep the resolution to standard industry practices. In recent times it has become a costly, cumbersome, and time-consuming process.

Individual claim disputes are better worked out between the parties; that requires communication, which unfortunately, is often not present. There are some individuals who can and often do function as informal mediators. The intermediary naturally has the kind of position and relationship to perform such a function. For direct writers, the account executive holds a similar position. Yes, the account executive is an employee of the reinsurer; however, he or she also happens to have close working relationships with the cedent. Both the intermediary and account executive share a compelling interest in resolving a dispute equitably and amicably.

When the treaty is in force, the ongoing relationship helps create compromises. If the treaty has been terminated, and there is no other existing business, the situation does not benefit from an ongoing business relationship.

Another feature is the fact that many reinsurance claims develop for years and close after a long tail of activity. A disputed case may not have outstanding payment requests, and thus, there is no urgency to resolve the dispute.

CEDENT VERSUS ASSUMER DUTIES

Because the reinsurance contract, treaty or facultative, is a contract of indemnity (see Chapter 3), the reinsurer does not make any payments until after the cedent has paid a portion of the claim within the reinsurer's portion. The cedent is responsible for the entire policyholder claim and seeks recovery after the fact from its reinsurers. Obviously, very large claims create a situation where the cedent seeks swift remuneration from its reinsurers.

Thus there are differences in the duties of primary and reinsurance claim handlers. The cedent is the controlling decision maker. The reinsurance treaty binds the reinsurers to settlements made by the cedent. As the ceded capacity grows and reinsurers begin to hold an increasing dollar share in the claim settlements, they tend to follow the cases quite closely.

It is possible that an aggressive settlement posture may increase the upside potential of the claim. If, for example, the case is one of questionable liability and the cedent is pressing hard to close the claim without payment, they may actually pass by interim settlement options in their effort to win the entire case. Because cases tend to increase in value over time, this effort can have a deleterious effect on the reinsurers' position, while the cedent's net position is capped by the treaty attachment point. Reinsurers may exert significant pressure in such situations. If the beliefs are strong on both sides, problems can arise that test the relationship.

Reinsurers typically hold a contractual right to participate in any settlement, as an interested indirect party and at their own expense. In doing so, the cedent maintains its duties. Typically, the reinsurer only gains closer monitoring of the situation. However, if one is on the scene and close to the negotiations, the advices have a greater hearing and impact. Thus, even in an extreme situation, the cedent's duties and the reinsurer's duties remain normal.

EXPENSES

Almost always, expenses allocated to individual cases include costs of litigation and independent adjusters, but not staff expenses of the cedent. The latter are considered to be covered by any commission applicable to the business. The independent adjusters are considered to be professional handlers who try to effect the best result possible; thus such costs are shared by reinsurers.

The expenses can be handled as an amount included within the total loss. Alternatively, they can be shared *pro rata,* in addition to the incurred amount of the claim. The appropriate method for the particular treaty or certificate is specifically outlined in the written contract.

At several points in this text, reinsurance has been described as a contract of indemnity rather than a contract of liability. Primary policies are contracts of liability in that they respond to the assertion of loss or damage by a third party, even though the loss or damage may not be visible. They provide funds for defense to prove an allegation false. Treaty and facultative reinsurance are designed to respond only to the actual payments of loss by the cedent. This sets the full accountability in the hands of the cedent. It also prevents policyholder suits from naming reinsurers in suits against an insurer. Yet, cedents often bill reinsurers for portions of expense payments on cases that are not payable for indemnity. For example, if the cedent spends a lot of money in defense against a frivolous claim with a large demand, the cedent's staff often feels that in winning, they saved reinsurers money. Therefore, they submit billings for a share of the expenses. Similarly, if a claim is reserved into the layer, the cedent's staff will apportion expenses and bill reinsurers. In both cases, reinsurers are likely to deny the expense payment request. There are two standard expense handling methodologies.

Expense as Part of Ultimate Net Loss

On an ultimate net loss basis, reinsurer payments are not due until the paid loss (including LAE) exceeds the retention. It does not distinguish between expense items and indemnity items. Thus, the cedent should not look to recover expenses along the way.

The words "in addition" that are part of the definition seem to confuse the cedent's staff. In the case of ultimate net loss, the expenses are included with the indemnity amount as one figure. So "included" is perhaps a better term than "in addition."

Expense Added on a *Pro Rata* Basis

Under this method, expenses are split in proportion to the amount of paid indemnity on the claim. Reinsurers will reject payment requests that are submitted before the treaty responds to indemnity payments.

The calculation is as follows: If the reinsurer's portion of the paid indemnity is zero, its portion of the paid expense is zero multiplied by the paid expense total, which is zero.

For a nontrivial example, let us consider an $82,500 claim to a treaty with a $50,000 retention; let us assume further that expenses of an outside adjuster amounted to $18,000. The reinsurer's portion would be $32,500 and the cedent's net $50,000. The claim would be split 60.6 percent net and 39.4 percent ceded. In this situation, the $18,000 expenses would be split as follows:

$$\text{Cedent } \$18,000 \times 0.606 = \$10,908$$
$$\text{Reinsurer } \$18,000 \times 0.394 = \$\ 7,092$$

The above calculation is well defined in the reinsurance contract language. However, every so often cedents submit requests for expense payments that are not warranted. Because the amounts are small, some do pass through the reinsurer's inspection process. Such sporadic payments probably exacerbate this problem by creating confusion or doubt, but they do not follow the contractual language of when expense payments are justified.

CASE RESERVING

A case reserve is an amount set aside in reserve for a specific filed claim. Reserves that are case based are often differentiated from those that are posted in bulk for anticipated claim payout that is not related to specific cases.

The cedent's initial evaluation is hard to analyze, because the judgment is one where assorted facts and circumstances are assigned a numerical reserve. The reinsurer's position is to oversee that judgment, offer constructive criticism on occasion, compliment good work as appropriate, etc. It is a helpful, indeed vital, service if the cedent and reinsurer work effectively in tandem. Obviously, it can be difficult if the mechanism has friction or the relations are strained.

The applicability is direct and equivalent for proportional claims. The difference is that excess claims typically are reported individually, while proportional claims are usually reported in a monthly or quarterly bordereau. Proportional treaties typically specify a point beyond which all large claims are specifically and individually reported. The reinsurer attempts to complete the same process when reviewing claim bordereaux, tests for suitability to the treaty; recognizes the claim, tests for adequacy of reserving, looks for coverage concerns, etc.

The posting of a reserve by a reinsurer does not necessarily mean that the reinsurer believes the claim is wholly valid. The reinsurer may still want to question the claim and perhaps deny coverage or payment. The reserve is a measure of the liability presented within the report, but it may not totally reflect the reinsurer's belief about the merits of the case. The process of reserving is procedural and important as the reinsurer undertakes its fiduciary responsibility to its owners to be sure the event meets all the terms and conditions of the policy. It is the reinsurer's goal to be sure any amount ultimately paid is warranted, appropriate, and reasonable.

Reserves may be posted for indemnity amounts and also as budgeting of expenses. Reinsurers are particular about separating these categories. In fact, reinsurers require that ceded expenses be split between internal and external expenses. Generally, the reinsurance does not apply to internal expenses such as company claim staff and file maintenance costs. Such costs are covered by any commission allotted in the reinsurance terms. On the other hand, expenses of outside adjusters and legal counsel are charged to the specific claim and incurred as indemnity by reinsurers.

CLAIM DEVELOPMENTAL ANALYSIS

Chapter 11 related some claim developmental measurement techniques that are used in pricing treaty reinsurance. Developmental evaluation is a key matter for assessment by the claim department.

Developmental measurements are typically the work of actuaries; indeed, they are required to be attested to by an actuary. Other departments have perspectives on the amount of development to be expected. Exposure amassed within the portfolio has a direct impact on the type and amount of claims that can arise; thus, underwriters' opinions should be incorporated in the developmental analysis. Individual claims can be assessed for developmental potentials, so claims handlers should be involved in the analysis. The entire process is a very complex forecasting calculation; thus actuaries should control the calculating. How all these parties fit together varies widely by company. Creating a procedure that includes the perspectives of each department is best.

A mathematical forecast can be skewed for a variety of reasons. Let's consider some of them.

1. Facultative claim portfolios tend to have larger claims on average but a fewer number of claims than do treaty situations. This is mainly due to greater use of excess of loss but also to the limits accepted. Thus, for facultative portfolios the forecasting may lack credibility.

2. Projecting claim totals does not consider the fact that many of the individual claims will be limited by the limit of the treaty or certificate. There should be some linkage to policy limits; often this factor is neglected.

3. Underwriters may apply exclusions, sublimits, or pricing techniques that eliminate, reduce, or control certain kinds of exposures. For example, in worker's compensation, the guideline may stipulate that no classification be written with a class rate above $40. That eliminates many high-rated, high-exposure employee classes. Thus, without using the term *asbestos,* this condition may effectively reduce asbestosis exposures. If the actuaries' focus is just on the numbers, they might incorporate factors for asbestosis into their forecast and overstate the situation.

Guidelines such as the worker's compensation rate illustrated above may be subtle and not readily visible to those not directly involved. It is important that the underwriters be involved for their perspective on how the portfolio is composed and for particular efforts affecting long tail exposures. Claim handlers are in a position to observe just how effective those underwriting efforts might be. They should be in a position to attest the kind, count, and severity of classes of claims that may produce uncomfortable development.

Both the underwriting and claims areas can use some data processing techniques to maintain measures by class, kind, quality, etc., which can be used to make the developmental forecasting more accurate. This is one of the important corporate functions that is best accomplished through a team effort, combining several areas of specialty. Further, many of the techniques illustrated earlier in this text can be, and often are, put to good use.

BULK RESERVING

Bulk reserves are those amounts set aside by insurers and reinsurers for future payments that cannot yet be tied to any specific case. For example, if the carrier believes that one of 20 claims will mushroom in ultimate value, it should set aside a reserve for that anticipated amount. This would be a bulk reserve because it was not posted for a specific claim. Later, if one of those

20 claims does arise, the bulk reserve would be decreased, while the case reserve is increased, not necessarily for identical amounts. The carrier may feel some bulk potential exists for the 19 remaining cases; however, due to the passage of time, this may be assessed at a different amount.

Both the cedent and reinsurer set bulk reserves on their business, as required statutorily. The process is the end result of the developmental analysis, coupled with other management financial decisions. Reinsurers use the term "incurred but not reported" (IBNR) for bulk reserves. This includes 1) amounts that are anticipated to arise from claims that happened during the accident year period, but which have not yet been reported to the cedent and 2) amounts that are estimated to arise from the existing or known claims, but where current reserves may be insufficient. Theoretically, this could be a redundancy as well as an increment. In practice, redundancies are quite rare.

As mentioned earlier, these developmental patterns can span more than 20 years. How does this happen?

1. Some policies cover exposures that take longer to materialize and evaluate. Architects' and engineers' errors and omissions policies is one such example. The accident or event may be held to have happened when the architects put their pens to the drafting paper. Years later, the claim arises and is charged back to the date of occurrence, which is in some past policy period.

2. Cases that are litigated take longer to settle. The courts are backlogged, and the development of facts takes time under the legal methodology. It is appropriate to consider this as time taken to get the facts right.

3. Although the statute of limitations blocks some old incidents from being filed, it does permit plaintiffs to file suits when the timing works to their advantage, which may mean waiting until facts are forgotten.

4. Some cases involving children are postponed until they reach 18 or 21 years of age.

5. Some bodily injuries are not set with the medical effort immediately following the accident. The injury may be of a progressive nature. It may not be possible to predict how this will play out. For example, the care may develop from home family care to daily nurse visits to round-the-clock nursing, and beyond. Just how much this might cost and the timing of the costs are often impossible to predict.

6. The entire process of moving from the initial report of the accident or event through the investigatory process and through negotiations to settlement can be exacerbated by the circumstances of the event or the personalities of the parties. The process is never swift. Even settlement does not always mean closure.

7. Complexity adds to the time factor. If the case is international or technically complex there will be considerable time spent in sorting out the situation.

8. Serious cases often have disastrous financial implications that force one party into bankruptcy. An entirely different set of laws and procedural actions that arise in the bankruptcy has direct impact on how fast the case will close.

Given that several of these factors might exist a given claim and thereby complicate the process, one should not be surprised at the long tail of development.

No Case-Based IBNR for Facultative Reinsurance

Bulk reserves apply to blocks or portfolios of business. Because facultative reinsurance applies to individual policies, one will not find cedents reporting such reserves to facultative reinsurers.

Infrequent Treaty-Based IBNR Reports

Because bulk reserves are typically set for an entire portfolio, they may not apply to that segment of the portfolio that is subject to a specific treaty. As a result, cedents do not always supply IBNR for individual treaties.

Credibility is another consideration. Small treaties do not possess a statistically credible amount of data and thus might not warrant forecasting IBNR.

Our interest has been in demonstrating why the long tail exists and how it impacts treaty versus facultative reinsurance. We have in Chapter 11 demonstrated one very common technique for forecasting IBNR. We also have stressed how the perspectives from underwriters and claim handlers can be used as supportive methodology.

AUDITING

There are many aspects or targets for an audit by reinsurers. Reinsurers frequently review the books on site at the cedent's offices as a prebinding audit. In addition, they make a practice of visiting troubled companies. Because many of the cedent's reports are brief or summary in nature, it is advisable that they undertake routine audits for most accounts. There will be some exceptions where the percentage is small, the distance great, and the necessity of an audit low.

A prebinding audit will focus on measuring the exposures to be ceded, but it will also gather information about the history of the subject business. It should be understood that the reinsurer is assessing the abilities of the cedent to manage, underwrite, process accounts, and handle/settle claims and ascertaining the cedent's moral fiber. These criteria are fundamental to the decision to authorize any submission. A significant amount of time in a prebinding audit will be spent analyzing claims.

A renewal audit involves the same measurements, but more attention is focused on the claim files. First, with some exposure on the books, the reinsurer will want to review the perspectives that the claim files offer to understand the account. Second, claims are the area where problems arise.

Suppose for example that a treaty excluded marine business and that the cedent wrote contractors of many kinds. A painter would be an appropriate type of contractor for this business. Would the underwriter consider a policy on a painter who happened to have accepted long-term contracts to paint offshore oil drilling rigs to be an appropriate cession? Some might feel this is appropriate since the painter is not engaged in the shipping business. Others may feel the cession is entirely inappropriate, since the painter is exposed to the perils of the sea in carrying out his daily business. If there is no claim, was the cession in error?

The above example is a very specialized situation, yet it demonstrates how normal business may fall into "gray" areas of interpretation of a reinsurance contract. Just how literally should the exclusions be taken? That question might inspire debate among reinsurers or cedents. One way to look at the situation is that if the reinsurance excluded marine business, it did so to avoid ocean-related claims. Thus, since the offshore painter was exposed to such claims, the business should not be ceded or should be declined if cessions were automatic. The theory is that one wants to write business that is acceptable and to avoid business that can be construed as unacceptable. One should avoid controversial business or discuss the cession before binding the business.

Following is an outline of some matters to look for in an audit. Note that this particular outline encompasses a broad scope, not just claims. Often, however, because claims is an area of particular focus, the reinsurer's auditors will be claims handlers. Further, this outline has greater applicability for a renewal since it doies not include much of the exposure analysis characteristic of a pre-binding audit.

The claims department budgets for auditing and coordinates its audit teams by bringing younger staff along to show them how the audit is accomplished. In doing so, the claims staff is better educated. Teaching is a broadening experience and the exposure helps the younger staff members. In addition, the claims auditors quite often review premium and underwriting matters while at the cedent's location.

Inspection of Records

In reinsurance, auditing is often called "inspection of records." This reflects the subject matter limitation. Auditing is considered the specialty of accountants and CPAs. The sophistication and testing methods are well defined for CPA auditors who face testing for standard practices. Reinsurance inspectors have more limited, industry specific goals; thus, the reinsurance process is casually defined.

Audits are focused in just one direction. The activity is confined to assuming reinsurers observing cedents. A given reinsurance contract may be one of a thousand assumed by a reinsurer in a given year. Because the audit is confined to the subject business, the scope precedents would be narrow with little overall credibility. Cedent audits of reinsurers are rarely done.

The assumer's perspective is motivated by a desire to learn more about the activities of the cedent and the developing results within the terms of the treaty. Thus, the subject business restriction is not viewed as limiting to reinsurers.

Reinsurers audit for many reasons:

1. *Prebinding Data Collection.* Developing information for pricing and understanding exposures.
2. *Underwriting Compliance Testing.* Is undertaken to make sure proper methods were employed and that the policies afforded coverage that was entirely permissible within the reinsurance contract.
3. *Accounting Checks.* Reports received are compared with appropriate cedent base documents, commonly referred to as "footings." Cash flow timing is observed.
4. *Claims Reviews.* Taken and often repeated annually to observe settlement and handling practices, to monitor case development, to measure and profile the spread and composition, and to check reserve levels.

Inspection Checkpoints

The following is a list of inspection checkpoints. The language may seem judgmental or biased. However, the test or question itself is neutral. Checking to see if commissions were excessive is due diligence. Finding such is another matter.

If a company is operating in an honest, ethical manner it should not resist a fair inspection by an interested, subscribing reinsurer. Typically both gain by the visitation. The reinsurer gains a better understanding of the cedent's subject business. In the course of the review, the reinsurer may observe an inefficiency or inappropriate case reserve. Because reinsurers see hundreds of situations each year, they may be in a position to suggest alternatives or improvements. Simply pointing to a shortcoming in procedures allows the cedent to address the matter, perhaps before a problem arises.

These checkpoints are intended to illustrate the scope and target perspectives. Some are quite specific, others are broadly stated.

1. Coverage Checks
   A. Was the contract wording ambiguous?
   B. Did the submission contain inaccurate data?
   C. Did the net retention meet representations?
      How was the net defined in the submission and contract?
      Was the net automatic and consistent?
      Was any part of the net ceded elsewhere?
      Were there proportional cessions within the net retained line?
   D. Is there evidence of business ceded 100 percent?
   E. Were there any circular cessions?
      Did the company cede to subsidiary companies?
      Was intercompany pooled business ceded to the reinsurance?
      Were any accounts ceded twice—double dipping?
      Did dummy frontings exist?
2. Underwriting Checks
   A. Did the company fail to underwrite as represented?
      Did all cessions match the exclusion guidelines?
      Did any claims arise from excluded business?
   B. Was any excluded business ceded?
      Were casualty exclusions double checked?
      Was any pool and association business ceded?
   C. Were exposures understated?
      Did law firms have more than 10 percent securities and exchange work?
      Did subcontractors have certificates of insurance?
      Did contractors perform work offshore in violation of a marine exclusion?
   D. Was binding authority delegated?
      Does the contract permit delegating of underwriting?
      Does the contract permit semiautomatic treaties?
      Does the contract permit programs?
      Are all MGA agreements available for inspection?
      Are any MGAs or programs unprofitable; if so why?
      Did the company audit MGAs and delegated authorities? If so, the audit should be reviewed.
   E. Were any cessions ceded retroactively?

   F. Did any policies have limits higher than allowed?

   G. Did any business violate written or implied warrantees?

   H. Did the profile of kind, class, and line of business match original representations?

3. Accounting Checks

   A. Did reports match base data or footings?

   B. Did subject premium tie to the annual statement?

   C. Did GNWPI and GNEPI match original representations?

       Were booking procedures appropriate?

       Did the UPR match that estimated in theory?

       Was any premium ceded from prior years?

   D. Did bookings preserve calendar and accident years properly?

   E. Was acquisition cost reasonable?

       Does a cap exist and was it met?

       Were overrides included as underlying commissions?

       Did any individual accounts deviate from the norm?

       Have associated companies or agents padded commissions?

       Was any business churned?

       Did any evidence exist of pyramided commissions?

       Were accounts booked on a net or nett basis?

   F. What can be learned from a profile of the source of the business?

   G. Were bookings delayed?

       Did cash flow swiftly after receipt?

       Did cash flow meet the contract schedule?

   H. Did the contract have a contingent of profit commission?

       Was the timing of the contingent commission proper?

       Was the sliding scale calculated correctly?

   I. Did ceded accounts have contingencies from third parties?

       Were such contingencies properly included as subject premium?

       Were commissions deducted from profit commissions received?

   J. Was earned interest included in the reports?

       How was interest on funds addressed in the contract?

       Was interest added to GNWPI?

   K. Did the contract include incoming or outgoing portfolios?

       Were accounts booked to the wrong year?

       Were extensions to prior year policies included in the current year?

   L. Were subrogations processed properly?

   M. Did effective and expiration dates lie within permissible dates?

   N. Will the company release internal audit reports?

       Were corrections evident?

       Were net corrections permitted?

       How were accounts reconciled?

4. Claim Checks
   A. Did the filed payment requests match abstracts?
   B. Did the cause of loss fall within the exclusions?
   C. Did the date of loss fall within policy effective dates and reinsurance effective dates?
      Were claims applied to the correct treaty year?
      Does the loss follow the ceded premium?
   D. How were aggregate claims handled?
   E. Was claim handling consistent by policy type?
   F. Was the caseload appropriate for the staff size and experience level?
   G. Was in-house loss adjustment expense passed off as if outside expense?
   H. Were any claims phoney?
   I. Was reserving proper?
   J. Were settlement practices appropriate?
   K. Was subrogation processed properly?
   L. Were multiple claim event controls appropriate?
      What controls were in place?
      Did catastrophe claims include liability losses?
      Did the cedent capture all accumulated claims within an event?
5. Data Processing
   A. How was EDP controlled?
      Is access restricted?
      Who can affect changes and corrections?
      How are accounts reconciled?
      How is cash matched to reports?
   B. Do sample file abstracts match EDP records?
   C. Do unusual items exist?
      Are there negative premiums?
      Are there negative payments?
      Does any negative subrogation exist?
   D. Were transactions codes proper?
      Do code conflicts exist?
      Does the summary by code type match the overall total?

SUMMARY

Chapter 12 stressed the flow of information from the accounting staff to underwriting and management. The claims staff has a similar position and responsibility.

In the course of assessing claims, any unusual, serious, large, or objectionable event should be reported to underwriting and management. Single events may be important. Early recognition of trends is also vital. Perhaps the key word is "probable," for the claims staff is in a position to observe developing situations and can project from early information what will evolve in time.

We have also focused on matters that cause disputes between cedents and reinsurers. These are pivotal situations where fundamentals can be illustrated. Typically a disagreement will arise in the interpretation of a procedure or intent. A clear understanding of the fundamentals often leads to a resolution. At times arbitration is necessary to resolve the dispute. However, in the normal course of processing claims, there is excellent cooperation between cedents and reinsurers. For example, they discuss divergent assessments over potentials and often reach agreement as to the appropriate amount for reserves. Reinsurers offer effective suggestions on handling specific cases. Since they are in a position to observe many claims and many techniques, reinsurance claims administrators hold the appropriate expertise and perspective to offer help with a difficult situation.

14

FINANCIAL EVALUATION

COMPANY
- **Ownership**
- **Affiliated Companies**
- **Structure**
- **Key Staff**

CAPITAL AND SURPLUS
- **Shareholders Equity Profile**
- **Change in Shareholders Equity Relativity**
- **Change in Assets Relativity**
- **Policyholder's Surplus Profile**
- **Change in Surplus Test**
- **Net Liabilities to Surplus Test**
- **Net Writings to Surplus Test**
- **Net Leverage Test**
- **Ceded Leverage Test**
- **Gross Leverage Test**

WRITINGS
- **Production Source Profile**
- **Line of Business Profile**
- **Change in Mix of Business Profile**
- **Long Tail Business to Total Writings Relativity**
- **Geographic Distribution Profiles**
- **Change in Net Written Premium Test**
- **Direct Written Premium to Policyholder's Surplus Test**

REINSURANCE
- **Schedule F Profile**
- **Five Largest Reinsurers Profile, Based on Losses**
- **Reinsurance Recoverable to Surplus Test**
- **Maximum Net Retained Line to Surplus Relativity**
- **Surplus Aid to Surplus Test**

RESULTS
- **Combined Ratio Test**
- **Operating Ratio Test**

RESERVES
- **Reserve Change Test**
- **Reported Loss Reserve to Surplus Test**
- **Reserve Development to Surplus Tests**
- **Estimated Reserve Deficiency to Surplus Test**
- **IBNR to Total Loss Reserve Relativity**

EXPENSES
- **Internal Expense Profile**
- **Other Expense Profile**

INVESTMENTS
- **Investment Profile**
- **Yield Test**
- **Net Investment Relativity**
- **Return on Policyholder's Surplus Test**
- **Quick Liquidity Test**
- **Current Liquidity Test**
- **Overall Liquidity Test**
- **Liabilities to Liquid Assets Test**
- **Agents Balances to Net Policyholder's Surplus Test**

SUMMARY

There are two sides to reinsurance: ceding and assuming.

The ceding reinsurer is concerned about the staying power of each reinsurer. Will a catastrophic loss bankrupt the reinsurer so that each paid claim into the reinsurance contract is only partially recovered? Or will bad business practices over time force the reinsurer out of business before the cedent's needs are fully met?

Cedents pay reinsurance premiums in full by about 24 months. However, they recover paid losses slowly over a period of many years. For example; following a large property catastrophe, the reserves are typically posted to 95 percent within two years and perhaps to 99 percent in three years. However, payments might not reach the highest layer for five to seven years (see Exhibit 14.1). The casualty developmental tail extends five to seven years for automobile claims, longer for general liability and worker's compensation claims, and possibly beyond 20 years for some er-

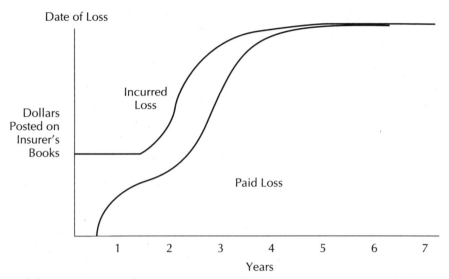

Exhibit 14.1.   Sample Property Development

rors and omissions or professional liability claims. Payments are even slower (see Exhibit 14.2).

Thus, any prudent buyer or cedent will check to be sure each reinsurer will be sufficiently financially healthy to survive beyond the anticipated tail of the particular reinsurance contract. The object is to build long-lasting cedent/assumer relationships that will extend through many renewals, such

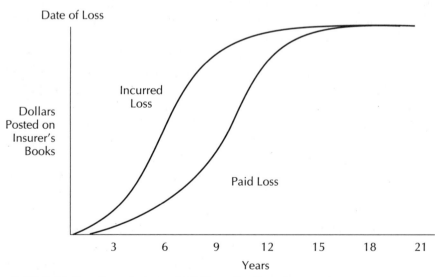

Exhibit 14.2.   Sample Long Tail Casualty Development

that the total premium will exceed the total recovered, while providing the cedent a vehicle to transfer some of its concerns from year to year. The reinsurer gains a reasonable profit and the carrier gains a satisfactory cost/recovery ratio over the term of the transfer.

The cedent's review is a detailed, continuous, and objective solvency analysis.

The assuming reinsurer's review may be more subjective. Will the subject business be profitable? The reinsurer may not be concerned about exposures not covered by their contract. For example, a property reinsurer may not be concerned about a risky liability segment written by the cedent, as long as the reinsurer is satisfied that the property business holds an attractive profit potential.

The subjective measures deal with potentials for the business and may not have a prior historical basis for assessment. If the line or type is new to the cedent or if the exposure is perceived to be different, then objective calculations are not possible, or perhaps not sufficiently credible. Thus the assessment is judgmental rather than calculated.

The assuming reinsurers are concerned about the ability of the cedent to produce, select, underwrite, price, and administer the business. They will also closely review how the cedent handles claims.

Given these two different perspectives, are there common tests or questions in the financial review? One must appreciate the fact there is great variance among different companies in the methods used for financial review. This chapter shall describe some of the commonly used measurements.

Good and bad scores are relative. Each of the tests or measures should be compared to a known standard. Because the insurance business is cyclical, the norms shift from year to year. Understanding today's norms requires a substantial amount of research.

Benchmarks separate acceptable scores from unacceptable ones. They exist as minimal acceptable levels. Many companies may exceed the benchmark of a particular test. The company will make a decision based on the overall analysis.

The hard part of financial evaluation is assessing these matters at the onset, before the relationship provides time to work together and observe the stature of the cedent company.

There are several rating organizations that undertake in-depth financial reviews of the major insurers and compile overall ratings of financial strength and claim payment ability, including A. M. Best & Company, Standard & Poor's Corporation, Demotech, Inc., Duff & Phelps Credit Rating Company, Moody's Investor Services, Insurstat, Insurance Solvency International, and others. Tech Financial Corporation is an example of a small company that provides in-depth analysis of individual companies with an effort to show

how that company works and how its results compare to recent industry averages. The following sample analysis has been provided by Tech Financial Corporation.

1. COMPANY

1a. Ownership
Who owns the company? Has this ownership been stable? If it is a stock company, has the price been stable? Have there been large blocks of stock traded? Do the senior officers have a significant ownership position?

1b. Affiliated Companies
List all companies. Do they pool experience? How do they prohibit circular transfers?

1c. Structure
Is the company a stock, mutual, or other? Does the company operate with a strong home office core? Do regional offices hold significant self-governing authority?

1d. Key Staff
List leaders: senior management, head underwriter, head financial executive, head claims, etc. What is their experience? How long have they been at this company? What is their reputation inside and outside the company?

2. CAPITAL AND SURPLUS

2a. Shareholders Equity Profile
Shareholders equity is available from the company's audit report. It is applicable only to stock companies.

Profile Shareholders Equity	Stock value	Paid in capital	Retained earnings	Equity
# _____ Shares at 12/___ Dividends to parent prior year Net income prior year # _____ Shares at 12/___ Dividends to parent current year Net income current year # _____ Shares at 12/___				

Remark: Look for stability.

2b. Change in Shareholders Equity Relativity

This measure is one part of total assets. It is sometimes valuable to compare the growth in equity to the overall growth in assets.

Relativity Shareholders Equity Growth	
Equity at 12/31/___	=
Equity at 12/31/___	=
Relativity as a %	=

Remark: Look for patterned growth. If any significant swings exist, upward or downward, inquire.

2c. Change in Assets Relativity

Growth in the asset base is an indicator of overall financial improvement.

Relativity Asset Growth	
Current assets	=
Prior assets	=
Relativity as a %	=

Consolidated industry relativity . . . . _____%

    Remark: Does this track growth in shareholders equity?

2d. Policyholder's Surplus Profile

The following profile displays the changes in policyholder's surplus (Phs) over the year. These should be reviewed for unusual items and details of unusual size.

Profile Policyholder's Surplus Detail	
Prior Policyholder's surplus	=
Net income	=
Net unrealized capital gain	=
Change in nonadmitted assets	=
Change in unauthorized reins	=
Change in foreign exchange	=
Excess of statutory over statement reserves	=
Paid in capital	=
Transferred to policyholders surplus	=
Transferred from policyholders surplus	=
Paid in surplus	=
Transferred to surplus	=
Transferred from surplus	=
Net home office remittances	=
Dividends to stockholders	=
Change in treasury stock	=
Extraordinary taxes	=

Aggregate write-ins	=
Current policyholders surplus	=
Change in policyholders surplus	=

2e. Change in Surplus Test

This IRIS test is the main measure of improvement in a company's total financial picture. A small drop may occur from time to time, thus the failure point has been set at −10 percent, a significant drop. The test is also said to fail if the growth is above 50 percent. Such large increases are considered an indication of instability. It is sometimes related to changes in ownership.

| IRIS Test
Change in Surplus		Current Year	Prior Year
Underwriting expenses	a		
Underwriting aggregate write-ins	b		
Underwriting comm and brokerage	c		
Underwriting tax, licencing, and fees	d		
Subtotal .5 (a + b) + c + d	e		
Net written premium	f		
Ratio (e/f)	g		
Unearned premium reserve less credits	h		
Equity (g × h)	i		
Policyholder's surplus	j		
IRIS formula (j1 + i1 − g2 − i2)/j2			
Change in surplus	=		

Remark: Compare the pattern and trend of policyholder's surplus with the growth in assets and equity.

2f. Net Liabilities to Surplus Test

This test is a measure of leverage of unpaid obligations to surplus, after assumed and ceded reinsurance.

| Test
Net Liability to Surplus	
Net liabilities	=
Policyholder's surplus	=
Test relativity as a %	=

Normal range . . . . _____%
Test failure . . . . .above 470%
Consolidated industry relativity . . . . _____%
Remark: Look for consistency and check severe fluctuations.

2g. Net Writings to Surplus Test

This IRIS test reflects the leverage of the company's net volume (after assumed and ceded reinsurance) to surplus. A low, conservative leverage provides a cushion of financial strength to absorb a period of above average losses.

IRIS Test Net written premium/Surplus	
Net written premium =	
Policyholder's surplus =	
Test relativity as a % =	

Normal range . . . . _____%
Test failure . . . . .above 300%
Consolidated industry relativity . . . . _____%
Remark: Graphing this test provides excellent perspective, suggest doing so with the company's measures shown against the industry averages.

2h. Net Leverage Test

This test is the sum of tests 2e and 2f, NWP/Phs and Net Liability/Phs. It measures the company's net accumulated exposures from pricing errors and errors in estimating liabilities, as related to surplus.

Test Net Leverage	
Net written premium/policyholder's surplus (Test 2g) =	
Net liability/policyholder's surplus (Test 2f) =	
Test relativity as a % =	

Normal range . . . . _____%
Test failure . . . . .above 750%
Consolidated industry relativity . . . . _____%

2i. Ceded Leverage Test

This test measures the proportion of the company's premiums and liability ceded to nonaffiliated reinsurers and foreign affiliates, net of any funds held. It reflects the dependence of the company on such reinsurance.

Test Ceded Leverage	
Ceded reinsurance premiums	a
Ceded to U.S. affiliates	b
Adjusted cessions (a−b)	c
Adjustment ratio (c/a)	d
Ceded IBNR	e
Ceded agents balances due	f
Ceded agents balances deferred	g
Subtotal (e + f + g)	h
Adjusted sum (h × d)	i
Ceded unearned premium	j

Unpaid loss recoverable	k
Reinsurance funds held	l
Total (i + j + k + l)	m
Policyholder's surplus	n
Test relativity as a %	=

Normal range . . . . _____%
Test failure . . . . above 100%
Consolidated industry relativity . . . . _____%

2j. Gross Leverage Test

This test measures overall leverage and should be considered in relation to the net and ceded leverage.

Test
Gross Leverage
Net leverage (Test 2g)   =
Ceded leverage (Test 2h) =
Test relativity as a %   =

Normal range . . . . _____%
Test failure . . . . above 850%
Consolidated industry relativity . . . . _____%
Remark: Compare all three leverage tests in concert and individually. One can learn by studying the parts as well as the whole.

3. WRITINGS

3a. Production Source Profile

A questionnaire varies by line and is, therefore, beyond the scope of this book.

3b. Line of Business Profile

Profile	Direct and Assumed		
Line of Business	Total	Percent	Industry %
Liability and reinsurance 30B =			
Property and reinsurance 30A =			
Combined property and casualty =			
Other and reinsurance 30C + 30D =			
Total =			

Remark: This display is particularly meaningful, as it shows the four main segments available in the annual statement. Reinsurance lines 30A, 30B, 30C, and 30D refer to assumed reinsurance lines of business in the annual statement.

3c. Change in Mix of Business Profile

The mix of business within the company's portfolio is a key component of the analysis of a company. It is vital to understand the change in mix, particularly in recent years.

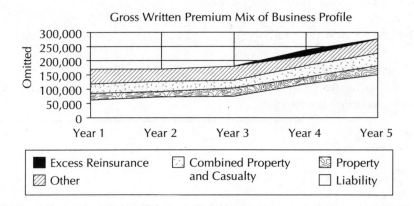

Gross Written Premium Mix of Business Profile

■ Excess Reinsurance	▨ Combined Property and Casualty	▨ Property
▨ Other		☐ Liability

Remark: The above style graph is particularly good for showing trends in mix. It is important to understand that the liability component has grown significantly industrywide, thus many companies display increases in this component.

3d. Long Tail Business to Total Writings Relativity

This measure is displayed here as one indication of the kinds of business written. This focus is on the liability exposures where claims take a long time to reach ultimate or final payout. This perspective is important when reviewing reserves.

Relativity Long Tail Business	Direct and Assumed Total	Percent	Industry %
Medical malpractice	=		
Worker's compensation	=		
Other liability	=		
Reinsurance 30B	=		
Subtotal long tail	=		
Total all business	=		

Remark: This relativity is interesting to observe over time. Reinsurance 30B is long tail/liability reinsurance assumed.

3e. Geographic Distribution Profiles

The following are two displays of geographic distribution. Assumed reinsurance is not included, since the reinsurance geographic designation often refers to the location or source of business rather than to the exposure.

Profile Zone Distribution	Direct written premium	Percent	Industry %
New England	=		
Atlantic Coast	=		
Southeast	=		
Mideast (East of Mississippi River)	=		
Midwest (West of Mississippi River)	=		
Southern Plains	=		
West Coast	=		
Canada and other	=		
Total all territories	=		

Remark: There are many ways to set the zones; it is best to do it consistently. One important perspective here is whether the company is a regional carrier or national carrier. What is its growth trend? Is it increasing its market share in existing territories or expanding to new territories? Another measure is to look at the size and distribution of the five largest states.

3f. Change in Net Written Premium Test

This IRIS test is a measure of aggressiveness, and a high score is considered to be a sign of lack of restraint. Since premiums are one indication of underwriting exposure, rapid growth may be a concern. This is one of the early warning tests of financial trouble, since a pressing need for cash may drive a company to relax its underwriting standards.

IRIS Test Net written premium growth	Net written premium	% Change
1986 =		
1987 =		
1988 =		
1989 =		
1990 =		

IRIS test failure . . . . .above or below range 25% to +25%
Consolidated industry relativity . . . . ._____%
Remark: This is another test that is well suited for graphing. Compare four- to five-year patterns of the company with the overall industry.

3g. Direct Written Premium to Policyholder's Surplus Test

This test reflects the position before reinsurance is assumed or ceded. It is a leverage indicator, where higher relativities are considered aggressive and therefore uncomfortable.

IRIS Test DWP/Surplus	
Direct written premium	=
Policyholder's surplus	=
Test relativity as a %	=

Normal range ...._____%
Test failure .... above 280%
Consolidated industry relativity ...._____%
Remark: Compare with the net written premium test illustrated above.

4. REINSURANCE

4a. Schedule F Profile
This profile is offered as information about preferences in placing reinsurance.

Profile Type of Reinsurer		Recoverable on paid losses	Unpaid losses	Total	Percent
Non-U.S. affiliates	=				
U.S. affiliates	=				
U.S. reinsurers	=				
Pools and associations	=				
Other reinsurers	=				
Totals	=				

Remark: If several annual statements are available, look for consistency. Also look for reinsurers in financial difficulty or those in transition financially. Are reinsurers leaving the business should be noted.

4b. Five Largest Reinsurers Profile, Based on Losses
This section is important since the largest reinsurers represent the core of the ceded program. One should consider the proportion ceded, plus the reputation and ratings within this key group.

4c. Reinsurance Recoverable to Surplus Test
This test measures amounts recoverable from reinsurers, which is a credit or reduction of liabilities (rather than an asset) in statutory accounting. Reinsurance recoverable is exposed to credit or security risk. This has been a major factor in insolvencies. The ratio to policyholder's surplus is one way to put this item into perspective.

Test Reinsurance Recoverables to Surplus	
Unearned premium	=
Unpaid reinsured loss	=
Reinsured IBNR	=
Funds held	=
Sum less funds held	=
Policyholder's surplus	=
Test relativity as a %	=

Test failure .... above 50%

4d. Maximum Net Retained Line to Surplus Relativity

This measurement has the basic premise that in order to make the law of large numbers work, the company should not take up any single risk or exposure that amounts to more than a couple of points of surplus. Scores above 3 percent indicate aggressiveness; too much of that is negative. Worker's compensation statutory limits are excluded from this measurement.

Relativity Maximum Net Retained Line to Surplus	
Maximum net line	=
Policyholder's surplus	=
Test relativity as a %	=

Normal range . . . . _____%
Consolidated industry relativity is not available.

4e. Surplus Aid to Surplus Test

This IRIS test measures the use of reinsurance to bolster surplus. Since surplus is the key to many financial tests, any action to mask deficiency is a concern. This test is an estimate of the amount of such aid secured. High scores may indicate that other tests should be recalculated.

IRIS Test Surplus Aid to Surplus	
Ceded Commission and brokerage	a
Unearned premium reserve U.S. reinsurance	=
Unearned premium reserve pools and association	=
Unearned premium reserve other nonaffiliates	=
Total unearned premium reserve ceded nonaffiliates	b
Gross written premium ceded affiliates	=
Gross written premium ceded nonaffiliates	=
Total gross ceded premium	c
Surplus aid (a $\times$ b/c)	=
Policyholder's surplus	=
Test relativity as a %	=

Test failure . . . . above 25%
Consolidated industry relativity . . . . _____%

5. RESULTS

5a. Combined Ratio Test

This test is the standard trade ratio or combined ratio used to measure underwriting profitability. Dividends are not included in this section. The test is the two-year result.

Test Combined Ratio		Current year	Prior year	Two-year total
Net written premium		a		
Net earned premium		b		
Incurred loss		c		
Loss adjustment expense		d		
Underwriting expense		e		
Policyholder's dividends		f		
Loss ratio	(c/b)	g		
LAE ratio	(d/b)	h		
Expense ratio	(e/a)	i		
Policyholder's dividend ratio	(f/a)	j		
Combined ratio	(sum)	=		

Test failure . . . . .above 115%
Consolidated industry relativities . . . . _____%

Remark: The above chart displays a two-year calculation. It is far better to review this over a longer period. Again compare this company to the industry averages.

5b. Operating Ratio Test

This IRIS test adds to the combined ratio relativities of other major profit/ loss factors, taken as ratios to written premium. It is a measure of overall profitability. Investment income and dividends are put into perspective in this test. The IRIS test is the two-year ratio.

IRIS Test Operating Ratio	Current year	Prior year	Two-year total
Combined ratio (5a)	a		
Stockholder's dividends	b		
Dividends/new written premium (b/net written premium)	c		
Net investment gain	d		
Gain as a credit (−1) x d	e		
Net gain/Net written premium (e/Net written premium)	f		
Other income and charge-offs	g		
Charge-offs as a credit (−1)	h		
Charge-offs/net written premium (h/net written premium)	i		
Taxes	j		
Taxes/net written premium (j/net written premium)	k		
Operating ratio (a + c + f + i + k)	=		

IRIS test failure . . . . .above 100%

Remark: There is so much emphasis within the industry on the combined ratio that often the broad perspective is subordinated. How does the company make its money? The operating ratio is a good test for conservatism. Does the company hold its authorization of exposures in line with its investment potential? Another consideration is whether the dividends are rewards from profit or kept high even if the year is in loss.

6. RESERVES

6a. Reserve Change Test
This test expresses the growth in reserves during the year. Any variance that is sizeable should be noted, with an explanation sought. Our measure assumes that reductions are better than increases, but large decreases should be investigated.

Test Change in Reserves	
Loss reserves ending	=
Loss reserves starting	=
Test relativity as a %	=

Test failure . . . . above 15%
Remark: How does this measure compare with the growth in premium?

6b. Reported Loss Reserve to Surplus Test
This test displays the amount of reserve carried for past events as a ratio to surplus. A high score reflects potential problems. If the reserves are substantially understated, a high score then indicates recovery will be harder due to adverse leverage.

Test Reported Loss Reserves to Surplus	
Net outstanding loss	=
Net outstanding LAE	=
Total reported reserves	=
Policyholder's surplus	=
Test relativity as a %	=

Test failure . . . . above 200%

6c. Reserve Development to Surplus Tests
These IRIS tests relate the reserve development reported in Schedule P to surplus. Since the change may be an increase or decrease, the two-year statistic is more credible. On the other hand, the current year relativity is an earlier indicator of potential problems. A high score indicates the company is adjusting its view of past exposures upward, obviously not a positive sign.

IRIS Test One-Year Loss Development
Current year development =   Policyholder's surplus   =   One-year relativity as a % =

IRIS test failure . . . . .above 25%

Consolidated industry relativity . . . . _____%

IRIS Test Two-Year Loss Development
Development two years   =   Policyholder's surplus   =   Two-year relativity as a % =

IRIS test failure . . . . .above 25%

Consolidated industry relativity . . . . _____%

6d. Estimated Reserve Deficiency to Surplus Test

This IRIS test measures the change in loss reserves to NEP. If the current period is different than the past two years, that amount is the estimated deficiency. Positive numbers indicate deficiency, while negatives reflect redundancy.

IRIS Test Estimated Reserves		Current year	1st prior year	2nd prior year
Loss reserves	a			
Loss expenses	b			
Reinsurance loss payable	c			
One-year reserve development	d1			
Two-year reserve development	d2			
Earned premiums	e			
Reserve ratio (a + b + c + d)/e	f			
Prior year's ratio (f1 + f2)/2	g			
Estimated deficiency g(e) − a − b − c	h			
Policyholder's surplus	i			
Test relativity as a %				

IRIS test failure . . . . .above 15%

Consolidated industry relativity . . . . _____%

6e. IBNR to Total Loss Reserve Relativity

This relativity is sometimes referred to as the "IBNR" loading. It relates the portion of reserved for unknown events and understated case reserves to total reserves. This score should be higher for a company writing a significant portion of long tail business. IBNR is an estimate, and the industry has experienced considerable volatility in such reserves.

Relativity IBNR Loading	
Direct case reserves	a
Assumed case reserves	b
Ceded reserves as a credit	c
Net loss adjustment reserves	d
Direct IBNR	e
Assumed IBNR	f
Ceded IBNR as a credit	g
Net IBNR (e + f + g)	h
Net reserves (a + b + c + d + h)	i
Relativity as a %	=

Remark: This should be reviewed over several years, for perspective on trend.

7. EXPENSES

7a. Internal Expense Profile

Expenses have been separated into two parts for ease in analysis. The first part relates to staff, equipment, rent, and associated expenses.

Profile Internal Expenses		Expenditure	Percent	Industry %
Salaries	=			
Other wage-related expenses	=			
Travel	=			
General	=			
Rent	=			
Equipment related	=			
Legal and auditing	=			
Total internal expenses	=			

Remark: Salary is one focal point. Does the company carry high salaries compared to the industry averages, and is this problematic?

7b. Other Expense Profile

This section displays all other expenses.

Profile Other Expenses		Expenditure	Percent	Industry %
Net claim adjustment expenses	=			
Net commission and brokerage	=			
Taxes, licenses, and fees	=			
Real estate expenses	=			
Real estate taxes	=			
Reimbursement of accident and health	=			
All other	=			
Total other expenses	=			

8. INVESTMENTS

8a. Investment Profile

The format for these profiles flows directly from the annual statement.

Profile Investments		Valuation	Percent	Industry %
Cash	=			
Short-term investments	=			
Unaffiliated bonds	=			
Unaffiliated stocks	=			
Affiliated bonds	=			
Affiliated stocks	=			
Real estate	=			
Other	=			
Total	=			

Profile Bond Quality		Valuation	Percent	Industry %
Highest quality	=			
High quality	=			
Medium quality	=			
Low quality	=			
Lower quality	=			
In or near default	=			
Total bonds	=			

Profile Bond Maturity Scale		Valuation	Percent	Industry %
1 Year	=			
1–5 Year	=			
5–10 Year	=			
10–20 Year	=			
20+ years	=			
Total	=			

Remark: Do these graphs display a straightforward investment plan? Is there a preference for unaffiliated bonds? How much was short-term investment as opposed to long-term? Have they selected high-quality issues, with good spread in maturity? If time permits, look over the selection of individual stocks and bonds. Are there highly speculative issues? Are junk bonds evident?

8b. Yield Test

This IRIS test displays income from investments as a percentage of cash plus invested assets less borrowed money. The higher the yield, the better the result of the company's investment strategy. This test is an important measure of the financial operations of the company.

IRIS Test Yield		Current year	Prior year
Total investments + cash	=		
Interest, dividend, and real estate income	=		
Borrowed money	=		
Total net of borrowed money	=		
Average net holdings	=		
Net investment income	=		
Test relativity as a %	=		

IRIS test failure . . . . .below 5%
Consolidated industry relativity . . . . _____%
Remark: Review this over time if possible. Has the result been consistent? Is it likely to improve?

8c. Net Investment Relativity

This measure is part of the operating ratio test. The ratio of yield to written premium puts investment gains into perspective in a manner similar to that used for underwriting.

Relativity Net Investment Gain		Current year	Prior year
Net investment yield	=		
Net written premium	=		
Test relativity as a %	=		

Consolidated industry relativity . . . . _____%

8d. Return on Policyholder's Surplus Test

This test relates the total return of underwriting and investments, after taxes and dividends, to the company's net worth at the beginning of the year.

Test Return on Surplus		Current year	Prior year
Net income	=		
Policyholder's surplus	=		
Test relativity as a %	=		

Test failure . . . . .below 3%

8e. Quick Liquidity Test

This test relates those assets that can be readily turned into cash to net liabilities. These "quick assets" can be converted into cash with little effect on surplus. The test indicates the company's ability to reduce its outstanding liabilities without borrowing money or selling long-term investments in an untimely fashion.

Test Quick Liquidity	
Cash	=
Short-term investments	=
One-year unaffiliated bonds	=
Five-year government bonds	=
Unaffiliated stocks	=
Discount stocks 20%	=
Total quick assets	=
Total liabilities	=
Amounts to/from affiliates	=
Negative liabilities	=
Net liabilities	=
Test relativity as a %	=

Test failure . . . . .below 15%

8f. Current Liquidity Test

This IRIS test measures the proportion of cash, unaffiliated investments, and encumbrances on other properties to net liabilities plus ceded balances payable. This measures the proportion of liabilities covered by nonaffiliated investments. When the ratio is under 100 percent, the company must rely on investments in affiliates or its ability to turn premium balances into material assets, in order to maintain solvency.

Test Current Liquidity	
Net investments (Test 8a)	=
Net liabilities	=
Reinsurance balance payable	=
Adjusted net liabilities	=
Test relativity as a %	=

Test failure . . . . .below 90%
Consolidated industry relativity . . . . _____%

8g. Overall Liquidity Test

This test relates total admitted assets to the total liabilities less conditional reserves. This measure does not consider the quality or marketability of assets and assumes the collectability of all amounts recoverable from reinsurers on UPR, O/S, and IBNR. In this respect, it is like the tests for current liquidity;

however, this test includes assets that were not invested. This test also relates to leverage.

Test Overall Liquidity	
Total admitted assets	=
Net liabilities (Test 8d)	=
Test relativity as a %	=

Test failure . . . . .below 120%
Consolidated industry relativity . . . . _____%
Remark: As with leverage, compare these individually as well as overall.

8h. Liabilities to Liquid Assets Test
This IRIS test is a measure of the company's overall ability to meet its financial demands. It provides a rough indication of the possible implications for policyholders if the company must be liquidated.

IRIS Test Liabilities to Liquid Assets	
Total Liabilities	=
Agents balances ceded	=
Premium balances ceded	=
Adjusted total balances	=
Cash + invested assets	=
Deferred agents balances	=
Deferred ceded agents balance	=
Real estate encumberances	=
Interest, dividends, and real estate	=
Investments in parent	=
Liquid assets	=
Test relativity as a %	=

Test failure . . . . .above 105%
Consolidated industry relativity . . . . _____%
Remark: This is another test of liquidity in that it measures total potential need as compared to assets that may be readily liquidated or sold.

8i. Agents Balances to Net Policyholder's Surplus Test
This IRIS test takes premium and agents balances collectable and relates this to policyholder's surplus, which has been reduced by the amount of premium and agents balances. A high ratio reflects a loss of investment potential on funds that have not been collected. Poor scores have been common in insolvencies. It also may be indicative of problems or disputes within the unpaid balances.

IRIS Test Agents Balances/Net Surplus	
Premium and agents balances	=
Reinsurance balances	=
Total balances	=
Policyholder's surplus	=
Premium and agents balances	=
Net surplus	=
Test relativity as a %	=

IRIS test failure . . . . .above 40%
Consolidated industry relativity . . . . _____%

SUMMARY

This chapter outlines several of the tests used in assessing an insurer's solvency and ability to pay claims. Weaknesses should be investigated.

Remember, reinsurers are in the business of making profits while helping insurers do their business better. Thus a weakness may indicate a problem that is merely motivating the insurer to seek assistance from a reinsurer. On the other hand weakness may mean the company has a poor foundation, inadequate pricing concepts, or an inability to handle day-to-day problems. Most companies have problems from time to time; sometimes it is necessary to note the single poor score and wait to observe the result of the same test a year later.

In one case, the client may only need a boost to overcome its situation. In another the weakness may preclude the reinsurer from any chance of providing its services in profit.

Just calculating the test scores is not sufficient. One must have sufficient understanding of the test to ascertain what is being measured and then how to proceed once the score is known.

Research is quite important. In order to grasp the meaning of a particular score, it is necessary to understand the trends within the industry. What might have been standard or normal a few years ago might not be average today. Some insurance people feel they have a handle on these matters, so they apply their gut feelings in decisions. This text has supplied 48 commonly used tests; there are many others. Is it reasonable to assume one can grasp the criss-crossing trends in so many tests and separate a good score from a poor one? No, that is simply not practical. Research into the industry norms is quite necessary to complete the assessment.

Further, interpretation of the scores varies according to the use of the test. For example, a ceding reinsurer may require that its casualty reinsurers be A rated, or better, with at least $250 million in capital. The benchmark for property reinsurers may be \$100 million in capital and a B or better rating. The longer developmental tail of casualty reinsurance motivates a higher standard. Also, property catastrophe reinsurance tends to be taken in small shares, so it may be that greater numbers of property reinsurers are necessary, and the same high standard does not permit sufficient capacity. There are not enough of the highest ranking reinsurers to cover the full catastrophe need for all companies.

The solvency and financial testing is typically accomplished with publicly available information or with prepared detail transferred in confidence. Some of the items, such an inquiry into capabilities of certain management functions are the direct result of visits to the cedent company.

15

CONTRACT WORDING

IMPORTANT CONSIDERATIONS
INTERESTS AND LIABILITIES AGREEMENT
- Preamble
- Business Covered
- Limit and Retention
- Follow the Fortunes
- Term and Cancellation
- Territory
- Exclusions
- Original Conditions
- Accounts and Remittances
- Ceding Commission
- Commission Adjustment
- Notice of Loss and Loss Settlements
- Loss Adjustment Expense
- Extra-Contractual Obligations
- Losses in Excess of Policy Limits
- Honorable Undertaking
- Offset
- Access to Records
- Errors and Omissions
- Taxes
- Currency
- Federal Excise Tax
- Security and Unauthorized Reinsurance
- Insolvency
- Arbitration
- Service of Suit
- Third-Party Beneficiary

- **Intermediary**
- **Waiver**
- **Conflict of Law and Severability**
- **Assignment**
- **Negotiated Agreement**
- **Surplus Cession**
- **Limit and Retention (for Excess of Loss Treaties)**
- **Net Retained Lines (for Excess of Loss Treaties)**
- **Definition of Ultimate Net Loss (for Excess of Loss Treaties)**
- **Notice of Loss and Loss Settlements (for Excess of Loss Treaties)**
- **Summary**

FACULTATIVE CERTIFICATE

SUMMARY

This chapter is not intended to be a definitive text on contract wording. Rather, it is intended to illustrate clauses that have been in use and are time tested, each with a brief description of the target concept.

If you are entering the reinsurance field, you would be well advised to collect various examples of each category. This suggestion is of benefit regardless of your area of specialization, as the contract language flows from the underwriter who negotiates and sets the terms and conditions to the accountant who books the statistics, to the claims person who oversees the primary carrier's handling to the account service representative who assists the cedent through the reporting process and to others who help these specialists perform.

IMPORTANT CONSIDERATIONS

The reinsurance contract must enunciate and clearly define, as far as practical, the essence of the negotiations, intent, and agreed terms so as to encompass the full understandings of the parties to the agreement.

It must be written to withstand the test of time and the potential of destructive evaluation of the content in an adversarial environment. Contracts with few losses and no disputes simply fade into history. Contracts with high activity and long developmental claim tail may emerge subject to interpretation many years in the future. Problems may fester over time to create departure of understanding and a hostile or adversarial dispute. Thus the contract must be comprehensive and painfully accurate.

Chapter 4 addressed the role of authorship. In the case of a direct writer, the contract is written by the reinsurer. In the broker market, the contract is written by the intermediary. The position of the author, whether one of the parties or an independent contractor, has a bearing on the terms, style, and perspectives of the contract wording.

INTERESTS AND LIABILITIES AGREEMENT

This agreement is applicable to broker market contracts and to contracts where several reinsurers participate in concert. The interests and liabilities agreement, commonly called the I&L, is a separate document attached to and forming a part of the reinsurance treaty. Typically it accomplishes the following:

1. Identifies the reinsurance contract to which it applies.
2. Sets shares of each subscribing reinsurer.
3. Sets the term applicable to the subscribing reinsurers.
4. Announces whether the subscribing reinsurers are participating on a joint or several basis.
5. Permits mutually agreed amendments or endorsements.

The I&L is typically just a single page, perhaps two, and serves as a signature page. It is the only page that specifies the subscribing reinsurers and their respective participations. It does so one or two pages at a time.

The subscribing reinsurers may know of the main reinsurer or lead underwriter, but they may or may not know of the entire list of reinsurers. If their share is joint they will indeed know the entire list. If their share is several, they may not know this information. In most situations, all parties with visible share sizes are known.

One of the more important terms in this clause is *several and not joint* applicability. In a joint agreement, the reinsurers would be obligated to respond to co-participants' payments that were not made. For example, in a joint agreement, if one reinsurer were to go bankrupt, the remaining reinsurers would have to pay their own part plus a prorated portion of any amount owed by the bankrupt reinsurer. In a several agreement, each reinsurer stands only for its respective share and is in no way obligated for shares held by other reinsurers. This is commonly called the joint and several clause, but the appropriate wording is "several and not joint." It is appropriate to incorporate severability in the I&L, because this is the point where each reinsurer signs.

INTERESTS AND LIABILITY AGREEMENT
for the
PROPERTY QUOTA SHARE REINSURANCE AGREEMENT
(Reference number J-99)
between

The MYTHICAL COMPANIES, which shall include:
ZEUS INSURANCE COMPANY, Hollywood, California
MYTHOS INDEMNITY, Salem, Massachusetts
(hereinafter together referred to as the "Company")

and

SPHINX REINSURANCE COMPANY, New York, New York
(hereinafter referred to as the "Subscribing Reinsurer")

The Company and the Subscribing Reinsurer agree as follows:

1. The Subscribing Reinsurer shall have a 2.0%, being $240,000 part of $12,000,000, participation in the interests, liabilities, and premiums of the "Reinsurer" as set forth in the Property Quota Share Reinsurance Agreement attached hereto and incorporated herein in its entirety by this reference.
   This individual participation shall be several and not joint with the participation of any other subscribing reinsurer.
2. The term of this Agreement shall commence on July 1, 19XX and shall be subject without limitation to the Term and Cancellation Article of the documentation attached hereto.
3. This agreement may be changed, altered, and amended as the parties may agree, provided such change, alteration, and amendment is evidenced by endorsement signed by authorized representatives of both the Company and the Subscribing Reinsurer.

In witness whereof, the parties hereto have caused this Agreement to be signed in duplicate by their representatives,

In Salem, Massachusetts, this ___day of _____, 19XX
By:_____ , On behalf of
ZEUS INSURANCE COMPANY, Salem, Massachusetts
MYTHOS INDEMNITY, Hollywood, California

and in New York, New York, this ___day of ___ , 19XX
By:_____ , On behalf of
SPHINX REINSURANCE COMPANY, New York, New York

Exhibit 15.1. Treaty Interests and Liabilities Agreement

Preamble

This clause names and identifies the contract. It names the cedent by its full corporate name and may specifically list each corporately owned entity that will be ceding business to the treaty.

Generally, the preamble will include wording to automatically extend coverage to new entities added to the corporate fleet. This applies to newly created subsidiaries as well as newly secured entities. (An endorsement adding a new entity, thereby changing the preamble, is unique in that it is one endorsement that is agreed upon in advance, or automatically agreed, yet in due course an endorsement will be submitted for signature. It is the only "automatic" coverage extension that requires an endorsement.)

The business of newly acquired companies that fits the definition of subject business is therefore automatically included at the time of its acquisition or formation. However, if the portfolio is sizeable or nonhomogeneous, it is likely that reinsurers will object to not having advance notice. The intent is to make the reinsurance contract flexible but not necessarily unbounded in its flexibility.

PROPERTY QUOTA SHARE REINSURANCE AGREEMENT
(Document reference number J-99)
between

The MYTHICAL COMPANIES, which shall include:
ZEUS INSURANCE COMPANY, Hollywood, California
MYTHOS INDEMNITY, Salem, Massachusetts
(hereinafter together referred to as the "Company")

and

the companies subscribing to the respective
Interests and Liabilities Agreements to which this Agreement is attached.
(hereinafter collectively referred to as the "Reinsurer")

Any additional companies established by the Company shall be deemed as automatically forming part of the Mythical Companies, the reinsurers being informed of their creation by way of endorsement as soon as practical.

Business Covered

This clause must clearly define the line, class, type, and kind of business to be covered. This is a hierarchical definition in that it typically begins with the annual statement line of business and is further described by successive limiting remarks. This format permits the reinsurers to confirm reports against published materials, differentiated from excluded business.

The clause will specify the type of policy or policies to be covered and in doing so it typically sweeps in "all policies, binders, contracts of insurance, coinsurance, coindemnity, oral or written, or other evidence of liability issued or contracted by the cedent." Use of a broad definition is specifically intended to include liability or risks that might arise for the cedent before a policy is formally issued, or perhaps arising out of an error, as long as the exposure otherwise conforms to the definition of subject business. For example, a casualty or liability exposure cannot surface under a property contract because such exposure is not permitted within the annual statement line of business, even in error.

For casualty contracts the business covered clause defines the basis of coverage, whether "claims made," "occurrence," or "losses discovered" policy forms are applicable and whether the company has the option to cede facultative or other treaty reinsurance. It is possible that such information is included elsewhere, such as the exclusions clause.

Generally this clause provides linkage to other specific defining clauses, which may include the limit and retention clause, exclusion clause, and others. This separates the core defining clauses from the operational clauses.

Note also that the contract is acknowledged to be a contract of indemnity (see Chapter 1). This means the reinsurers respond to payments made by the company rather than to liability accrued. This is perhaps the most crucial aspect of the reinsurance contract, and it appears quite subtly in this first article.

BUSINESS COVERED

In consideration of the premium to be paid by the Company to the Reinsurer, the Reinsurer agrees to indemnify the Company, as set forth in the Limit and Retention Article, in respect of the liability which may accrue to the Company under all policies, binders, contracts of insurance, coinsurance, coindemnity, oral or written, or other evidences of liability (hereinafter referred to as "policy" or "policies") issued or contracted by the Company and attaching (new or renewal) during the term of this

Agreement in respect to business classified by the Company as commercial property business to include but not limited to Fire, Extended Coverage, Allied Lines, Earthquake, Special Multiple Peril, Inland Marine, and Automobile Physical Damage ascribed to an underwriting year covered hereunder or renewed during the term of this Agreement, subject to the terms of this Agreement.

This Agreement shall cover losses whether arising on an "occurrence," "claims made," or "losses discovered" policy form basis, as original, for the full original policy period plus odd time (not to exceed eighteen (18) months in all) including any run-off provision or any extended reporting period option, or any discovery period contained in the original policies.

Risks otherwise excluded from this Agreement may be submitted by the Company to the Reinsurer for special acceptance.

Risks otherwise subject to cession hereunder may be submitted to the lead Reinsurer for exclusion from cession.

The Company may at its option, purchase reinsurance which, in its opinion, inures to the benefit of the Reinsurer hereon.

The last three sentences are quite interesting. The first two deal with risks that may be marginally included or excluded, but for which the company wants special consideration. Consider, for example, a very large property for which the company may be able to secure facultative reinsurance for the entire amount of additional capacity; size alone may make the risk atypical but otherwise homogeneous with the permitted cessions. The company may prefer to take this policy out of the treaty.

The last provision permits the company to purchase facultative reinsurance which reduces the limit exposing the treaty. In a commercial portfolio, the company may wish to restrict its capacity, net and treaty, for a specific class, such as restaurant business, to half that generally available through the treaty. Its comfort level may be less for the class, and it may prefer to handle the class differently. Reinsurers generally respect and permit such administration by the cedent. If the practice becomes all too common, the reinsurers may object to the fact that the treaty is not being used.

Limit and Retention

This clause is sometimes called the reinsurance coverage article, because it describes just how the reinsurance applies.

LIMIT AND RETENTION

The Company shall cede, and the Reinsurer shall accept as reinsurance, a quota share of the Company's net retained liability:

a) up to $10,000,000 each and every loss, each and every risk, of all business ceded hereunder, and
b) associated allocated loss adjustment expenses.

The Company shall be the sole judge of what constitutes one risk.

The Company shall participate for ten percent (10%) in the interests and liabilities of this Agreement to be retained net and unreinsured in any way other than property per occurrence catastrophe reinsurance.

Follow the Fortunes

This clause emphasizes the concept of an indemnity agreement by stipulating that the reinsurer's interests shall match those of the company. This clause may appear as a separate article or it may be included within the business reinsured article.

FOLLOW THE FORTUNES

The liability of the Reinsurer shall follow that of the Company in every case and shall be subject in all respects to all the general and specific stipulations, clauses, waivers, extensions, modifications, and endorsements of any of the Company's aforementioned policies, subject to the Exclusions Article and other terms and conditions of this Agreement as set forth herein.

Term and Cancellation

This clause is also called commencement and termination. Beyond the obvious specification of the contract period, this clause permits regulatory extensions imposed by one or more state insurance departments and specifically outlines how a reinsurer or the cedent can cancel the contract. A single-year contract may hold the option of quarterly cancellation, and a continuous contract may hold the option of quarterly cancellation at any quarter. Some contracts offer cancellation at any time, with 90 days or 180 days notice. Some only permit annual cancellation.

In the event of cancellation, the clause will address if, and how, coverage might continue for those policies issued during the in-force period of the contract. Two options predominate:

1. Cutoff with return of unearned premium reserves along with unexpired exposures
2. Runoff where the original terms apply until each issued appropriate policy is fully earned and each and every claim is concluded.

Briefly, a cutoff termination stops the exposure, however the reinsurer remains exposed to developments from business covered up to the time of termination. In a runoff situation, the existing policies are covered until expiration, or to the next anniversary, with the caveat that no coverage exists after a specified date.

Contracts commonly include a statement of extended expiration. Should a loss be in progress at the time of termination or cancellation, it shall be covered as though it occurred entirely within the contract period. Sometimes this appears as a separate article called *extended termination*. In the following sample it is included within the term and cancellation article.

TERM AND CANCELLATION

This Agreement shall take effect on and from 12:01 a.m., Standard Time, January 1, 19XX, at the location of the subject original policy and shall remain in force continuously thereafter subject to termination as of 12:01 a.m., Standard Time, at any January 1st, at the location of the original policy by either party giving the other not less than ninety (90) days written notice of its desire to terminate. The Reinsurer shall continue to participate in all insurances and reinsurances coming within the terms of this Agreement granted or renewed by the Company during the ninety (90) days aforesaid.

In the event of termination, coverage shall remain in force for all subject original policies in force at the date of termination until their natural expiration but not exceeding twelve months from the date of the termination, plus odd time, any run-off provision, any extended reporting period, or any discovery period contained in the subject original policies.

However, should any subject original policy to which this Agreement applies be extended, continued or renewed due to regulatory, or other legal restrictions, this Agreement shall automatically provide extended coverage until such original policies are actually terminated by the Company.

Alternatively, at the option of the Company, coverage hereunder may be terminated as respects subject original policies in force as of the date of termination and the reinsurer will return all unearned reinsurance premium in respect of such policies, notwithstanding any minimum premium provision contained elsewhere herein and cash (U.S. currency) in that amount.

Should the Company terminate this Agreement on a cutoff basis and this Agreement terminates while a loss covered hereunder is in progress, it is agreed that, subject to the other conditions of this Agreement, the Reinsurer shall indemnify the Company as if the entire loss had occurred during the time this Agreement is in force provided the loss covered hereunder started before the time of termination.

Note, if coverage is automatically extended by regulative authority, the reinsurers follow the cedent's fortune and also automatically extend the reinsurance coverage. The regulator would only make such a pronouncement if such was in the public interest, and both cedent and reinsurer wish to meet the needs of the public, however hard the effort may be to achieve that obligation.

Territory

While this is a necessary clause, it is typically very broad. Because many policies carry provisions for travel, it is typical to see worldwide capabilities.

TERRITORY

This Agreement shall apply wherever the Company's original policies apply.

Exclusions

This is a crucial section, because it further defines the covered business. The following illustration contains examples, and does not intend to display a typical listing.

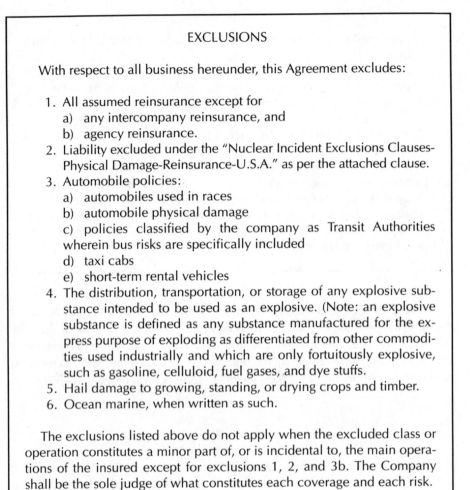

EXCLUSIONS

With respect to all business hereunder, this Agreement excludes:

1. All assumed reinsurance except for
   a) any intercompany reinsurance, and
   b) agency reinsurance.
2. Liability excluded under the "Nuclear Incident Exclusions Clauses-Physical Damage-Reinsurance-U.S.A." as per the attached clause.
3. Automobile policies:
   a) automobiles used in races
   b) automobile physical damage
   c) policies classified by the company as Transit Authorities wherein bus risks are specifically included
   d) taxi cabs
   e) short-term rental vehicles
4. The distribution, transportation, or storage of any explosive substance intended to be used as an explosive. (Note: an explosive substance is defined as any substance manufactured for the express purpose of exploding as differentiated from other commodities used industrially and which are only fortuitously explosive, such as gasoline, celluloid, fuel gases, and dye stuffs.
5. Hail damage to growing, standing, or drying crops and timber.
6. Ocean marine, when written as such.

The exclusions listed above do not apply when the excluded class or operation constitutes a minor part of, or is incidental to, the main operations of the insured except for exclusions 1, 2, and 3b. The Company shall be the sole judge of what constitutes each coverage and each risk.

Original Conditions

This clause ties the reinsurance to the same conditions faced by the company.

ORIGINAL CONDITIONS

All insurances falling under this Agreement shall be subject to the same terms, rates, conditions, and waivers, and to the same modifications, alterations, and cancellations as the respective policies of the Company (except in the event of the insolvency of the Company, the provisions of the Insolvency Article of this agreement shall apply) and the Reinsurer shall be credited, with its exact proportion of the original gross premiums received by the Company.

Accounts and Remittances

This clause outlines how the premiums and losses are to be reported and paid.

ACCOUNTS AND REMITTANCES

Within sixty (60) days following the end of each calendar quarter, the Company shall render a net account to the Reinsurer for each Underwriting Year based on the following:

1. Gross net written premium accounted for the quarter; less
2. The ceding commission as provided for in this Agreement; less
3. Loss and loss adjustment expense paid; plus
4. Subrogation, salvage, or other recoveries.

Within sixty (60) days following the end of the quarter, the debtor party shall remit to the creditor party any balance due. Should the balance be in favor of the Reinsurer, the balance due shall accompany the account; should the balance be in favor of the Company, the Reinsurer shall remit within thirty (30) days after receipt and verification of the account.

This account shall also bear a notation advising of the outstanding loss and loss adjustment expense reserve at the end of the quarter separately for each Underwriting Year, any special payment handled in accordance with the Notice of Loss and Loss Settlements Article and the unearned premium reserve at the end of the quarter separately for each Underwriting Year.

Ceding Commission

This article presents the method of calculating commissions within quarterly reports, subject to later adjustment.

CEDING COMMISSION

In the quarterly accounts, the Company shall deduct a provisional ceding commission equal to 32.5% of the gross net written premium ceded hereunder.

On return premiums, the Company shall return to the reinsurer the provisional commission of 32.5%.

The provisional ceding commission allowed shall include provision for all brokerage, original commissions, premium taxes, board and bureau fees and adjustments, and all other expenses of the Company whatsoever except losses and loss adjustment expenses, and except Federal Excise Tax.

Such provision ceding commissions shall be subject to adjustment, in accordance with the terms of the Commission Adjustment Article.

The types of commissions are outlined in Chapter 9, Reinsurance Proportional Pricing. The above clause varies in its content depending on the terms and structure of the agreed commission scheme.

Commission Adjustment

The adjustment methodology is outlined in this article. This clause varies widely, depending on the terms of the ceding commission clause. Typically it is lengthy. The reader should review Chapter 9 to learn the typical variations: flat commission, flat commission with profit contingency, and sliding scale.

Notice of Loss and Loss Settlements

This article sets forth the methodology for reporting and handling claims.

NOTICE OF LOSS AND LOSS SETTLEMENTS

Any loss settlement made by the Company, whether under strict policy conditions or by way of compromise, shall be unconditionally binding upon the Reinsurer in proportion to its participation, and the Reinsurer shall benefit proportionally in all salvages and recoveries.

The Reinsurer's share of losses, loss expenses, and loss recoveries shall be carried into the quarterly account for which provision is hereby made. Provided however, that when, as a result of any one loss, the anticipated amount recoverable under this Agreement exceeds $300,000, the Company shall advise the Reinsurer by separate report, continuing to keep the Reinsurer advised as the loss progresses. Should the ultimate disposition of a loss under this Agreement exceed $300,000, the Company shall have the option of requiring a special payment. The Reinsurer shall, upon demand, remit its proportion forthwith upon receipt of proof of loss. Should a special payment be demanded, a notation should appear on the next account in accordance with the Accounts and Remittances Article.

In the event the Reinsurer fails to pay within sixty (60) days of the date due under this Agreement, any amount of paid loss or allocated loss adjustment expense that is due to the Company under this Agreement and which amount is not in dispute, then within thirty (30) days thereof, but never later than December 31 of each year, the Reinsurer shall deliver to the Company a clean, unconditional, irrevocable evergreen letter of credit in the total amount of all such amounts of undisputed paid loss or allocated loss adjustment expense that are in excess of sixty (60) days overdue by the Reinsurer to the Company.

The Letter of Credit so provided under the above paragraph shall (a) meet the applicable standards for Letters of Credit required for credit for reinsurance authorized reinsurance purposes and be acceptable to the Company, and (b) the provisions of the Article entitled Security and Unauthorized Reinsurance (or the Article applicable to Letters of Credit in respect of unauthorized Reinsurers, howsoever entitled herein) shall fully apply to such letter of credit and any actions thereunder as if the Reinsurer were an unauthorized Reinsurer.

In the event that the Reinsurer fails to timely provide and maintain such Letter of Credit in the required amount, then thereafter, all amounts of paid loss and allocated loss adjustment expense due from the Reinsurer to the Company, whether in dispute or not, shall bear interest to the benefit of the Company at the rate of one and a half percent (1.5%) per month on the unpaid balance of the amount overdue from the date such amounts were originally due to the Company by the Reinsurer.

"Dispute" means either (a) the Company or the Reinsurer has initiated arbitration or litigation over the issue of the recoverability of such loss or loss adjustment expense, or (b) the Reinsurer has sent to the Company a formal written communication denying the validity of coverage for the loss or allocated loss adjustment expense.

Loss Adjustment Expense

Typically reinsurance contracts permit recovery of expenses in settling specific cases that have arisen through outside adjusters or experts and exclude recovery of internal expenses of the carrier. The latter are considered the cost of doing business for the primary carrier.

There are two methods: proportional recovery and inclusion of the expense within the loss amount. The following sample article is an "inclusion" clause. The LAE is recovered in the same manner and percentage as is paid loss. Please refer to the ultimate net loss clause for an alternative sample, one where recovery of LAE is proportional to the amount of paid loss to be recovered.

Loss adjustment expense is an important part of the reinsurance coverage. Reinsurers wish to promote full investigation, tough but fair negotiations, expert handling, and frequent review of potentials. The in-house work, that accomplished by employees of the ceding company, is considered covered by the commission or rate. Outside experts, legal fees, and associated costs are the subject of this article. Some contracts merge LAE expenses with loss and respond on that basis. Proportional treaties offer two options; *pro rata* additional or included within the loss amount. This clause relates the *pro rata*, or proportional, contribution toward these expenses in addition to the limit permitted for losses.

LOSS ADJUSTMENT EXPENSE

Loss adjustment expenses shall be in addition to Reinsurer's limit of liability. Loss adjustment expenses shall include all expenses (except for salaries, benefits, and unallocated traveling expenses of Company Directors, Officers, or employees, office expenses, overhead or other fixed expenses of the Company) relating to the adjustment of losses under original policies including appellate expenses and expenses and fees associated with Extra-Contractual Obligations, policy coverage, and declaratory judgment actions, prejudgment and postjudgment interest. The Reinsurer shall receive its prorated share of any recoveries of such expenses.

Extra-Contractual Obligations

This clause defines a term used in the previous article and extends the concept of following the fortunes. The clause addresses obligations that may arise outside of the policy coverage due to claim handling. For example, an aggressive posture, pressing to keep payments as low as possible, may result in the court penalizing the carrier. Since the effort would benefit the reinsurers if successful, the reinsurers should contribute in the downside risk.

Extra-contractual obligations are included as covered costs within the same philosophy derived from "follow the fortunes" for adverse results within the normally covered, subject business. Another such extension is for losses in excess of policy limits, which follows this article.

Note, in reading the following article, that extra-contractual obligations are not specifically defined. The intention here is to follow the fortunes of the ceding company if something unforeseen arises, specifically out of and related to a covered exposure. It is not completely open and must be related to subject business and covered exposure. The best definition is that included within the article itself.

EXTRA-CONTRACTUAL OBLIGATIONS

This Agreement shall protect the Company, subject to a limit of liability to the Reinsurer not exceeding the limit of liability appearing in the

Reinsurance Coverage Article of this Agreement, where such loss includes any extra-contractual obligations for eighty percent (80%) of such Extra-Contractual Obligations. "Extra-Contractual Obligations" are defined as those liabilities not covered under any other provision of this Agreement, and which arise from handling of any claim on business covered hereunder, such liabilities arising because of, not limited to, the following: failure by the Company to settle within the Policy limit or by reason of alleged or actual negligence, fraud or bad faith in rejecting an offer of settlement or in the preparation of the defense or in the trial of any action against its insured or in the preparation or prosecution of an appeal consequent upon any such action.

The date on which any Extra-Contractual Obligation is incurred by the Company shall be deemed, in all circumstances, to be the date of the original loss, and the Reinsurer's limit of liability referred to in the preceding paragraph shall include both Extra-Contractual Obligations and any other covered loss of the Company, other than prorated expense, arising out of the same loss.

However, this Article shall not apply where the loss has been incurred due to the fraud of a member of the Board of Directors or a corporate officer of the Company acting individually or collectively or in collusion with any individual or corporation or any other organization or party involved in the presentation, defense, or settlement of any claim covered hereunder.

Losses in Excess of Policy Limits

This clause extends the above concept for situations where the obligation is in excess of the original policy limit.

LOSSES IN EXCESS OF POLICY LIMITS

In the event the Company is held liable for an amount in excess of the Company's Policy Limit, one hundred percent (100%) of the amount of such loss in excess of the Company's policy limit shall be added to the amount of the Company's Policy Limit, and the sum thereof shall be considered as one loss, subject to the Reinsurer's limit of liability for one risk appearing in the Reinsurance Coverage Article of this Agreement. Coverage under this Article extends only to loss that would have been covered had the limit of liability of the insured's policy been adequate.

What are losses in excess of policy limits? Again, the article encompasses multiple possibilities, without specificity. Let us consider one of the more typical cases.

Suppose that in the course of handling a claim, the ceding company assumes a very hard line and stridently denies a claim, thereby failing to agree to a settlement offer at the policy limit. The claimant may sue if the ultimate settlement exceeds the policy limit. The claimant will hold the perspective that the matter could have been settled within the coverage it had purchased. The policyholder will assert that its insurer operated in bad faith, which was the proximate cause of the additional amount owed in the final settlement. It is an uncomfortable situation to be sure, but one that is covered by application of this clause. The reinsurer will stand behind the insurer by following its fortunes within the extensions provided by this clause.

Honorable Undertaking

Both ceding insurers and reinsurers want to hold the agreement to standards of the industry. Thus it is necessary to specify that interpretations shall be considered apart from constraints on details required by the U.S. legal system. This is an extension of the follow the fortunes clause, with a focus on legal technicalities.

HONORABLE UNDERTAKING

This Agreement shall be construed as an honorable undertaking between the parties hereto not to be defeated by technical legal constructions, it being the intention of this Agreement that the fortunes of the Reinsurer shall follow the fortunes of the Company. Nothing herein shall in any manner create any obligations or establish rights against the Reinsurer in favor of any third parties or any persons not parties to this Reinsurance Agreement.

Offset

Essentially this clause permits both cedent and reinsurer to subtract losses from premiums when making payments. There have been problems with liquidators pressing offset provisions skewed to their benefit, leading to the specific mention within the reinsurance agreement.

OFFSET

All amounts due to either the Company or the Reinsurer, by reason of premiums, losses or otherwise under this Agreement shall be subject to recoupment and to offset, the rights to which may be exercised at any time and from time to time by either party and, upon exercise thereof, only the balance shall be due. In the event of insolvency of the Company, offset shall be in accordance with governing law.

It is important to understand the concept of the offset clause. Offsets must be of like kind. This _may_ imply that facultative balances may not be offset against treaty balance. *May is underlined because* in some situations such offset is permitted and in others it has been resisted.

Consider, for example, that a reinsurer is obligated to pay losses when the cedent is unable to pay premiums. Under such circumstances, the reinsurer should be able to offset unpaid premiums against possible payments due. Consider further that the reason the insurer is unable to pay premiums is because it has been declared insolvent by state regulators. The offset should still hold, but in this specific case special bankruptcy laws apply. The Article stipulates that such laws may set the rulings in those situations.

Access to Records

The reinsurer provides broad coverage and in turn requires access to records so that it might monitor the handling of business ceded under the agreement. It may exercise this right on short notice or years after the policies have been fully earned.

Questioning the handling of business is an exercise in due diligence. Disputes may arise in narrow or in broad context. Expressing or raising a point of dispute does not in itself constitute a violation or breach of the reinsurer's duty or rights. Such situations represent times of confusion where the access to records is necessary to either resolve the dispute or to prove and measure the impact of the matter.

ACCESS TO RECORDS

The Reinsurer, by its duly appointed representatives, shall have the right at any reasonable time to examine all policy, claim, and administrative papers in the possession of the Company referring to business effected hereunder.

Errors and Omissions

This clause relieves either party from penalty in the event of error in handling this account. It is another extension of the Follow the Fortunes concept.

ERRORS AND OMISSIONS

Inadvertent delay, errors, or omissions made in connection with this agreement or any transaction hereunder shall not relieve either party from any liability which would have attached had such delay, error, or omission not occurred, provided always that such error or omission shall be rectified as soon as possible after discovery.

Taxes

The intent of this clause is to permit the entity that pays any tax to take credit for that amount within its own accounting.

TAXES

In consideration of the terms under which this Agreement is issued, the Company shall not claim a deduction in respect of the premium hereon when making tax returns, other than income or profits tax returns, to any state or territory of the United States of America, the District of Columbia, or Canada.

Currency

The following is a clause that converts every transaction to U.S. currency. Some worldwide covers specify two or three currencies.

CURRENCY

All retentions and limits hereunder are expressed in United States dollars, and all premium and loss payments shall be made in United States currency. For the purposes of this Agreement, amounts paid or received by the Company in any other currency shall be converted into United States dollars at the rate of exchange at which such transactions are converted on the books of the Company.

Federal Excise Tax

This tax is paid by the cedent but apportioned to reinsurers, with appropriate credits for return premium and return tax.

FEDERAL EXCISE TAX

If the Reinsurer is subject to the Federal Excise Tax, the Reinsurer agrees to allow, for the purpose of paying such tax, up to the applicable percentage of the premium payable hereon to the extent such premium is subject to the tax. In the event of any return premium becoming due hereunder, the Reinsurer shall deduct from the amount of the return premium the same percentage as it allowed, and the Company or its agent should take steps to recover the tax from the United States Government.

For many years the excise tax has been a 1 percent surcharge against non-admitted insurers and reinsurers. It is specifically addressed in the reinsurance treaty.

Security and Unauthorized Reinsurance

This clause addresses the licensing of reinsurers as outlined in Chapter 7. Reserves ceded to appropriately licensed reinsurers can be recorded within the annual statement as authorized reinsurance. Foreign and unauthorized reinsurance is not automatically considered as such, and typically cedents require Letters of Credit for reserves hereunder (sample document not provided).

Insolvency

This article addresses insolvency of one or more reinsurers or the cedent itself. It is typically a very long article and is generally worded in a standard or consistent format (sample document not provided).

Arbitration

The following clause is one used historically. Arbitration has become a complex remedy, it used to be simpler than litigation. There are changes currently being suggested to eliminate some of the difficulties without reducing rights of either party. Because there is lack of uniformity in the current language, an older sample is shown here for illustration.

This version outlines the selection of the third arbitrator using the American Arbitration Association. Other versions suggest that each party submit three names, whereby two shall be rejected by the other party and the third arbitrator shall be determined by drawing lots. This version does not specify the expertise of the two named arbitrators. It is normal to require that all arbitrators be current or former officers of insurance or reinsurance companies, or underwriters at Lloyd's of London. Further, this version sets the three arbitrators as equals. Other versions set the third as an umpire, to decide if the two do not agree. Some give the umpire authority to lead the arbitration.

ARBITRATION

1. If any dispute shall arise between any interested parties to this Agreement, either before or after its termination, with reference to the interpretation of this Agreement or the rights of either party with respect to any transactions under this Agreement, the dispute shall be referred to three arbitrators as a condition precedent to any right of action arising under this Agreement. One arbitrator is to be chosen by each party and the third by the two so chosen. If either party refuses or neglects to appoint an arbitrator within thirty (30) days after the receipt of written notice from the other party requesting it to do so, the requesting party may nominate two arbitrators who shall choose the third.

2. In the event the arbitrators do not agree on the selection of the third arbitrator within thirty (30) days after both arbitrators have been named, the reinsured shall petition the American Arbitration Association to appoint the third arbitrator. If the American Arbitration Association fails to appoint the third arbitrator within thirty (30) days after it has been requested to do so, either party may request a Justice of the Court of general jurisdiction of the state in which the arbitration is to be held to appoint an officer or retired officer of an insurance or reinsurance company as the third arbitrator. In the event both parties request appointment of the third arbitrator, the third arbitrator shall be the soonest named in writing by the Justice of the Court.

3. Each party shall submit its case to the arbitrators within thirty (30) days of the appointment of the arbitrators. The arbitrators shall consider this Agreement to be an honorable engagement rather than merely a legal obligation and may abstain from following the strict rules of law. The decision of a majority of the arbitrators shall be final and binding upon both the Reinsured and Reinsurer. Judgment

may be entered upon the award of the arbitrators in any court having jurisdiction.

4. Each party shall bear the fee and expenses of its own arbitrator, one half (1/2) of the third arbitrator and one half (1/2) of the other expenses of the arbitration. In the event both arbitrators are chosen by one party, the fees shall be equally divided between the parties.

5. Any such arbitration shall take place in _____ , _____ unless some other location is mutually agreed upon by the parties. It is agreed that for all purposes, this Agreement shall be deemed by the parties to be subject solely to the laws of the State of

_____ .

Service of Suit

Most legal contracts contain a clause that specifies when and how a dispute or legal processing is legally served against the other party and under which law the dispute will be contested. Given that the company has a known address, but that there may be multiple reinsurers, it is appropriate to specify how the company may serve legal papers.

SERVICE OF SUIT

A. In the event of a dispute arising out of or in connection with this Agreement, or if the Reinsurer fails to pay any amount claimed to be due under this Agreement, at the request of the Company, the Reinsurer shall submit to the jurisdiction of any court of competent jurisdiction within the state of _____ , comply with all requirements necessary to that court's jurisdiction, and all matters arising under this Agreement shall be determined in accordance with the law practice of that court and jurisdiction.

B. Service of process of suit in any suit may be made upon the firm of _____ at _____ ("Firm"), and in any suit instituted, the Reinsurer shall abide by the final decision of that court or any appellate court in the event of an appeal.

C. The Firm named above is hereby expressly authorized and directed by the Reinsurer as its true and lawful attorney to accept service of process of suit on behalf of the Reinsurer in any suit by the Company and, upon the request of the Company, to give a written undertaking to the Company to enter into a general appearance upon behalf of the Reinsurer in the event a suit shall be instituted.

D. Furthermore, pursuant to any statute of any state, territory or possession of the United States which makes provision therefore, the Reinsurer hereby further designates the Superintendent, Commissioner,
or Director of Insurance or any officer specified for that purpose in
the statute, or his successor or successors in office, as true and lawful attorney of the Reinsurer upon whom may be served any lawful
process in any action, suit, or proceeding instituted by or on behalf
of the Company and any beneficiary arising under this Agreement,
and hereby designates the Firm as the person to whom the said officer is authorized to mail such process, or a true copy thereof.

Third-Party Beneficiary

This clause underscores the fact that policyholders, or others, cannot use the
existence of a reinsurance agreement to cut through or sue the reinsurer.

THIRD-PARTY BENEFICIARY

Except as specifically and expressively provided elsewhere in this
agreement, the provisions of this Agreement are intended solely for the
benefit of the parties to and executing this Agreement, and nothing in
this Agreement shall in any manner create or be construed to create any
obligations to or establish any rights against any party to this Agreement
in favor of any third parties or other persons not parties to and executing
this Agreement.

Intermediary

Obviously this clause will not appear in a direct reinsurance contract. As discussed in Chapter 4, the intermediary stands between the parties in all matters,
except for disputes. The brokerage is paid by the reinsurers and is not mentioned in the contract. The payment consideration has been included as standard language following an intermediary bankruptcy where funds in transit
became the subject of numerous discussions between the parties at that time.

INTERMEDIARY

_____ of _____ ("Intermediary")
is hereby recognized as the intermediary, or broker, negotiating this

Agreement for all business hereunder. All communications (including but not limited to notices, statements, premiums, return premiums, commissions, taxes, losses, loss adjustment expenses, salvages, and loss settlements) relating thereto shall be transmitted to the Company or to the Reinsurer through the office of the Intermediary. Payments by the Reinsurer to the Intermediary shall be deemed only to constitute payment to the Company to the extent such payments are actually received by the Company.

The above articles constitute a single contract of reinsurance, a property quota share reinsurance agreement, interspersed with explanatory comments. The following are several other clauses one might find in treaty reinsurance contracts.

Waiver

This is a fairly standard clause for legal contracts, not always present in treaties. One use, for example, is to permit a reinsurer access to records, even if it did not inspect records while the policies were in force. The reinsurer does not lose its rights by not exercising them.

WAIVER

The failure of the Company or the Reinsurer to insist on strict compliance with this Agreement, or to exercise and right or remedy hereunder, shall not constitute a waiver of any rights contained herein, nor stop the parties from thereafter demanding full and complete compliance nor prevent the parties from exercising such remedy in the future.

Conflict of Law and Severability

Any legal imposition applies only to the particular item or conflict and not to the agreement as a whole.

CONFLICT OF LAW AND SEVERABILITY
If any provision of this Agreement should be invalid under applicable laws, the latter shall control but only to the extent of the conflict without affecting the remaining provisions of this Agreement.

Assignment

Reinsurers choose to assume business from cedents that are able to write the business successfully. Thus they will not permit the administration of the business to be transferred automatically to others. A new owner may not pass muster, indeed would need prior review. This clause works for both reinsurer and cedent.

ASSIGNMENT

This Agreement shall be binding and inure to the benefit of the Company and the Reinsurer and their respective successors and assigns, provided, however, that this Agreement may not be assigned by either the Company or the Reinsurer without the prior written consent of the other, which consent may be withheld by either party in its sole unfettered discretion.

Negotiated Agreement

This is another clause often found in contracts through an intermediary.

NEGOTIATED AGREEMENT

This Agreement has been negotiated by the parties, and the fact that the initial and final draft shall have been prepared by the Intermediary shall not give rise to any presumption for or against any party to this Agreement to be used in any form in construction or interpretation of this Agreement or any of its provisions.

Surplus Cession

This is a standard article used for a property surplus treaty. This specifies a maximum and minimum cession and the percentage split. Thus the cedent is able to use discretion by policy in apportioning the amount of cession to the treaty.

Note, this clause does accomplish the requirements of a surplus treaty by permitting the ceding carrier to vary its cession risk by risk. The reader is directed to review the surplus treaty requirements in Chapter 5.

SURPLUS CESSION

1. Cessions made hereunder shall not exceed five (5) times the Reinsured's net retention on any one risk, subject to a maximum cession of $5,000,000 on any one risk.
2. The Reinsured's minimum net retention hereunder shall be $250,000 as respects any one risk.
3. The Reinsured shall be the sole judge of what constitutes one risk and the net retention appropriate thereto. However, the Reinsured will not knowingly cede to this treaty more than the $5,000,000, where there is an identifiable accumulation of limits which are subject of one loss.

Limit and Retention (for Excess of Loss Treaties)

To appreciate the structure to which this clause applies, the reader should review Chapter 5, Excess of Loss Treaties.

Ultimate net loss is the end result. When a claims arises with reserves exposing the excess layer, the reinsurer posts its own reserves. Normally, excess claim payments are only due after settlement and payment by the primary carrier. At this point the amount of the claim will be at its ultimate, or concluding amount. Any subsequent adjustments will be considered to be interim until the ultimate amount is finally determined. It is then that the retention and limit are successively applied to determine the amount owed by reinsurers.

LIMIT AND RETENTION

The Reinsurer shall be liable to and shall reimburse the Company for one hundred percent (100%) of a) the amount of Ultimate Net Loss incurred by the Company in excess of two hundred fifty thousand dollars ($250,000) in respect of each coverage/each risk/each occurrence, but the sum recoverable hereunder shall not exceed two hundred fifty thousand dollars ($250,000) of Ultimate Net Loss in respect of each coverage/each risk/each such occurrence, and b) Allocated Loss Adjustment Expenses provided for in the Definition of Ultimate Net Loss Article of this Agreement.

The Company shall be the sole judge of what constitutes each coverage/ each risk.

Net Retained Lines (for Excess of Loss Treaties)

This clause defines the amount of loss that constitutes the net the cedent retained for its own account.

NET RETAINED LINES

This Agreement applies only to that portion of any insurance or reinsurance, amount of Loss in Excess of Original Policy Limits and Extra-Contractual Obligations which the Company retains net for its own account, and in calculating the amount of any loss hereunder and also in computing the amount or amounts in excess of which this Agreement attaches, only loss or losses in respect of that portion of any insurances or reinsurances, amounts of Loss in Excess of Original Policy Limits and Extra-Contractual Obligations which the Company retains net for its own account shall be included.

The amount of the Reinsurer's liability hereunder in respect of any loss or losses shall not be increased by reason of the inability of the Company to collect from any other reinsurers, whether specific or general, any amounts which may have become due from them whether such inability arises from the insolvency of such other reinsurers or otherwise.

Intercompany reinsurance between the Companies, collectively called the "Company," shall be disregarded for all purposes of the Agreement.

Definition of Ultimate Net Loss (for Excess of Loss Treaties)

This clause defines the manner in which the loss will be settled once the particular loss is settled and all potential recoveries are collected.

DEFINITION OF ULTIMATE NET LOSS

A. The term "Ultimate Net Loss" shall mean all amounts paid or payable by the Company under its policies (including one hundred percent (100%) of all amounts of loss in excess of original policy limits as provided for in the Loss in Excess of Policy Limits Article, eighty percent (80%) of Extra-Contractual Obligations as provided for in the Extra-Contractual Obligations Article, and one hundred percent (100%) of all amounts of Allocated Loss Adjustment Expenses as set forth below), after deducting all recoveries, all salvages and all amounts due under any other reinsurances, whether collected or not, except those to be disregarded as set forth in the Net Retained Lines Article, and those in excess of this layer.

All salvages and recoveries received subsequent to a loss settlement under this Agreement shall be applied as if received prior to the said loss settlement and all necessary adjustments shall be made between the Company and the Reinsurer.

Nothing in this Article shall be construed to mean that losses hereunder are not recoverable until the Company's final Ultimate Net Loss is ascertained.

B. The term "Allocated Loss Adjustment Expenses" shall mean all expenses (except for salaries, benefits, and traveling expenses of the Company's directors, officers, employees, or consultants, office expenses, overhead or other fixed expenses of the Company) relating to the adjustment of loss under subject original policies including appellate expenses, expenses and fees associated with policy coverage actions, declaratory judgment actions, prejudgment interest where not part of contractual indemnity and postjudgment interest, and legal costs.

Allocated Loss and Adjustment Expenses of the Company shall be covered hereunder in the same manner as the Company's subject original policy, as follows:

1) Where subject original policies on business covered written by the Company cover expenses in addition to the limit of liability then the Reinsurer shall be liable hereunder, in addition to the limit of liability for Ultimate Net Loss of this Agreement, as specified in the Limit and Retention Article, for its proportionate share of Allocated Loss Adjustment expense in the same ratio as ultimate net loss payments made under the Company's policy.

In the event a verdict or judgment is reduced by an appeal or settlement, subsequent entry of the judgment, resulting in an ultimate saving on such verdict or judgment, or a judgment reversed outright, the expense incurred in securing such final reduction or reversal shall be prorated between the Reinsurer and the Company in the proportion that each benefits from the reduction or reversal and the expense incurred up to the time of the original verdict or judgment shall be prorated in proportion to each party's interest in such verdict or judgment.

2) Where the original policies on business covered written by the Company include expenses as part of the limit of liability, the Reinsurer shall be liable for the ultimate net loss in excess of the Company's retention hereunder for such subject original policies; such ultimate net loss under both the limit and retention hereunder consisting of either indemnity payments or expenses or any combination of indemnity payments and expenses and loss in excess of original policy limits and Extra-Contractual Obligations as provided for in paragraph A above.

Notice of Loss and Loss Settlements (for Excess of Loss Treaties)

This clause supplies the outline for reporting claims under an excess of loss treaty.

NOTICE OF LOSS AND LOSS SETTLEMENTS

The Company shall give notice to the Reinsurer, as soon as reasonably practical, of an occurrence which in the opinion of the Company is likely to result in a claim against this Agreement, and the Company shall keep the Reinsurer advised of all subsequent developments.

The Company alone and at its full discretion shall adjust, settle, or compromise all claims and losses. All such adjustments, settlements, and compromises shall be binding on the Reinsurer. The Company shall likewise, at its sole discretion, commence, continue, defend, compromise, settle, or withdraw from actions, suits, or proceedings and generally do all such matters and things relating to any claims or losses as in its judgment may be beneficial or expedient.

The Reinsurer agrees to abide by the loss settlements of the Company, such settlements to be construed as satisfactory upon receipt of a proof of loss which contains the following information:

1. Claim number	8. Claim type
2. Policy number	9. Name of insured
3. Policy limit	10. Name of claimant
4. Policy period	11. Loss description
5. Loss location	12. Gross loss reserve
6. Date of loss	13. Paid loss to date
7. Date reported	14. Paid expense to date

Amounts falling to the share of the Reinsurer shall be immediately payable to the Company by the Reinsurer within fifteen (15) days of the Reinsurer's receipt of Proof of Loss.

Summary

The above clauses constitute a fundamental selection of the various articles that comprise a reinsurance treaty. Some of these are special clauses, designed for certain kinds of treaty structures, which are described in Chapter 5.

FACULTATIVE CERTIFICATE

Exhibit 15.2 is a sample of a complete property facultative certificate. It normally appears as a single page, printed on both sides. The clauses have

CERTIFICATE OF PROPERTY FACULTATIVE REINSURANCE

Certificate #: _____Renewing or Replacing #:_____
Policy #:_____

Reinsured Name and Address: _____
_____

In consideration of the Declarations and payment of the reinsurance premium and subject to the General Conditions attached, each of the reinsurers listed in Declaration Number 12 agrees to assume its stated share of the reinsurance limit hereon:
   1. Name of Original Insured:
   2. Location(s) Insured:
   3. Original Policy Term:
   4. Reinsurance Term:
   5. Coverage(s) Reinsured:
   6. Perils Reinsured:
   7. Original Policy Limit(s):
   8. Reinsured(s) Net and Treaty Retention:
   9. Reinsurance Limit Hereon:
10. Reinsurance Premium:
11. Ceding Commission:
12. Reinsurance as described in these declarations has been placed with and accepted by the following reinsurers (each for its own part and not one for the other):

REINSURER(S)	PARTICIPATION (Dollar Line or %)	REINSURANCE PREMIUM	REFERENCE NUMBER

Intermediary: _____
Brokerage:_____
   The Undersigned does hereby acknowledge and confirm its participation as indicated in Declaration Number 12 and authorizes the Intermediary to notify the Reinsured of its participation, and agrees that this signed Certificate may be retained by the Intermediary or may be delivered by it to the Reinsured at the Reinsured's request.
   Reinsurer: _____
   Date:_____ By: _____
   Please examine this document carefully and advise us immediately if it is incorrect or does not meet your requirements. If the above space is insufficient, please attach further detail as may be necessary. The underwriting information pertaining to this reinsurance is considered to form part of this certificate.

Exhibit 15.2. Property Facultative Certificate

Certificate of Property Facultative Reinsurance

General Conditions

The liability of the Reinsurer(s) named in this Certificate shall follow that of the Reinsured and, except as otherwise specifically provided in this Certificate, shall be subject to the terms and conditions of the policy(ies) reinsured. In no event shall anyone other than the Reinsured or, in the event of the Reinsured's insolvency, its liquidator, have any rights under this agreement.

A. The Reinsured *warrants to retain for its own account,* subject to any treaty or other facultative reinsurance, whether collectable or not, the limits of liability as specified in the Declarations. The Reinsured shall advise the Reinsurer of any other facultative reinsurance applicable to its retention.

B. The Reinsured *shall make available for inspection* and place at disposal of the Reinsurer at all reasonable times all records of the Reinsured relating to this Certificate or claims in connection therewith.

The Reinsured *shall furnish the Reinsurer with a copy of its policy*(ies) and all endorsements thereto. All changes which in any manner affect this Certificate are subject to prior approval of the Reinsurer.

C. The Reinsured *shall promptly notify the Reinsurer of any loss or claim and any subsequent developments* which involve or may involve this reinsurance based on injuries alleged or damage sought without regard to liability.

All loss settlements made by the Reinsured provided they are within the terms, conditions, and limit(s) of the original policy(ies) and this Certificate, shall be binding upon Reinsurer. Upon receipt of an acceptable proof of loss, the Reinsurer shall promptly pay its proportion of such loss as set forth in the Declarations.

The Reinsured has an obligation to investigate and defend against claims or suits to final determination. The Reinsurer does not undertake to investigate or defend claims or suits, however, it shall have the right and be given the opportunity with the full cooperation of the Reinsured to associate with the Reinsured and its representatives at its own expense, in any claim, suit, or proceeding involving this reinsurance.

The Reinsured *agrees to enforce its rights of recovery.* The Reinsurer will be paid or credited by the Reinsured with its proportionate share of salvage, that is, reimbursement obtained or recovery made by the Reinsured, less all expenses paid by the Reinsured in making such recovery (excluding Reinsured overhead and salaries, or any subsidiary, related or wholly owned company thereof). If the reinsurance afforded by this Certificate is on an excess of loss basis, salvage shall be applied in the inverse order in which liability applies.

D. In addition to the payment of loss, *the Reinsurer shall pay its proportion of allocated loss expenses* which are within the terms of the Reinsured's policy(ies) (other than office expenses and payments to any salaried employee of the Reinsured, or any subsidiary, related or wholly owned company thereof) incurred by the company in the investigation and settlement of claims or suits under the same terms of the policies reinsured, including the salaries and expenses of staff adjusters, and its proportion of court costs and any interest on any judgment or award, in the same ratio as that the reinsurer's loss payment bears to the Reinsured's gross loss payment under the policy(ies) reinsured by this Certificate.

E. The *Reinsured will be liable for all taxes on premiums ceded* to the Reinsurer under this Certificate.

Exhibit 15.2. *continued*

F. In the *event of insolvency of the Reinsured,* the reinsurance provided by this Certificate shall be payable by the Reinsurer on the basis of the liability of the Reinsured under the Policy(ies) reinsured, without diminution because of the insolvency, directly to the Reinsured or its liquidator. The Reinsurer shall be given notice of the pendency of each claim against the Reinsured on the policy(ies) reinsured hereunder within a reasonable time after such claim is filed in the insolvency proceedings. The Reinsurer shall have the right to investigate each such claim and interpose, at its own expense, in the proceeding where such claim is to be adjudicated, any defenses which it may deem available to the Reinsured, or its liquidator. The expense incurred by the reinsurer shall be chargeable subject to court approval, against the insolvent Reinsured as part of the expense of liquidation to the extent of a proportional share of the benefit which may accrue to the Reinsured solely as the result of the defense undertaken by the Reinsurer.

G. The *Reinsurer may offset any balance*(s) whether on account of premiums, commissions, claims, losses, adjustment expenses, or any other amount(s) due or to become due from any party to the other under this Certificate or any other agreement entered into between the Reinsured and the Reinsurer, whether acting as assuming reinsurer or as a ceding company.

H. Should the Reinsured's policy(ies) be cancelled, this Certificate shall terminate automatically at the same time and date. This *Certificate may be cancelled by the Reinsured or by the Reinsurer upon not less than thirty days prior written notice,* one to the other, stating when such cancellation shall be effective. Proof of mailing shall be deemed proof of notice and calculation of the earned premiums shall follow the Reinsured's calculation in the use of short rate or *pro rata* tables.

In the event this provision is prohibited or unenforceable in any jurisdiction it shall be ineffective to the extent of such prohibition or unenforceability.

I. The terms of this Certificate *shall not be waived or changed except by endorsement* issued to form a part hereof executed by a duly authorized representative of the Reinsurer.

J. Any difference of opinion between the Reinsurer and the Reinsured with respect to interpretation of this Certificate or the performance of the obligations under the Certificate shall be submitted to arbitration. Each party shall select an arbitrator within one month after written request for arbitration has been received from the party requesting arbitration. These two arbitrators shall select a third arbitrator within ten days after both have been appointed. Should the arbitrators fail to agree on a third arbitrator, each arbitrator shall select one name from a list of three names submitted by the other arbitrator, and the third arbitrator shall be selected by lot between the two names chosen. The arbitrators shall be officials or former officials of other insurance or reinsurance companies. They shall adopt their own rules and procedures, and the decision of the majority of arbitrators shall be binding on the parties.

In WITNESS WHEREOF, _____ Reinsurance Company has caused this certificate of reinsurance to be signed by its President at _____, but same shall not be binding upon the Reinsurer unless countersigned by an authorized representative of the Reinsurer.

_____, President, _____ Reinsurance Company

Exhibit 15.2. *continued*

not been separated with commentary as in the treaty sample above. A close reading will show that many of the same concepts apply. However, the facultative certificate is quite concise because it is written to apply to a single policy, on an indemnity basis. It covers the ceding company for economic loss from claims arising from the specific policy. It does not directly extend to the exposure of the policy, which is why the policyholder has no access to the reinsurer. Even though this linkage is indirect, it makes the certificate dependent on the terms of the underlying policy. Payments are linked to claims of the original policy. This close linkage permits the certificate to be a concise contract.

The underwriting information contains a lot of statistical detail that is omitted from the certificate. One example is the amount of deductible for the policy. Generally the certificate will only list the key location of a schedule, but the underwriting material will supply all locations.

Compare the terms of the facultative certificate with that of the treaty contract. You will note some core similarities that are concisely stated in the certificate and elaborated in the treaty. Some of the extra language in a treaty is explanation of the more complex structure or of a commission scheme that has profit-sharing features.

One could say that the articles and language within the certificate are minimum requirements for any reinsurance contract. One should check to see that these clauses are present and further that the language of each includes the basic points. Obviously some clauses will be necessarily different for a treaty. The tax clause of a certificate is quite brief, stating that the ceding company is fully responsible. The tax considerations of a treaty are more complex, and the assuming reinsurer may want to have the credit for tax payments pass through to their books, for example.

There is one noteworthy difference in the service of suit clause. The facultative certificate does not have such a clause. It assumes the two parties can contact each other. The treaty clause specifies just how the cedent can service suit papers on the reinsurers. Since many treaties have foreign as well as domestic security, this contractual treatment is desirable. Many facultative certificates do have a service of suit clause; if not, it can be added as necessary by endorsement to certificates of foreign reinsurers participating on a specific account.

SUMMARY

This chapter has introduced the basic elements of reinsurance contract wording. The length of a treaty increased significantly during the 1980s and 1990s as the business became more formalized. The "handshake" agreements between parties in the past had simply less complex wording. With the advance of our society the technicalities of contract language have expanded. Whether this is good or not is debatable. However, it is now quite essential that contract wordings be complete, without loose ends that might be wrongly interpreted.

In the past, people tended to stay with a company for their entire career. Thus the cedent and assuming reinsurer knew how the other party interpreted phrases and thought about the business. Today, one must be precise so that new staff and new leadership will not turn a contractual partner from the original intent. There is no question that reinsurance has become more complex.

GLOSSARY

Accident Year is the recording on a matching basis of all losses occurring during a given 12-month period of time, regardless of when the losses are reported, with all premium written during the same period.

Acquisition Costs are all expenses incurred by an insurance or reinsurance company that are directly related to acquiring business.

Additional Case Reserves are reserves posted by reinsurers on specific case files apart from those posted by the cedent; generally these are in addition to reserves of the primary carrier, where the reinsurer has a more pessimistic appraisal. Generally ACRs do not constitute a denial or resistance of claim recognition and are posted by reinsurers to better reflect their expectations of ultimate liability.

Adjustable Rate or Adjustable Commission refers to pricing schemes that contain a provision for an increase or decrease from the provisional basis, based on either the volume or profitability of the subject business.

Annual Statement is a regulatory requirement that summarizes the financials of an insurer or reinsurer as of December 31 each year. It includes a balance sheet supplemented by exhibits and schedules that measure status and performance. For contrast, see GAAP methods.

As If is a term used to refer to a recalculation of past results based on conditions proposed for the future, for example, the results of an excess of loss treaty with an increased retention.

Assumption is the taking up or binding of a contract of reinsurance.

Attachment Point is the specific amount of loss, per occurrence or in the aggregate as the case may be, above which excess of loss coverage becomes operative.

Auditing is an inspection of records by reinsurers that does not necessarily include standard practices of a Certified Public Accountant and often encompasses other tests and measures created by reinsurers to monitor the business assumed.

Authorized Reinsurance is that portion of reinsurance placed with reinsurers who are licensed or otherwise recognized by the applicable regulatory authority.

Benefit-to-Cost Ratio is the relativity between the cost of reinsurance and its benefit, not including subjective benefits (see Chapter 4).

Binder is a formal, written acceptance of a contract, which can apply to an insurance policy, a reinsurance treaty, or a facultative certificate.

Bordereau (Bordereaux plural) is a detail reporting form that supplies activity within all subject policies and their premium and all claims reported to reinsurers.

Broker Market or Brokerage Market is the class of reinsurers who write business expedited by the reinsurance intermediaries.

Bulk Reserves are amounts the insurer or reinsurer establishes as reserves which are not tied to a specific policy or reported claim; examples of bulk reserves are unearned premium reserves and IBNR.

Burning Cost is the ratio of claims to premium for several prior years' experience of a reinsurance treaty. In general usage, it does not include expenses.

Calendar Year is the recording of all premiums earned from January through December of any year, regardless of the year written, and all loss amounts reported or changed during the same period.

Carrier is used in this text to refer to an insurer; it can also be used to refer to reinsurers.

Casualty Insurance is insurance that is primarily concerned with losses of the policyholder caused by injuries to other persons or to the property of others and the legal liability imposed on the insured therefrom.

Catastrophe is loss comprising a number or frequency of claims arising out of a single event or cause, such that they are properly aggregated within a single reinsured event.

Cedent or **Ceding Company** is the party that is reinsuring all or part of its business with another carrier. The outbound transfer is ceded to the assuming reinsurer.

Cession is the outward transfer of a reinsurance transaction.

Combined Ratio is the combination of underwriting expenses to written premiums plus losses related to earned premiums; it is a combined loss plus expense ratio.

Commutation is the act of negotiating the conclusion to a reinsurance treaty or certificate before all losses have been closed and fully paid. It estimates future liabilities, provides a discount for early payment, and achieves a complete discharge of all future obligations under a contract by either party.

Contingent Commission is a commission that is contingent on there being a profit. It is a mechanism designed to share profit with reinsurers.

Contract of Indemnity, as used in reinsurance, is one that responds to economic loss, not merely damage.

Cover Note is a binder for a treaty which outlines the agreed terms (see also **Slip**).

Credibility is a relative term which refers to the value or weight that is attached to a statistical calculation or statement. Greater credibility is associated with better odds, higher frequency, or routine occurrences.

Cutoff is a term that applies to terminated treaties stipulating that the assuming reinsurer is not liable for loss occurrences taking place after the date of termination. It may require a return of unearned premium.

Direct Writer is a reinsurer that provides reinsurance directly to primary insurers without the assistance of intermediaries.

Direct Written Premium is the gross premiums written by an insurance company on primary business and specifically excludes assumed reinsurance.

Earned Premiums comprise that portion of premium representing the expired portion of the policy or contract term and, as such, has been exposed to the possibility of loss.

Excess of Loss Reinsurance is the class of reinsurance cessions such that the cedent is protected for recognized claims that exceed a preset retention, or deductible, commonly referred to as the attachment point, and responds thereafter until the amount incurred exceeds the stated limit of liability. This is sometimes referred to as nonproportional reinsurance.

Exclusions are designated types of insurance, risks, perils, or exposures that are not covered by the insurance policy or reinsurance treaty or certificate, irrespective of the other terms of the contract.

Facultative Reinsurance is reinsurance of all or part of the insurance provided by a *single* risk, exposure, or policy (see Chapter 3). While this description is simplistically true, there are considerations beyond this definition.

Financial Reinsurance is reinsurance with focus on the financial function of reinsurance, which includes cessions of asset risk, credit risk, interest rate risk, and payment timing risk, among others (see Chapter 6).

Finite Risk a term synonymous with Financial Reinsurance or Financial Insurance—some use this word to describe just the exposure to which these two types of coverage apply.

Flat Rate or **Flat Commission** is a pricing scheme that applies a fixed rate or percentage without any subsequent adjustment.

Following Reinsurer is a participating reinsurer that agrees to the terms negotiated between the cedent and the lead reinsurer.

From Ground Up is a reinsurance phrase that applies to a particular claim and the amount applicable to the covered perils or risk, which includes all amounts apportioned to the primary carrier and excess or surplus lines insurance, as well as all reinsurance. It specifically includes any deductible amount.

Functions of Reinsurance refer to specific needs of the reinsurance buyer arising out of the risk management considerations about the portfolio of business or perhaps an individual policy it has written or plans to write. Primary functions are capacity, catastrophe, stabilization, and financial. Secondary functions include market intelligence, advice, margin, etc.

GAAP or Generally Accepted Account Principles are those financial measures common to other industries, which assign income and disbursements to the proper period, as distinguished from the statutory accounting required by insurance regulators.

Gross Line is the total amount of liability written on a specific risk, or exposure, by an insurer including the amount it cedes to reinsurers. Likewise, a reinsurer may have a gross line, including amounts it cedes to retrocessionaires. The gross line is the sum of the net line and amount reinsured.

Gross Net Premiums Written is the gross written premium less premiums ceded to reinsurers during a given period.

Gross Premiums Written is the total premium for insurance and insurance assumed during a given period before deduction of all reinsurance ceded, brokerage, commission, and other acquisition costs.

Header is the term applied in this book to the block of information characterizing a specific claim or treaty, which is linked to the accounting or claim records detailing the premiums, commissions, brokerages, payments, reserves, LAE, and other expense items processed for that account or claim. The linking of such information with the accounting records enables the reinsurer to statistically analyze its business.

Incurred but not Reported (IBNR) is the reserve for estimated losses that have been incurred but which have not yet been reported to the insurer or reinsurer, and specifically includes unknown future developments on known losses. This amount is typically defined as the difference between the losses that will ultimately be reported and the losses reported to date.

Incurred Loss is the total loss sustained by an insurer or reinsurer under a policy or group of policies whether paid or unpaid, including any provision for losses that have occurred but which have not yet been reported to the carrier.

In Force is the period when coverage is applicable. A bound policy is in force during its specified term. This term is often used to refer to the period when the policy was exposed to loss, as differentiated from the developmental tail of the losses arising within the in-force period.

Inspection of Records is an audit by reinsurers that does not necessarily include standard practices of a Certified Public Accountant, and often encompasses other tests and measures created by reinsurers to monitor the business assumed.

Intermediary is the reinsurance broker who serves as the agent to facilitate the transfer of reinsurance. The fee or commission for this service is called brokerage.

Investment Income is money earned from invested assets and may include realized capital gains less capital losses during the period.

IRIS Test(s) comprise a set of early warning tests for insurance solvency and performance maintained by the National Association of Insurance Commissioners in their Insurance Regulatory Information System (see Chapter 14).

Layer is the interval between the retention, or attachment point, and the maximum limit of indemnity for which a reinsurer is responsible.

Lead Reinsurer is one of the participating reinsurers who has been involved in negotiating the terms of the particular cession.

Leveraging is a process that obtains a disproportionate effect or result. It may be achieved by cleverly arranging one's business, however there is typically an associated or resulting cost.

Loading is an index of a pricing component that is included as a factor or multiplicand in building a rate.

Line is a term with more than one definition.

1. It refers to the classes of business within the annual statement which include fire, homeowner's, worker's compensation, etc.
2. It applies to the amount of limit accepted on a specific risk.
3. With respect to a surplus share treaty, line pertains to the multiple that the surplus reinsurance applies to the net retained portion, i.e., a two-line treaty permits reinsurance cessions of up to twice that retained by the cedent.

Loss Adjustment Expenses (LAE) is the expense of settling claims, including legal and other fees and the portion of general expenses allocated to claim settlement costs.

Loss Development is the difference between the total amount incurred in a policy or accident year measured at two different points in time. As a year matures more is known about the various claims, thus estimates can be improved, either increased or decreased. Because the number of claims reported may also change from one measure to the next, loss development includes IBNR.

Loss Reserves are the amounts of liability established by insurers and reinsurers to reflect the estimated costs of claim payments and related expenses that the insurer or reinsurer may be required to pay with respect to insurance or reinsurance it has written. Reserves are established for losses and for loss adjustment expenses.

Margin is the remainder after deducting known or itemized costs.

Net Line is the amount of liability written on a specific risk or exposure by an insurer, excluding the amount it cedes to reinsurers. Likewise, a reinsurer may have a net line, excluding amounts it cedes to retrocessionaires. The gross line is the sum of the net line and amount reinsured.

Net Premiums Written is the gross premium written for a specific period, less all premiums ceded to reinsurers during the period, less brokerage, commission, and other acquisition expenses.

Pari Passu—can be literally translated as "at an equal pace." It is used in reinsurance to specify that following reinsurers are treated "equally without preferance" with lead reinsurers, irrespective of share sizes. A counter example would be that foreign reinsurers are *pari passu* with the domestic reinsurers, but for, as the case may be, the requirements to prepay excise tax or to post funds held.

Portfolio is a collection of policies or reinsurance treaties, or facultative certificates, which comprises all or part of the business written by a specific carrier. A treaty applies to all or part of a class or type of policies, collectively referred to as the subject business or portfolio of the cedent. Likewise, a retrocession applies to all or part of the portfolio of a reinsurer, which consists of the collective reinsurance assumed by that reinsurer.

Primary Insurer is a licensed insurance carrier, or approved insurance entity, that contracts with the consumer to provide insurance coverage.

Priority is a term which reinsurers use to denote the order in which various treaties apply. (Some foreign markets use this term to apply to the retention, a practice not adopted within this text.)

Probable Maximum Loss (PML) is an estimate of property loss likelihood within the limit of liability afforded by the insurance policy. It has applicability on a policy basis for facultative reinsurance and is estimated on a portfolio basis for treaty reinsurance. Its definition varies widely and may or may not include considerations for quick response by the fire company, working sprinklers, adequate water pressure, etc.

Property Insurance is insurance that indemnifies a person with an insurable interest in tangible property for loss related to damage to such property or the loss of use of such subject property.

Proportional Reinsurance is arranged on a proportional or percentage sharing basis; such sharing may be fixed or variable. This specifically includes the following structures: *pro rata* reinsurance, participating reinsurance, quota share reinsurance, and surplus share reinsurance.

Pro Rata Reinsurance is a synonym for proportional reinsurance.

Prospective Rating Plan is a formula based on the past history of an account to project the necessary price for the coming year. Because negotiation is involved, the ultimate rate may include other considerations.

Pure Premium is that part of the premium that is sufficient to pay for loss and loss adjustment expenses, but not other costs or expenses.

Quota Share Reinsurance is a type of proportional reinsurance whereby a fixed percentage of a specific class or kind of business is ceded to reinsurers. A specific policy can also be ceded on a fixed percentage basis, commonly referred to as a facultative quota share.

Rate is a percentage factor applied in a pricing scheme.

Rate-on-Line is the amount of premium divided by the indemnity.

Reinstatement is the restoration of limit, applicable to a property excess of loss treaty after payment by the reinsurer of all or part of a total loss.

Reinsurance is a transfer that meets the following criteria:

1. An insurable interest must exist.
2. Risk must exist at the inception of the contract, although it may change during the period of the contract.
3. Transfer of some portion of the risk from cedent to reinsurer.
4. Some consideration must be passed from the cedent to the assuming reinsurer.
5. The parties offer utmost good faith throughout the transaction.
6. The agreement is one of indemnity.
7. The reinsurer is liable only to the cedent.

Relativity is the statistical comparison between two measures, often expressed as a quotient, which serves to enhance the perspectives one can gather from the data.

Retrocession is where a reinsurer is transferring all or part of the assumed reinsurance to another reinsurer(s), it is reinsurance of reinsurance.

Retrospective Rating Plan is a formula whereby the ultimate rate for a given term is determined by the results obtained in that term, such that the maximum and minimum were preset as well as the formula to be applied.

Runoff is a term that applies to terminated treaties stipulating that the assuming reinsurer is liable for loss occurrences taking place after the date of termination on policies ceded during the applicable effective period of the reinsurance contract. The reinsurer is therefore responsible for the unearned liability and retains the unearned premium.

Skewness is a mathematical term used within this text to refer to situations where an imbalance may exist within a portfolio of business, particularly one where a few policy limits do not relate to the majority.

Sliding Scale is a type of commission where the amount varies depending upon the ratio of losses to premium.

Slip is a binder for a treaty that outlines the agreed terms. See also Cover Note.

Special Acceptance is an agreement to include within a reinsurance contract a specific risk or exposure that is not included automatically.

Subject Premium is the gross written premium from all business to which a reinsurance treaty applies. Note the treaty may be rated on another basis, but subject premium applies to the premium of the portfolio actually ceded to the treaty. In the case of proportional treaties, it is 100 percent of the portfolio premium, before the cession. In the case of an excess treaty, it is the total primary premium from all policies in the subject portfolio which expose the treaty, regardless of the limit of the individual policy.

Summary Reporting is the general classification of monthly, quarterly, or annual reporting that lacks specific policy or claim data.

Surplus Share Reinsurance or **Surplus Treaty** is proportional reinsurance such that the cedent has a protocol for cessions by class or kind of policy and retains a limited right to vary the proportion to be ceded on an individual policy basis. (Because this is a single negotiation covering multiple risks, exposures, or policies, it is not a facultative concept.)

Tail as used within this text, refers to that period of time between the initial reserving of a specific loss or event and the ultimate payment thereof; during this period information about the claim is collected and settlement negotiations are undertaken, such that the evaluation of the claim progresses, thereby referring to the developmental tail of the claim. While many claims are ultimately settled within the initial reserves, the overall development is typically upward, because the knowledge of subsequent facts and measurements contribute to the reserving process.

Target Risks comprise a list of high-value, commonly reinsured structures that are specifically excluded from many property reinsurance contracts; they include many bridges, tunnels, and high-value art collections.

Treaty Reinsurance is a transfer of more than one risk, exposure, or policy on a bulk basis such that a single negotiation takes into account the minor variances within the group of policies to be protected. Typically the cedent is obligated to offer all such business, and the reinsurer is obligated to accept a specified portion of all such classified risks originally underwritten by the primary insurer.

Uberrimae Fidei, which literally translates as "utmost good faith," is an underlying characterization of reinsurance transactions. Among the concepts that might be considered a breach of utmost good faith would be the failure of a cedent to disclose the full, known particulars of a risk (see the Follow the Fortunes clause in Chapter 15).

Underwriting is the process of reviewing applications for insurance or reinsurance coverage, deciding whether to accept all or part of the coverage, and determining the applicable premiums.

Underwriting Capacity is the maximum amount that an insurance company can underwrite. The limit is generally determined by the company's retained earnings and investment capital. Reinsurance serves to increase a company's capacity by reducing its net exposure from particular risks.

Underwriting Expenses comprise the aggregate of policy acquisition costs, including commissions, and the portion of administrative, general, and other expenses attributable to underwriting operations.

Unearned Premiums comprise that portion of premium representing the unexpired portion of the policy or contract term and, as such, have not yet been exposed to the possibility of loss.

Utilization Ratio is the percentage of direct and assumed premiums that is spent on reinsurance (see Chapter 4).

INDEX